HACKER, INFLUENCER, FAKER, SPY

ROBERT DOVER

Hacker, Influencer, Faker, Spy

Intelligence Agencies in the Digital Age

HURST & COMPANY, LONDON

First published in the United Kingdom in 2022 by
C. Hurst & Co. (Publishers) Ltd.,
New Wing, Somerset House, Strand, London, WC2R 1LA

The right of Robert Dover to be identified as the author of
this publication is asserted by him in accordance with the
Copyright, Designs and Patents Act, 1988.

Distributed in the United States, Canada and Latin America
by Oxford University Press, 198 Madison Avenue,
New York, NY 10016, United States of America.

A Cataloguing-in-Publication data record for this book
is available from the British Library.

ISBN: 9781787384835

www.hurstpublishers.com

Printed in Great Britain by Bell and Bain Ltd, Glasgow

This book is dedicated to my wife, Chrissie.
Wife, life-partner, best friend. You have taught me the value of things outside the academy, the value of family time and holidays, the joy of running through muddy fields, and how cool our gang is. Thank you for putting up with me whilst I've been doing the dawn chorus starts and the witching hour finishes of writing this book, worked on impact case studies, marked papers, prepared lectures and supervised my large cohort of PhD students. If you are reading this it is finally over, and it's time for us to go and have more fun.

This book is also dedicated to our children. You are a fine product of our parenting(!)

CONTENTS

ACKNOWLEDGEMENTS

I like the Kremlinology of acknowledgements. Those who are thanked and noted, and those who are not. As a device, I think the negative-acknowledgements section has been long overlooked. Even so, I have been persuaded not to begin this trend.

I would like to thank my parents, Richard and Janet, for sparking a lifelong interest in security and politics and—as I can now see as a parent myself—the value in placing a strong emphasis on reading and lifelong learning. Without you, none of this would be possible.

I would like to thank Andrew Monaghan for his enduring friendship, his wise counsel, his studied irreverence and scepticism and his generosity in reading drafts and framing his critiques with precision and care. It is life affirming to know that a mutual admiration of *TMS* (*Test Match Special*), knowledge of the noble game, some mobile telephony and the occasional days at cricket grounds can amount to some of the very best in life.

I would like to thank Erik Jones, who has been a strong feature of my intellectual life since 1997. He has been—in turns—personal tutor, sparring partner, co-writer, provider of critiques, great dinner company, the right kind of bad influence and righter of wrongs.

I have some obscured acknowledgements I hope you will forgive. Many thanks to Mike Goodman for being a fine and longstanding research collaborator and to David Omand for wise counsel and sharp critiques. I would like to thank Tim for his abiding wisdom; Patrick, for our wonderfully vigorous exchanges of views; Mark

ACKNOWLEDGEMENTS

Laffey for being the vision thing; Richard Paterson for instilling early rigour, the Tapir, Hank, Roger and Linda for excessively good advice; Friedi for her valuable and wider insights; H&H for being jointly delusional that they are my favourite former students; and Mike Caine and Sarah Childs for making me a far better academic than I was when I respectively first met them.

INTRODUCTION
INTELLIGENCE IN THE UBIQUITOUSLY INTERCONNECTED
INFORMATION AGE

The case for intelligence:

If you know neither yourself nor your enemy, you will always endanger yourself.

Sun Tzu

Understanding the limits of intelligence:

Reports that say that something hasn't happened are always interesting to me, because as we know, there are known knowns; these are things we know we know. We also know there are known unknowns; that is to say we know there are some things we do not know. But there are also unknown unknowns—the ones we don't know we don't know.

Donald Rumsfeld

***

Many seek to make the business of government intelligence artificially complex. Those seeking complexity obsess about its architecture, its techniques and tradecraft, the technologies it utilises, the technologies it is threatened by and what it says about our place in the world (whichever *us* that is). But at its heart, intelligence is simple: it aims to avoid surprises. Defensive intelligence seeks to avoid damaging surprises. Offensive intelligence seeks to spring surprises on others, and to disrupt our adversary's attempts to surprise us.

Our sense that government intelligence is complex comes through in the popular and academic retelling of the work of these secret communities. These accounts attempt to map out how agencies function, their relationships with the political elites, and what legal, political and moral authorities they call upon. Such retellings often also highlight particular incidents: those that have played out well or, more frequently, those that have played out badly.[1] To sit alongside intelligence officials is to quickly lose the simplicity that characterises the mission, be it avoiding surprises, or identifying, containing and rolling back threats. It is to become immersed in the self-referential maze of their operating environment: from the impenetrable jargon, through to the difficulty of forming coalitions of the willing, bureaucratic turf wars and resource conflicts to enact reforms or transformation, to the political positioning of the agencies, the individuals within them, or the very business of intelligence itself.

This weight of complexity creates a fog of ambiguity for those trying to communicate what intelligence is, what it does, and how it does it. It prevents them describing what role and influence intelligence has on our politics and on the individual citizen's relationship with intelligence agencies.

The lengthy Cold War and the precarious deterrence provided by the balance of nuclear forces between the NATO and Warsaw Pact nations provided the perfect backdrop to the development of large and technologically innovative intelligence services and a keen public and political interest in how intelligence works. Whilst the Cold War is seen by many as the highpoint of 'intelligence games' and of espionage, the information era or internet age has come to be signalled by those concerned by governmental over-reach as a further high-water mark in intelligence activity and intrusions into the private lives of individuals. Both these statements contain some truths but they miss the extent to which the FANG companies (Facebook, Amazon, Netflix and Google) have created a surveillance society that is far more capable and intrusive than those of Western governments (Orlowski, 2020; Zuboff, 2019).

The books, documentaries, social media feeds and other information sources that that aim to improve the public's understanding of intelligence have been framed around two basic tropes: the first is a steady conservatism around the description of intelligence organisations and processes, whilst being accompanied by a drip-feed of positive and negative operational details.

The second is the show-stopper revelation that generates public discussion. In the 1980s, Peter Wright's memoir *Spycatcher* aimed to provide a hitherto unseen glimpse into the world of Cold War espionage, including grand plots and scandals, although it became better well known because of the failed attempts by the UK government to censor it. Similar efforts by David Shayler and Annie Machon had similar but diluted impacts. WikiLeaks created larger storms with their Cablegate release of diplomatic cables, touching upon some of the work of intelligence agencies and parallel diplomacy (Brevini, Hintz & McCurdy, 2013). More recently, Edward Snowden's whistleblowing (or treachery, depending on your view) showed us all the extent of American and British intelligence power and, with it, that these agencies could reach into the most intimate thoughts of the general public (Bruder & Maharidge, 2020; Harding, 2014; Snowden, 2019). Snowden's revelations, occurring as they did during the teenage years of the internet age, provided the space for commentators of all stripes to take a view, to suggest what it is that we do not know, or to offer words of calm reassurance that big government is protecting us (Gioe & Hatfield, 2020; Murata, Adams & Palma, 2017; Ruby, Goggin & Keane, 2017).

These conservative and showstopping tropes do have uses in describing steady evolution, and stark dislocation and transformation in turn, and they define the field I work in. These tropes miss two analytical elephants in the room: (1) that intelligence activity exists to defend and advance the status quo ante. It is a tool for protecting and projecting power and it has successfully managed the politics of the Global South for at least seventy years; and (2) that the vast majority of commentary about intelligence equates to retelling the partial stories of the British and American intelligence communities and that the academic and commentariat fields fail to acknowledge the aggressive centrality of the Anglosphere to the global intelligence picture: this is a reinforcing set of actors and narratives that seeks to entrench the dominance of the Global North. In the context of aggressive posturing from China, Russia and North Korea, amongst others, the role of the nexus of intelligence, security and entrenched economic and manufacturing interests is a defence of liberal plurality that is the hallmark of the Euro–Atlantic area. The role of intelligence is, therefore, a defence of ideas and a conception of politics. The disruption of threats to economic interests, to the development of security technologies and so on, is a smaller scale punctuation point in this contest of ideas.

A Softly Post-structural Turn in Intelligence Studies?

The British and American intelligence communities act as the white blood cells for the Anglosphere's dominance of global politics. These two communities have leveraged and continue to leverage their advantages in intelligence tradecraft and technology to advance the Anglosphere's political, economic and social interests over those of their competitors, and have defended the core institutions of power from attack by internal and external adversaries. This is, of course, what they are tasked to do. But, in doing so, these agencies and their governments have helped to subjugate the Global South, denying these regions and peoples voice by actively managing the domestic and international politics of these countries, by maintaining dysfunctional political systems in those nations, and contributing to a pattern of political behaviour and narratives that others and excludes the Global South from the information, financial and military elites of the Global North. More pertinently, and echoing the language of Véronique Pin-Fat, they have helped to create a westernised, and liberal 'picture of reason' through which to view the world: that is to create a universalised sense of 'how things are' (Pin-Fat, 2010). As I note through my review of popular culture and future technology (Chapter 8), the development of what is framed as political neutral technologies and artefacts are actually highly political. It is not necessary for an intelligence officer, a developer of technology, a video games developer, or a producer of television programmes to explicitly understand the politics of their role: the system in which they are operating makes their often unconscious political choices seem like the only natural thing to do.

In her work Pin-Fat suggests the successful creation and protection of this 'picture of reason' means that, whilst there should be multiple readings of the same system, political phenomenon or episode, we are trained to fixate on one aspect rather than another. Furthermore, when the structural conditioning or individual predilection is so trained to see only one aspect, then we are blind to other aspects and even their existence. Such insights help to explain the political divisions that at the time of writing are fracturing the UK, the US and Europe, around fundamental issues of identity, politics, the response to the COVID-19 pandemic and the international response to Russia's invasion of Ukraine. It is reasonable to assert, therefore, that the result of the actions of individuals, organisations and the collective effort of governments is to effectively hide important aspects, or episodes, in plain sight: consequently, we are blind to them. The effect of this conditioning and how and what we are able to see, can make a large difference to how we encounter and are able to relate to our world and the 'things' in it. Pin-Fat's essential conclusion is that even unveiling previously hidden aspects is a form of political and ethical change (Pin-Fat, 2010, pp. 4–30). But a picture of reason—a consistent world view—is not a sufficient condition, however, for the outsized influence in the world that the US and the UK enjoy.

So, how do we account for the impact that intelligence has on our domestic and international politics? How do we utilise the insights from international relations to illuminate these novel contributions? The post-structuralist turn in international relations was dismissed by positivist and realist scholars, and consequently by practitioners, as offering few insights into the real world of international politics. This assessment was buttressed by fairly lazy critiques that critical scholars were actually saying that there is no 'real world' and that consequently they were (for example) trying to undermine my lived experience of the pen, the paper and the table I am writing this chapter from. As with everything in life there were shards of truth to the critique and there are clearly examples of post-structural work that added very little to our understanding of politics and power.

Indeed, having begun my career at Bristol during this post-structural turn I, too, rejected it as having a cultish quality to it, which—in retrospect—had little to do with the intellectual endeavour that underpins it. So, it is with thanks to my former University of Leicester colleagues Jamie Johnson and Sana Rahim that, with our lengthy discussion about these concepts, I have returned to them as a way of understanding how the business of intelligence impacts on politics, and how unconscious the politics is behind many of the acts and developments we can observe. I should note, however, that any errors of interpretation remaining are, of course, mine alone.

As a result, one of my aims here is to provide an intelligence studies reading of the theoretical work that emphasises the importance of language and meaning in international relations. In utilising insights from Véronique Pin-Fat and Karin Fierke, I establish a set of principles through which to examine the role of intelligence. The principles rest upon some understandings of how language establishes the meaning of objects, rules and events, and in so doing sets boundaries around which actors can move and encounter the world. So, from this perspective it is the correspondence theory of truth that is useful to us: that is, we experience something to be 'more true' when it corresponds to our understanding of it. The persuasive charm of Donald Trump to his base of support was that they felt that his critique of liberal media accorded with their experience of their views being marginalised, of being despicable as Hillary Clinton infamously described them. Similarly, those who were ardent 'leavers' in the Brexit debate were constantly reaffirmed in their views of the EU as a malignant influence over their lives and our politics and, because it accorded so completely with their lived experiences, they could not see views that challenged it. One of the really interesting things we learned in the early phases of Russia's invasion of Ukraine in February 2022 was that the propaganda efforts of the Russian state, and their 'useful idiots' in the Euro–Atlantic area, were merely tolerated rather than actively consumed. The invasion itself acted to knock European citizens out of their complacency in this regard, producing accusations of Russophobia across Europe.

The rules that intelligence agencies help to make, reinforce and defend are, as Kenneth Waltz argued, the result of acting and reacting to each other, which in turn produces a structure of interactions that is larger than the sum of its parts (Waltz, 1979, pp. 75–76); in (re)producing the patterns of dominance, intelligence agencies constantly re-make and reinforce these rules. The rules do not remain static: the point is that they respond to the context in which they are placed. In this respect we can understand this phenomenon in the same way that Andrew Moravcsik went on to articulate 'preferences' (strategic positions that remain stable over time) and 'policies' (those day-to-day decisions that must remain largely consistent with the preferences) (Moravcsik, 1993). Preferences are the long-term framing, and therefore the stable paradigm through which short-term policies are articulated. Preferences are capable of changing, but only as a result of some form of shock or the sheer weight of accepted or enacted policies that stand in contrast to the over-arching preferences. It is in this mechanism that we can see that the spectrum of domestic and internationally focused agencies have some latitude to flex, to be agents of change, to work with a rule-set to maintain this hegemony—the example of the American use of torture and extraordinary measures in the War on Terror is a fine demonstration of this point (Fierke, 2002, p. 340).

The utility of examining episodes such as rendition and torture is persuasively argued by Pin-Fat, who says that they provide us with the opportunity to work forensically through the underpinning logics—in this case the experience of Western vulnerability versus the human rights of those from the Middle East (Pin-Fat, 2009). We might also apply a similar thought experiment in the domestic context to those who adhere to marginalised beliefs, which the government views as hazardous to the common good. The perceived threat posed by these people has been enough to suspend carefully curated human rights norms and protections. These thought experiments also allow us to reflect on our own response to hypothetical scenarios where a foreign power renders or tortures British or American citizens, and therefore the precise conditions and drivers for the rule-sets that we apply more generally. These experiments provide insights into who we are (individually and collectively), how we identify 'normal' and 'outsider', and the political and ethical room to manoeuvre.

So, far from these post-structural logics arguing that there is no *real world* (although some have argued there is), the key lesson for us is that these post-structural approaches are an incredibly helpful and under-explored way of understanding the business of intelligence. The logics provide a notion that boundaries of meaning are fluidly established in the context of the interaction of agencies with adversaries, or even with those who are surveyed. This is the gap the agencies work in when impacting upon the politics of third states or in the case of domestic policing, in the so-called 'Spy Cops' scandal of undercover policing against lawful protest groups. Meaning can be changed, which is why well-resourced and technically able intelligence agencies can have such a large impact upon our politics and society. We do not need to reach beyond the success of Russian intelligence agencies in the UK and US in 2015 and 2016 to understand the strategic shock that can be delivered to third countries in essentially changing the boundaries of meaning.

Following through the arguments of Wittgenstein, Fierke, Pin-Fat and others, logic and language are embedded within each other, so the way we describe events, and the way governments describe events, are imbued with logics drawn from prevailing pictures of reason and accepted community rules. This is why a small trader avoiding value added tax through cash-in-hand transactions is adorned with negative labelling, whilst a corporation avoiding corporation tax through heavily contrived structures is provided with the less-onerous label of 'aggressive tax planning', whilst there is an absolute moral equivalence to both sets of activities. Thus, to see beyond that which we are really comfortable with is both tricky and emotionally difficult. It is literally counter-intuitive. When senior scholars like Andrew Monaghan and Keir Giles question our received way of interpreting Russian politics they are often positioned by critics as outsiders, and yet even basic reflective engagement with their work shows a consistent underpinning logic that should cause us a pause for thought. Similarly, anarchist and Marxist readings of liberal governance are rejected by many as a reflex response, and, whilst it is very simple to reject Marxist prescriptions, it is far more difficult to argue with the underpinning critiques of politics and economics. The strength of this point should be self-evident to us through the events of 2021, with the jarring realities of what drove the Black Lives Matters campaign and the historical and contemporary injustices that surround the issue.

The example of how 'we' respond to Russia is useful in highlighting the potential analytical traction from post-structural insights around speech acts. The failure to act decisively on Russian state-sponsored assassinations on British streets has undermined the deterrent effect of the UK government's strong words condemning the Russian government. The British government's speech act has been undermined by the material reality: it is now cast as weakness. Consequently, the interaction between Russia and the UK has acquired a meaning and a set of rules that are currently being reproduced by subsequent interactions. But, as noted before, these rules are not fixed and are capable of being changed by motivated actors willing to reinterpret the rules against emerging facts. Russian aggression against their dissidents located in the UK is capable of being seen in various ways, and one reasonable response would be for the UK to stop providing a safe-harbour to these characters, as a means by which to re-set the current rule-set. Similarly, we can observe that Chinese inward investment into the UK was seen by the Conservative government led by David Cameron as an unalloyed positive, whilst the successor Conservative government of Boris Johnson has seen this inward investment in internet technologies as hostile. The change in grammar has been driven by the authoritarian turn in Hong Kong and the strong sense of Chinese culpability in the spread of the COVID-19 pathogen that has disproportionately impacted upon the UK. Thus, the ethical and political space that allowed Chinese participation in the UK's core infrastructure in 2015 no longer exists in 2020. So, throughout this book, I seek to describe the picture of reason that is being defended or pushed (the value-set), the 'picture of the subject' (the understanding of ourselves, our system of government, and our rule-set), and the picture of the ethico-political space, which covers the reality and the possibility contained within the situation.

In maintaining and extending a hierarchy of knowledge, material resource and advantage between the developed and developing worlds the Global North similarly maintains a narrative of superiority and superior opportunity and acts. In this regard modern states of the Global North are similar to mercantile states of two hundred years ago, the key difference being—this time—to extract human resources to service developed economies whilst seeking rents on knowledge and technologies that have facilitated the post-industrial development of the Global North.

There is, however, a paradox at the heart of this information age, which British and American intelligence officials have seen as key to them continuing to assert their dominance, but which has become a point of significant vulnerability for the political and economic systems they seek to protect and for how they themselves operate as institutions (Dover, 2020). The nub of the transatlantic imbroglio over the involvement of Huawei in Western internet infrastructures is located in it being a form of colonial entrapment by the Chinese state—which wilfully ignores the extent of Chinese colonial interference in Western economies and Western politics already (UK Defence Select Committee, 2020).

Standing on the Shoulders...

This book focuses on these two glaring omissions of intelligence's acutely political role in the active maintenance of a fluctuating status quo (which is not as oxymoronic as it might first seem), and in acting to maintain a dominance over the Global South. In doing these two things, the book sets itself apart from much of the existing intelligence studies field. It aims to describe how the agencies and commentators establish, advance and defend particular pictures of reason, the rules and structures that flow from them, whilst describing the impact this has had on domestic and international politics and social relations. Not only is intelligence the 'hidden wiring' of government: it is also vital and hidden wiring in the operation of economic relations, knowledge production and social relationships.

This book is also unique in another more marginal—but important—way. I see this work as a natural successor to two totemic volumes: Michael Herman's 1996 book, *Intelligence Power in Peace and War* (Herman, 1996) and Sir David Omand's 2010 book, *Securing the State* (Omand, 2010). It is closer to the latter than the former in the scope of its ambition to outline the contours of how intelligence works, but within the narrower field of view of the internet-enabled age and the impact upon the public. This book is also partly a competitor to Omand's most recent book, *How Spies Think* (Omand, 2020), which succeeds at drawing lessons from intelligence into a wider frame, and the first draft of this book was written—it would appear—at the same time Omand was writing his.

It should also be noted that Michael Herman and David Omand are very significant figures in the practitioner realm of intelligence: the late Michael Herman headed GCHQ's efforts against Russia for a significant portion of the Cold War, and subsequently played a large role in retirement assisting and mentoring intelligence studies scholars through his Oxford Intelligence Group at Nuffield College. In turn, Sir David was the first coordinator of British intelligence, as well as having been the Director of GCHQ and a Permanent Secretary of the Ministry of Defence. Like Michael he, too, has provided endlessly generous sharp-eyed and occasionally sharply written (but never sharply spoken) advice, guidance and mentoring to a generation of intelligence studies scholars. Importantly, both of them have written their important contributions to the field from the perspective of having been very senior insiders to the intelligence community.

I am—of course—not an insider in the way that Herman and Omand were. I have been fortunate to have been granted some glimpses inside the intelligence machine as part of research projects I have run, and from community insiders I have worked with. I feel I understand the machine better than most, but not in the same way as very senior former insiders would. This also means—of course— that I have a different pool of resources and experiences to call on to critique the business of intelligence, in a way that they might neither readily recognise nor accept. My humble suggestion to the reader is that they read both this and *Securing the State* as a double-header, to compare and contrast these respective assessments of the role of intelligence in our society.

The Structure and Key Themes of this Book

This book has two parts. Part 1 is titled 'Enforcing Liberal Hegemony', which sounds a little too close to journal articles from various critical schools of international relations theory. I am not using the term in this way; instead, I am seeking to describe what I have observed, which is that government intelligence effort has an acutely political underpinning, something that, whilst standing in plain sight, we have collectively chosen to ignore. So, Part 1 looks to flesh out how the advancement and defence of liberal hegemonies have and continue to occur. It is important to note that I do not argue from a standpoint that this liberalism is static; indeed, observations from political economists like Ian Bruff, that liberalism itself is undergoing an autocratic turn, seem persuasive to me (Bruff, 2014; Bruff & Tansel, 2019). So, it is the advancement and defence of a broad church of Anglophone liberalism that government intelligence agencies are engaged in, and the chapters in this first part of the book reflect this. These chapters examine the technological and political disruption of intelligence within a contemporary framework, the underspecified cultural understanding of intelligence—be it the culture of the agencies, and indeed how they treat difference and culture as they find it in the wider world. Part 1 then moves on to consider how intelligence agencies encounter and engage with external experts, the developing role of open source intelligence (OSINT) in intelligence, and the maturing arena of so-called hybrid warfare and disinformation conflicts.

Part 2 is titled 'The Public Consumption of Intelligence' and is a touch shorter than the first part. It focuses on the relationship between the public, different forms of media, and the depictions made of intelligence by these media sources. It makes use of insights from media and communications studies, film studies and the study of popular culture, as well as insights from intelligence scholars who have written on cultural portrayals, such as Jeremy Black, Pierre Lethier, Christopher Moran, Trevor McCrisken, James Der Derian and Christina Rowley. The central contention of the material in Part 2 is that, as Der Derian coined it, the MIME-NET (military–industrial media–entertainment network) creates and reproduces a value-set through its cultural artefacts that is so aligned it is co-produced, and this allows—in his frame of reference—the prosecution of virtuous wars (Der Derian, 2010). For this study, and as noted earlier, the MIME-NET has functioned to produce, advocate for and defend a particular picture of reason that frames our understanding of the world, producing endless different 'virtuous' outcomes.

Outside these formal sections and chapters, there are three other cross-cutting themes that I want to highlight, and which appear as golden threads through the book. These are: surprises (and how the efforts made to avoid them), the impacts of globalisation, and the very contemporary contest in our collective understanding of security. Because these themes sit beneath the main analysis, I will quickly address them here.

Surprises

Intelligence agencies are knowledge producers and actors on the domestic and international stage. Using a range of technical, technological and human techniques and sources, they seek to uncover unknown unknowns, and known unknowns, to be able to provide warning notices to their political leaders, thus providing competitive advantage. Furthermore, in identifying adversary activities they are also used to disrupt these activities using a variety of intrusive techniques, ranging from the psychological all the way up to the deployment of Special Forces. Of equal importance—but often overlooked—is the role of intelligence in providing early warnings about developing situations or competitors in the international system. This is the very heart of their mission in avoiding surprises but, as I argue later in this book, this role could be usefully reconceptualised as providing decision support to government. Indeed, it is in this decision-support role that the real value added of intelligence will come.

It is commonly assumed that the knowledge produced by intelligence agencies is certain—a Rumsfeldian known known—but it is contingent, fluid and subject to change. To paraphrase Philip Davies, 'if it was easy, it wouldn't be intelligence'. One of the things this book does is to explore how the business of intelligence has been impacted by the internet age—an age that has been recognised as disrupting and dislocating social and economic relations (Eraslan & Kukuoglu, 2019; van Dijck, 2020). It does this by looking at this central question of impact from different thematic vectors: of intelligence tradecraft, of globalisation, organisational culture and psychology, the challenge of populist politics, of hybrid warfare, of media relations, and of popular culture. In this sense it captures a development at the operational level—the use of informational technologies in intelligence activities—and draws them wider to show this much larger shift at the strategic level.

The book is written from the perspective of observing British and American intelligence communities, which are politically and operationally aligned. Whilst some scholars, like Philip Davies, have suggested that the two communities treat intelligence in a different way, there has been considerable evidence over the last ten years to suggest that in counterterrorism, communications and electronic intelligence the two have moved in lockstep. The Snowden revelations offered a tantalising glimpse of the extent to which the US National Security Agency and its British equivalent, GCHQ, are so close as to be synonymous. Earlier episodes, such as the work of Duncan Campbell and the European Parliament around the NSA's ECHELON interception programme similarly highlighted these important overlaps (Campbell, 1988). The common approaches they have taken to the major security challenges of the modern era means that I think it is not only justifiable but valuable to consider how in combination the US and UK intelligence communities have responded and shaped the operational environment and our politics. Where there are meaningful differences, I have drawn these out clearly and they create their own learning moments for us.

Christopher Andrew and David Dilks famously described intelligence as the missing dimension in international relations, but it is difficult to think this remains valid in the way they intended it today (Andrew & Dilks, 1984). At best intelligence might be described as misunderstood, underexplored and under-examined by the public, politicians and academics. This is unfortunate because intelligence frames our domestic and international security disposition, it has led to technological and policy developments that impact upon all that we do in society, which is why Peter Hennessy described it as 'the hidden wiring' of the state (Hennessy, 1996).

I would go further and argue that the role of intelligence in the formation of modern states is far more significant than even the description of hidden wiring implies. From the reign of Elizabeth I in England (1558–1603), intelligence has been proactively used to protect the respective heads of state and heads of government, to suppress sedition and subversion, to enforce the limits of dissent and political activity, to protect key infrastructure and the underpinning to trading success, to collect information on, and disrupt the activities of, international competitors and to advance and manage the state's interests abroad. Across the Atlantic, the fledgling United States was protected by an early machinery of intelligence that was vested in a private company called Pinkertons, established in 1850. The Pinkertons Company conducted close protection during the American Civil War, and had the good judgment or luck to be on the victorious side of Abraham Lincoln (O'Hara, 2016). Pinkerton's role in government enforcement diminished after the 1893 Anti-Pinkerton Act and it was replaced through the growth of government intelligence via naval and coastguard routes before the many disparate agencies were placed within a presentational wrapper of the intelligence community after the Second World War (Warner & McDonald, 2005).

The emergence of more muscular domestic and internationally focused intelligence agencies in America after 1945 came partly as a response to the necessities of the Cold War, both to protect but also to advance the US' hegemonic role in the international system. This convinced successive administrations that such a global role would only be secured by having an interventionist and entrepreneurial intelligence and security organisations. The role of intelligence has been pivotal to the development of US history and to America's place in the world, and to securing coherent ideological narratives that predominate across North America and Western Europe.

Globalised intelligence

Globalisation was a term, largely used positively, to describe the leaps forward in global interconnectedness. This 'ever closening union' was assisted by reductions in trading barriers, fast and cheap global communications, the rapid movement of capital and goods, cheap air travel and a general acceptability of global migration—certainly within post-industrial societies—with fewer barriers than ever before. Scholars like Justin Rosenberg correctly pointed out that globalisation was not a modern phenomenon at all and sought to demonstrate the deep historical antecedents of these practices to illuminate how the Anglosphere got to be where it is today (Rosenberg, 2003). Whilst globalisation saw the spread of American and European business practices and finance, cultural and social norms and Western-style democracy, it came with the perceived negatives of the dilution of local cultures, the stretching of local resources to cope with large numbers of incomers, and a growing divide between a small number of people becoming very wealthy and a large number of people who felt left behind and impoverished by globalisation. Threats and adversaries also made the most of the opportunities of globalisation: dangerous ideologies, training, communication and technologies could now all move around the globe quickly. The openness of globalisation was its biggest plus but also its greatest vulnerability. Roadside bombs in the Iraqi insurgency were said to be designed in Russia, manufactured in China, and financed and delivered by Iran: a form of globalisation that no-one in the Global North welcomed.

This book argues that some of the prominent challenges to intelligence from globalisation are—in effect—self-inflicted wounds. The decision made by both American and British signals intelligence agencies to collect and warehouse internet data has distracted them from more productive aspects of intelligence work. Not only has it been distracting but it is also fundamentally changing the relationship between the public, the agencies, politics and the media. If very little usable intelligence is coming from such intelligence, then more productive activities should be sought. As we will see, the agencies have struggled to transform quickly enough to keep up with the pace of this form of globalisation: they now need to adapt again to the transformation against globalisation and towards isolation, which places a greater emphasis upon strategic warning, counterintelligence and the mitigation of threats. The spectre of the

COVID-19 pandemic is likely to advance the moves towards the onshoring or reshoring of manufacturing to the Global North, and with it a period of economic and political turbulence as migratory flows has been disrupted and industries—such as my own higher education—go through periods of painful realignment.

Security policy and narratives in flux

The way the public is sold messages and policies about security has changed since 2001, and it continues to cause confusion. The paradoxes at the heart of the security narrative sound something like this:

> *Invasive security is good.*
> *Unless it is directed at 'us'.*
>
> *It is good when it is directed at 'them'.*
> *And 'they' would have nothing to fear if they were not doing anything wrong.*

Such logics continue:

> *Physical policing and intelligence levels should be reduced because they represent bad value for money, and they do not investigate the right things.*
>
> *But crime is going up because the undesirables are increasingly lawless and that is intolerable and needs something doing about it.*
>
> *The politicisation of security and surveillance has come through parallel developments in the advanced uses of data analytics and data-driven political marketing, and it is concerning.*
>
> *But advanced data analytics should be used to investigate and prosecute political opponents and people who hold dissenting views.*

In its international guise:

> *Collective defence is outdated because it is premised upon a rules-based order that does not take into account the special circumstances and unique history of our nation.*
>
> *But national defence and international influence are absolutely key. (But we do not want to pay any more in taxes for it.)*

Our contemporary debates about security have not been logically consistent, but these inconsistencies have been allowed to hang in the air and remain unresolved on the grounds that every opinion is as valid as the next, regardless of what the evidence suggests. This level of confusion also seems to be a deliberate tactic within the political elites to keep the narrative ground constantly shifting (Surkov, 2008). Within this fluidity there is an important constitutional question about the position and role of intelligence agencies within our democracies: former senior practitioners, like Sir David Omand, have been pivotal in positioning the role of intelligence in democratic systems of government (Omand, *Securing the State*, 2010). On the opposite side have been the efforts of various political leaders, often accused of engaging with foreign governments, to question the role and validity of intelligence agencies. In the case of the US, pointed challenges to the legitimacy of the intelligence community have coincided with agencies being asked to investigate foreign collusion, and the awkward realisation that it is the primary customers of intelligence who are being investigated. So, the disruption to our politics is as much about the hidden wiring of the state (the activities of security and intelligence services) as it is about conspiracies around the activities of the so-called 'deep state': a pejorative re-working of the activities of the same agencies and officers. As will become apparent through the book, I argue that, whilst the business of intelligence is having to rapidly adapt to meet the modern challenges of electronic globalisation, it remains more steady state than deep state, a term which is evoked by campaigners to distance government officials from the citizenry (Chaffetz, 2018; Fitzgerald, 2020). This is the paradox of all being the same, and yet very different.

Since the turn of the century a plethora of intelligence reforms has been introduced across the Western world that have the potential—if misapplied—to fundamentally change the relationship between the public and the state. Counterterrorism and counter-radicalisation laws look eminently sensible in the context of terrorism threats but look less sustainable or desirable when held up to the light of environmental activists holding sit-down protests on common land. Plans to end or ban encryption on communications again seems proportionate when considered in the midst of an ongoing attack, but would undermine e-commerce and all legal and appropriate communications, with little thought to the notion that committed terrorists have not been shown to be communicating on open or easy to intercept platforms. Similarly, the bulk collection of movement data from mobile phones and GPS devices would have been unthinkable and unacceptable twenty years ago, and yet these are accepted techniques used by private data brokers and intelligence and law enforcement agencies today, rendering it impossible for an individual to effectively opt out of contact with the state, to engage in teenage dreaming or peaceful activism without growing an analysable record (Zegart & Morell, 2019). Pre-2000, it was perfectly possible to go 'off grid' so long as the individual remained on the right side of the law and did not holiday abroad, for example. It is now almost inconceivable—even theoretically—to think of ways that a person could go 'off grid'. Consequently, the public collectively relies upon strong laws and effective oversight to protect them from government agencies over-reaching or overstepping. The chapters that follow should provide some pause for thought about whether these oversight mechanisms are currently match fit.

The connectivity, symbiosis and yet tension between the intelligence community and the now heavily digitised media is a prominent feature in how we should understand the developing business of intelligence and how intelligence helps to shape our understanding of the world and mitigate threats from our adversaries. The stand-out security moments of the last twenty years in the Global North have been media events, typified by striking visual images and rolling news analysis. From the attacks on New York in 2001 to those in Madrid in 2004, London 2005 and then onto the marauding attacks in Mumbai 2008, and then the multiple attacks on Australia, Belgium, France, Germany, New Zealand, Sweden and the United Kingdom, all have had prominent legacies and new-media exposure: a contest between sympathisers, troublemakers and the authorities across all forms of media outlet. A good intelligence officer will see shaping the operational environment as one of her key jobs, and that includes managing messages and the flow of information coming through the media. The relationship between journalists and intelligence officers is highlighted in Chapter 3, and with it examining the uneven topography of privileged relations and the continued evolution of antagonistic relationships with the diminishing number of well-funded investigative reporters. The economic realities of journalism and the emergence of a public that has a good deal of unearned confidence in their abilities to assess what looks like unedited information have created a complex information environment, one that is being exploited by international adversaries and domestic insurgents.

A diminution of the trust felt by the public for politicians and government agencies has been the other significant push factor behind the growth of alternative sources of information and for the doubts cast over sources of official information. To a great extent the British and American administrations helped to create these levels of distrust with their misappropriation of intelligence as a defining feature of their case for war against Saddam Hussein's Iraq in 2003. This and the failure to communicate adequately why they were taking the actions they took in response to the 2008 financial crisis seem to have created a long-term and fundamental breach in the relationship between governments and their publics. Such breaches prevented President Obama and Prime Minister Cameron from being able to create collective support for decisive action against the Syrian government's use of chemical weapons in 2015 and laid the platform for values-based voting (where evidence matters very little) in elections and referenda since (Gaskarth, 2016; Strong, 2015).

The demystification of the business of intelligence over the last hundred years has been a gradual process that has picked up speed the closer we get to the present day. The British government had a set routine of neither confirming nor denying the existence of intelligence agencies or the work they did for much of previous hundred years. The existence of the UK's Joint Intelligence Committee, which considers intelligence assessments, was accidently revealed at a talk at the Royal United Services Institute in 1938 and again in a published obituary in *The Times* in 1945: both of which were slips that suggested a growing machinery of intelligence, rather than deliberately providing the public with new information.

During the Cold War there was a little more openness provided about the intelligence world, with official histories being commissioned by the British government and across the Atlantic with a growing trend for investigative journalism and unofficial histories of the principle agencies. By the 1970s and 1980s, the US had seen its totemic Church Committee (named after Frank Church) reveal a considerable amount of information about the CIA, whilst the 1983 Franks Report (named after Lord Franks) examined the lessons to be learned about the Falklands crisis and made clearer the central role of the Joint Intelligence Committee and the way that the intelligence community provides warning notice to the government (National Archives, 1983). Franks was shortly followed by the fiasco surrounding the former MI5 Officer Peter Wright's book, *Spycatcher*, which the government had effectively blocked from publication in the UK (Wright & Greengrass, 1987). Wright managed to get the book published in Australia, but only after a legal contest in which the Cabinet Secretary—Sir Robert Armstrong— was forced to concede in court that MI5 had existed for the duration of Wright's employment but that he (somewhat ludicrously) could neither confirm nor deny that MI5 had existed before or after that employment (Burnet & Thomas, 1989). Such tight secrecy made for a permissive environment for very well informed and experienced fiction writers like John le Carré, Graham Greene, Frederick Forsyth and, more recently, from the former Director General of MI5, Stella Rimington, Mick Herron and Alan Judd, to shape the public's perception of intelligence through fictionalised accounts. These accounts have led directly to, or inspired, cinematic content and video gaming, as is explored later in Chapters 7 and 8 on popular culture.

In the post-Cold War era Western governments felt more comfortable with a measured degree of openness. Chapter 4 on open source intelligence and Chapter 6 on the relationship between intelligence and the media demonstrate that through official processes of declassification, through revelations and investigative journalism and—in the case of the UK with what was labelled avowal—the public came to know more about the purpose and activities of intelligence agencies. We should, however, note that the bulk declassification that occurred at the end of the Clinton Presidency was quickly reversed by the Bush Administration and millions of papers that had been released were reclassified. Regardless of this reclassification effort, the spate of memoirs, public lectures and documentary contributions from former high-ranking officials like Dame Eliza Manningham-Buller, Michael Warner, Richard Dearlove, and desk-officers like Richard Tomlinson and Tom Marcus, and former insiders of adversary groups like Omar Nasiri and Ed Hussain, has increased public connectivity with intelligence work. At the dawn of the internet age, the British government commissioned proper official histories of the agencies. The late and dearly missed Keith Jeffrey's book on MI6 was a fine history on the early years of MI6 (Jeffrey, 2010), Christopher Andrew has produced a lengthy and comprehensive official history of MI5 (Andrew, 2012), John Ferris has written an interesting and very sympathetic book on GCHQ (Ferris, 2020), whilst my long-standing co-writer Michael Goodman published the first of his 2-volume official history of the Joint Intelligence Committee in 2015, with the second due for publication in 2022–3 (Goodman, 2015). There have also been official histories on British defence economic intelligence (Davies, 2018) and on the D-Notice Committee (Wilkinson, 2009). There are also highly impressive unofficial histories, notably of GCHQ by Richard Aldrich (Aldrich, 2010) and in the pacey book on MI6 by the journalist Gordon Corera (Corera, 2012). Almost unbelievably, in the context of the secrecy that went before it, intelligence agencies across the Atlantic areas developed corporate websites and even joined mainstream social media sites. When the CIA officially joined Twitter in 2014 its inaugural tweet humorously read: 'we can neither confirm nor deny that this our *first tweet*', which received mixed reviews despite being a good effort. Information about intelligence feels simpler to get hold of, and yet considerable challenges remain around official secrecy and information warfare, which are explored at length during the remainder of the book.

The increase in circulating knowledge has also removed some of the mystique of intelligence work and given the public partial insights into the work of intelligence agencies and their officers. There is nothing inherently wrong with the normalisation of intelligence, but the consequences of it have been that the public feels that it can reject talk of 'what intelligence tells us' as being contested and often trumped by the views of online commentators who obviously do not have the same access to information as government actors.

The development of the hybrid media system, where traditional and electronic media outlets reinforce and buttress each other and dilute the desire for or need for quality and fact-checked journalism, has created apparent opportunities for intelligence agencies to gather 'glimpses into the souls' of the citizenry through what they share online, and some early warnings of developing angst and even violence in society (Chadwick, 2017; Haider *et al.*, 2020). It has produced divergent narrative realities (divergent pictures of reason) and yet greater cohesion to one variant or another. This interconnectedness has also created new vectors of vulnerability for the agencies, and is hastening the end of official secrecy, instead creating a system of—as Richard Aldrich and Christopher Moran termed it—delayed disclosure (Aldrich & Moran, 2019). Understanding the pressures on official secrecy is important because it should lead to changes in the ways that intelligence communities operate: protecting a smaller number of genuine secrets and reflecting upon the utility of the large system of official secrecy and classification that exists on both sides of the Atlantic.

Contributions

This book provides insights into how the digital age has impacted upon the relationships between governments, intelligence agencies, external expertise, new and legacy media outlets and the public. These complex relationships, which touch upon fundamental aspects of how our societies function, the rule of law, the regulation of and oversight over government actions and what we can reasonably expect our governments to do for us, are shifting, and shifting without either an adequate society-wide conversation or a meaningful way of distilling such a conversation into action. Many of these activities are hidden from view, but those we can see are often mischaracterised or misunderstood. We can see proxies for these public debates playing out in the online conversations—although conversation seems far too polite a term for actually happens online—and through popular cultural depictions, where screenwriters and novelists are distilling the contours of the debates and placing them within fictionalised scenarios: sometimes aided by intelligence agencies, often not.

The digital age has given rise to a democratisation of information exchange but, as will be demonstrated later, it has not given rise to effective intelligence oversight or to meaningful knowledge about what intelligence agencies are able to do. Nor—more importantly— has it improved the understanding of what the impacts have been on social relations or the (re)production of particular ideas, values and behaviours. Even less well described or accounted for are the impacts of privately owned data-brokers, including the near ubiquitous social media and advertising and selling platforms, whose impact is far less well regulated than that of state institutions, and more difficult to access. My analysis gives credence to those who have highlighted the developments and impacts of these technology companies on society and intelligence activities in particular. Ultimately, it is possible to read into the analysis of this book that modern government intelligence is struggling to cope with the demands of a rapidly changing society, of bifurcated forms of globalisation and its discontents, of the transnationality of threats, and that governments seem to be keener to make strategically important decisions without a solid evidence base. In the chapter on open source intelligence (Chapter 4), I provide what I think is the answer to these challenges, in the form of a refocusing of intelligence activity into decision support: something that does not diminish the important security role of the agencies, but which helps to improve government decision making and threat mitigation.

References

Aldrich, R. (2010) *GCHQ*. London: Harper.

Aldrich, R. and Moran, C. (2019) 'Delayed disclosure: National security, whistle–blowers and the nature of secrecy'. *Political Studies* 67 (2), 291–306.

Andrew, C. (2012) *The Defence of the Realm: The Authorized History of MI5*. London: Penguin.

Andrew, C. and Dilks, D. (1984) *The Missing Dimension. Governments and Intelligence Communities in the Twentieth Century.* London: Macmillan.

Brevini, B., Hintz, A. and McCurdy, P. (2013) *Beyond WikiLeaks: Implications for the Future of Communications, Journalism and Society.* London: Palgrave MacMillan.

Bruder, J. and Maharidge, D. (2020) *Snowden's Box: Trust in the Age of Surveillance.* London: Verso.

Bruff, I. (2014). 'The rise of authoritarian neoliberalism'. *Rethinking Marxism* 26 (1),113–129.

Bruff, I. and Tansel, C. (2019) 'Authoritarian neoliberalism: Trajectories of knowledge production and praxis'. *Globalizations* 16 (3), 233–244.

Burnet, D. and Thomas, R. (1989) 'Spycatcher: The commodification of truth'. *Journal of Law and Society* 16 (2), 210–224.

Campbell, D. (1988) 'Somebody's listening'. *New Statesman*, 12 August (pp. 10–12).

Chadwick, A. (2017). *The Hybrid Media System: Power and Politics.* Oxford: Oxford University Press.

Chaffetz, J. (2018) *The Deep State: How an Army of Bureaucrats Protected Barack Obama and Is Working to Destroy Donald Trump.* New York, NY: Broadside.

Corera, G. (2012) *MI6: Life and Death in the British Secret Service.* London: Weidenfeld & Nicolson.

Davies, P. (2018). *The Authorised History of British Defence Economic Intelligence: A Cold War in Whitehall, 1929–90.* London: Routledge.

Der Derian, J. (2010) *Virtuous War: Mapping the Military–Industrial Media–Entertainment Network* (2nd edition). Abingdon: Routledge.

Dover, R. (2020) 'SOCMINT: A shifting balance of opportunity'. *Intelligence and National Security* 35 (2), 216–232.

Eraslan, L. and Kukuoglu, A. (2019) 'Social relations in virtual world and social media aggression'. *World Journal on Educational Technology: Current Issues* 11 (2), 1–11.

Ferris, J. (2020) *Behind the Enigma: The Authorised History of GCHQ, Britain's Secret Cyber-Intelligence Agency.* London: Bloomsbury.

Fierke, K. (2002) 'Links across the abyss: Language and logic in international relations'. *International Studies Quarterly* 46 (3), 331–354.

Fitzgerald, I. (2020) *The Deep State: A History of Secret Agendas and Shadow Governments.* New York, NY: Arcturus Press.

Gaskarth, J. (2016) 'The fiasco of the 2013 Syria votes: Decline and denial in British foreign policy'. *Journal of European Public Policy* 23 (5), 718–734.

Gioe, D. and Hatfield, J. (2020) 'A damage assessment framework for insider threats to national security information: Edward Snowden and the Cambridge Five in comparative historical perspective'. *Cambridge Review of International Affairs* 34 (5), 704–738.

Goodman, M. (2015) *The Official History of the Joint Intelligence Committee. Volume 1: From the Approach of the Second World War to the Suez Crisis.* London: Routledge.

Haider, S., Ilyas, W., Anwar, A., Shahzad, H. and Yakub, U. (2020) 'Analyzing Brexit's impact using sentiment analysis and topic modeling on Twitter discussion'. *The 21st Annual International Conference on Digital Government Research* (pp. 1–6). 15–19 June 2020. Seoul: Association for Computing Machinery.

Harding, L. (2014) *The Snowden Files: The Inside Story of the World's Most Wanted Man.* New York, NY: Vintage Press.

Hennessy, P. (1996) *The Hidden Wiring: Unearthing The British Constitution.* London: Phoenix Press.

Herman, M. (1996) *Intelligence Power in Peace and War.* Cambridge: Cambridge University Press.

Jeffrey, K. (2010) *MI6: The History of the Secret Intelligence Service 1909–1949.* London: Bloomsbury.

Moravcsik, A. (1993) 'Preferences and power in the European Community: A liberal intergovernmentalist approach'. *JCMS: Journal of Common Market Studies* 31 (4), 473–524.

Murata, K., Adams, A. and Palma, A. (2017) 'Following Snowden: A cross-cultural study on the social impact of Snowden's revelations'. *Journal of Information, Communication and Ethics in Society* 15 (3), 183–196.

National Archives. (1983) *The Franks Report Archive.* Retrieved from National Archives: https://discovery.nationalarchives.gov.uk/details/r/C11760221, accessed 2 November 2021

O'Hara, S. (2016) *Inventing the Pinkertons; or, Spies, Sleuths, Mercenaries, and Thugs.* Baltimore, MD: Johns Hopkins University Press.

Omand, D. (2010) *Securing the State.* London: Hurst.

———. (2020) *How Spies Think: Ten Lessons in Intelligence.* London: Penguin.

Orlowski, J. (Director). (2020) *The Social Dilemma* [Film]. [Motion Picture].

Pin-Fat, V. (2009) 'How do we begin to think about the world?' In J. Edkins and M. Zehfuss, *Global Politics: A New Introduction* (pp. 22–44). Oxford: Oxford University Press.

———. (2010) *Universality, Ethics and International Relations: A Grammatical Reading.* London: Routledge.

Rosenberg, J. (2003) *The Follies of Globalisation Theory.* London: Verso.

Ruby, F., Goggin, G. and Keane, J. (2017) '"Comparative Silence" still?' *Digital Journalism* 5 (3), 353–367.

Snowden, E. (2019) *Permanent Record.* New York, NY: Macmillan.

Strong, J. (2015) 'Why parliament now decides on war: Tracing the growth of the parliamentary prerogative through Syria, Libya and Iraq'. *The British Journal of Politics and International Relations* 17 (4), 604–622.

Surkov, V. (2008) 'Russian political culture: The view from utopia'. *Russian Social Science Review* 49 (6), 81–97.

UK Defence Select Committee. (2020) *The Security of 5G.* London: HMSO.

van Dijck, J. (2020) 'Governing digital societies: Private platforms, public values'. *Computer Law and Security Review* 36, 105377.

Waltz, K. N. (1979) *Theory of International Politics.* New York, NY: McGrawHill.

Warner, M. and McDonald, J. (2005) *US Intelligence Community Reform Studies since 1947.* Washington DC: Center for the Study of Intelligence.

Wilkinson, N. (2009) *Secrecy and the Media: The Official History of the United Kingdom's D-Notice System.* London: Routledge.

Wright, P. and Greengrass, P. (1987) *Spycatcher.* Canberra: Heinemann.

Zegart, A. and Morell, M. (2019) 'Spies, lies, and algorithms: Why US intelligence agencies must adapt or fail'. *Foreign Affairs*, 98, 85–96.

Zuboff, S. (2019) *The Age of Surveillance Capitalism.* London & New York: Profile Books.

PART ONE

ENFORCING LIBERAL HEGEMONY

1

'NARRATIVE VIOLATION'
THE ROLE OF INTELLIGENCE IN TECHNOLOGICAL AND POLITICAL DISRUPTION

What You Need to Know…

Digital globalisation has made information easier to come by. The always-on-internet age has made the process of verifying and validating information more complicated and less certain. This form of globalisation has made keeping secrets and protecting strategically important assets far more difficult. Technological disruption has been a key tool in the political dislocation that has occurred in Europe and the United States since 2008. The growth of wealth disparity, of opinion as fact, and the speed at which misinformation can be distributed and impact upon public decision making and the public psyche, has heralded an era in information conflict. It has also resulted in an unseating of the public's trust in public institutions and in the notion of facts. Since the turn of the century, and on both sides of the Atlantic, there have been concerted attempts to politicise intelligence agencies and the business of intelligence. Intelligence agencies have been simultaneously pressured to engage in political activities whilst being publicly demonised as working against the interests of the people. This has unhelpfully highlighted intelligence work but has also placed agencies and officers in the difficult position of needing to assess the risks associated with their own political leaders and the international networks they sit in. We can reasonably predict that, for the future, the work of intelligence agencies will reach a further public prominence in being linked to unsettling important domestic political and international economic interests.

***

73% of internet users in the EU are concerned about online disinformation or misinformation during election periods.

(Eurobarometer Survey, October 2018)

85% of respondents perceive online fake news as a problem in their country and 83% perceive it as a problem for democracy in general.

(Eurobarometer survey, February 2018)

***

Impartial observers of Western politics might reflect the sense that logic is no longer an accurate guide to understanding domestic and international politics across much of North America and the European Union. Such a view would also be a commentary on the quality of political debate in the Euro–Atlantic area since 2015. For the purposes of this book and the argument it advances around the role of intelligence in information conflict, and that intelligence serves to marshall and reproduce certain types of political, social and economic interaction and beliefs, we can observe a considerable, recent disruptive challenge to that (constantly evolving) consensus. This disruption has come from so-called populist politicians, or as Jonathan Hopkin more accurately suggests, 'anti-system' politicians who have skilfully harnessed persuasive political themes and amplified them using networked devices (Davis, 2021; Hopkin, 2020).

The political disruption from 2015 to the present day has challenged the business of intelligence in both technical and fundamental ways. Intelligence agencies are both a reflection of, and serve, the societies they spring from, but anti-system politicians have been quick to paint intelligence agencies as being part of establishment forces that exist to frustrate the will of the people. So, whilst the dynamic of intelligence as being in competition with external forces and internal anti-state subversives is well established, the notion of subversion coming from *within the state apparatus* is new. The use of intelligence assets to investigate relationships with outside—and adversary—nations has placed agencies in the invidious position of directly and indirectly investigating those they are tasked by. Even worse, the anti-system politicians who have managed to gain a toe-hold in power have not been reliable with secrets and information that required discretion and they have occasionally tried to publicly task intelligence agencies to directly or indirectly investigate their opponents (Atkinson *et al.*, 2020; Hellinger, 2019). In this era of digitally driven populism, intelligence has become politicised by all sides in an unprecedented way.

The attempt to politicise intelligence is important, however. It is a common misconception to think of intelligence agencies as being apolitical. They are clearly not, because they seek to both protect and advance the state and its interests, both of which represent identifiable forms of political choice, with political, social and economic consequences. In the UK, and as Crown Servants, intelligence officers and the agencies they work for have their remits established by statute and are required to act impartially within the limits established by these statutes. So, for example, the protection of parliamentary democracy is a non-negotiable aspect of the role of British intelligence agencies, and there were developments—around proroguing parliament—during the Brexit farrago that should have exercised the minds of Crown Servants (Schleiter & Fleming, 2020; White, 2019). In acting impartially towards political parties, intelligence officers will occasionally cause friction. The stories around Harold Wilson's suspicions and Peter Mandelson and Jack Straw seeking access to their MI5 records are examples of such moments (Moran, 2014).

But the defence of parliamentary democracy and the political culture that comes with such a system is *political,* just not party political. This small, but crucial semantic is where the confusion arises in the minds of many. Intelligence agencies are not disinterested and unbiased arbiters: they are political actors in their own right. They create and defend narratives that align to the maintained existence of their state and the states' interests. When Peter Hennessy so correctly described them as the hidden wiring of the state, he could have extended this line to include that they are key to securing the underpinning rationale and framing logics of our ways of life: out-competing external and domestic adversaries has a fundamental impact on the physical and information battlespace. So, the attempt to politicise the business of intelligence by holding the agencies as an exemplar of forces reined against the public, or by trying to use the agencies for partisan purposes, is to foreground intelligence work in a way that is unhelpful to those carrying on sensitive and nearly always secret work and it damages the hidden wiring of our political, social and economic system. The disruptors should be careful what they wish for.

Part of the role and function of the intelligence community—as briefly noted above—is to scan the horizon for threats and to make sense of our domestic and the international political, economic and social system. This is complicated by the recent and continuous breaches of the conventions that have governed political behaviour, where even some key establishment players have set upon courses where breaking the rules (or stretching them to their very breaking point) is a key element of their modus operandi (Davis, 2021). That is not to say that our politicians have never lied or obscured awkward truths: it is that the contemporary hybrid media system has provided a seductive incentivisation for our politicians to tell the *truths* that they would like heard, whether or not they are supported by empirical evidence. In this context, this recent political disruption has been powerful because it has matched advanced computer-driven analytical capabilities with algorithmically driven online advertising on near ubiquitous social media platforms, against populations ill-equipped to assess the information they are receiving, regulated by legislative frameworks and judicial practices that are ill-equipped to deal with the consequences.

The great political disruptors of our time—characters like Donald Trump and Steve Bannon in the US, Luigi Di Maio and Matteo Salvini in Italy, Viktor Orban in Hungary, Nigel Farage, Jeremy Corbyn, Boris Johnson and Dominic Cummings in the UK[1]—and those who have worked to support them, have been astute operators, managing to harness myths, long-standing grievances and technology to disrupt the relatively comfortable and settled politics of the post-WW2 era. A good number of these characters have been accused of rule breaking, and some of them are still dealing with parliamentary and judicial inquiries into this alleged conduct. Where some have been found against, the consequences have been so light as to constitute a transaction cost at worst, or an incentive to repeat the activities. Most importantly, perhaps, these disruptive politicians (the majority of whom are anti-system politicians) have been electorally successful, and consequently are able to set the tone for our political debate.

There is a need to make a security-based assessment of this new politics, and in parallel to question the widespread—and almost unchallenged—view that disruptive consumer technologies have had positive results for society and our economics. We should also challenge the view that those tech-industry disruptors who have used technology to change society are at the cutting edge of modernisation, representing a vanguard of a new industrial revolution. These forms of disruption have not necessarily resulted in better results for business (in the round) as they have concentrated capital, and therefore influence, into a smaller group of business leaders and finance groups (Anderson & Rainie, 2021). These technology disruptors have also yielded little more than the shortest-term benefits to technologists and investors, rather than securing enduring value for consumers (Muller, 2020; Si & Chen, 2020): the 'tear-down' (as they term it) of existing industries will have long-lasting repercussions for the fabric of society and for the economic basis upon which our societies are currently founded (Williamson *et al.*, 2020).

In the political and security realm the rapid development of networked and always-on technology and information becomes positively dangerous because of what it implies about discourse, identity and security. We have already seen in both the US and the UK that as the public increasingly come to depend on online news aggregators and social media as their principal news outlets, the algorithmic curation of news for individuals means that what one person sees is radically different to what a second person sees, helping to cause a polarisation on emotive issues (Beam, Hutchens

& Hmielowski, 2016). The impact of these automated and curated news feeds is to try to appeal to the reader, to encourage them to continue viewing, and so the algorithms attempt to feed ever more confirmatory information. It is very easy to see how individuals who are fed a steady diet of confirmatory information end up concluding that their views are the only rational ones that can be held. Why wouldn't they? Given that both sides of the major issues of our time are fed different but confirmatory information that ends up creating totalising viewpoints (on issues such as Brexit, Covid vaccines and the attempts to impeach President Trump), this will—barring unforeseen interventions—result in some level of political violence.

The electoral systems of the West are entirely unsuited to this level of polarisation, as they condense issue salience across the full gamut of policies into one blunt mark upon a ballot sheet every four or five years. These electoral systems also seem unsuited to dealing with the challenge of people who have sought to reshape, remake and bend and break conventions and rules in the search for power (and have done so). In the case of the UK, in December 2019 the people delivered decisively in favour of Boris Johnson's brand of right-wing and softly nationalist populism over Jeremy Corbyn's brand of left-wing populism, at least breaking the deadlock that had existed over British politics since 2016. These disrupters have been described as a new generation of Maoists. They have come to their political activism mostly with a brand of free-market economics, and a socially conservative underpinning that would set them apart from authentic Maoist predecessors. For most of these political disruptors, the disruption in and of itself—aside from their personal elevation— is the end that they seek. They want to break the settled order, and all are—in their own ways—against the forms of globalisation that have heralded economic gains and political stability since the Second World War.

If this chapter makes a small contribution to the burgeoning study of populism or anti-system politics, then it adds to that literature in being able to expand and highlight the security impacts of this disruption and the role of what disruptors often pejoratively describe as 'the deep state' in the development of, participation in, and push-back against populist politics (Dover, 2022).

Intelligence and Transnational, Populist Politics

As noted above, the technology-led disruptions to North American and European political systems can be traced to moments where a significant number of political and media participants chose to step outside the established 'rules of the game' (Davis, 2021). The notion of there being established rules of the game is itself contested, because populists often contend that not only are they working within certain rules, but also, they argue, they are the only remaining defence. The caveat they employ is that in the course of serving the popular will—a will that only they represent—this demands that they sometimes circumvent the rules or processes they see as acting as a barrier. In the case of a small clique of President Trump's supporters on 6 January 2021, this included violence against the legislature. There has been a degree of soul searching and relativism for commentators, who have also polarised between those declaring anti-system politicians as necessary correctives to our politics and those declaring the end of politics as we know it.

The critiques made about President George W. Bush and Prime Minister Tony Blair during their respective periods in office were as equally scathing as the ones endured by President Trump and Prime Minister Johnson: on the posters of protestors Blair is still referred to, somewhat harshly, as 'Bliar' (*sic*). Casting back forty years, President Reagan and Prime Minister Thatcher were also accused of ripping up politics as we knew it. These four prominent leaders can be said to have reshaped politics, and to have done so with both controversy and friction within their parties and on national and international scales: Reagan and Thatcher effectively broke the trade unions, placed the individual and choice at the heart of politics and society, and mainstreamed neoliberal economics. Bush and Blair were responsible for the era of muscular liberalism, enhanced measures in the global war on terror and modified evidence and truths in pursuit of that war.

Although accused of having broken established conventions and domestic and international law, both Bush and Blair have been scathing about the conduct of President Trump, and Blair has used his experience to highlight where the 'Vote Leave' campaign and the Conservative government broke electoral and parliamentary conventions in the Brexit debate. Interestingly, Thatcher, Blair and Bush were all also accused of having politicised their intelligence agencies (Coletta, 2018). In Thatcher's case this involved fighting unionisation in GCHQ, and engaging intelligence officers in muscular defences against anti-nuclear campaigners, and in fighting the mining unions: the latter of which were said to have taken financial support from hostile third countries. In Bush and Blair's respective cases, politicisation was noticeably seen through the preparation of the case for war against Iraq in 2003, and in the prosecution of physical counterterrorism campaigns following 2003, which included kidnapping and torture.

Whether Bush and Blair's condemnation of Trump will ultimately be seen to be hypocritical or evidence of changes to political practice will be the subject of a considerable number of future debates. There is sufficient evidence, however, to suggest that there have been many breaches of established political conventions, matched to a highly sophisticated understanding of how the hybrid media environment operates and the role that data analytics and targeting can play within that system. It seems self-evident that there has been a shift in political culture, and the creation of a new political grammar that is associated with insularity and populism. For the voting public, this disruption has allowed it full access to their more basic instincts, instincts that had been constrained by a mesh of norms and laws around acceptability of language and views from the late 1960s to the present day. The public has been told over the last decade, but particularly since 2015, that any ill-founded opinion has the worth, weight and value of validated evidence and fully thought through assessments: if the public believes something to be true, it is (Foster & Feldman, 2021).

The public has been further sold the line that bad policy outcomes only happen if there is a failure of collective belief, rather than that these bad outcomes might be the most likely consequences of poor policy choices. Even worse, and harking back to the populist extremism of the 1930s, populists have adopted the line that bad policy outcomes might also be generated by bad actors 'over there' working against the collective will, reviving divisive and dangerous 'them' and 'us' narratives. The bad actors in populist rhetoric are often acting to undermine the state, they are enriching themselves in the process of doing so, and are seeking—in a sense—to enslave the state. This is somewhat ironic in the British context of the pandemic, where party donors and supporters have been conspicuous recipients of lucrative protective equipment contracts. For some senior British politicians, such the MP Jacob Rees-Mogg and the former MEPs Nigel Farage and Ann Widdecombe, leaving the EU was akin to being a slave liberated from a slave owner, or akin to Eastern Europe being liberated from the vassalage of the Soviet Union: two sentiments that could be seen as insensitive due to incomparability of the lived experiences of actual slaves and that the then European Council President Donald Tusk had actually fought for genuine liberation, in fear of his life, from the Soviet state during the 1980s (Tusk, 2005). Such narratives have persisted into the second year of the pandemic, with mask wearing also being likened to slavery by some politicians, which also showed a scant understanding of the lived experiences of slaves (Clulow, 2021).

For intelligence agencies, who are empowered to protect the democratic functioning of the state and to protect key infrastructure against the actions of hostile powers, the challenge presented by populists and anti-system politicians has been complex. The challenges have come from inside the state but are accused of being assisted and funded by hostile powers (a clear concern for counterintelligence and organised crime directorates). Those who have been investigated are very close to, or deeply embedded within, the political establishment and the referenda and elections that are punctuation points have changed the strategic direction of the states involved. If such influence was ever proven would it be better to nullify a tainted election or to manage its consequences, to work to avoid a recurrence and maintain the perceived sanctity of electoral politics? Whilst intelligence agencies have been highly resistant to the effects of politicisation, certainly since the damaging and publicly aired claims around the approach to the Iraq War in 2003, they have had a measure of control through managing the pacing of investigations. The slow pace at which the combination of the UK Electoral Commission, the Metropolitan Police Service and the National Crime Agency moved in relation to the alleged irregularities around the EU Referendum in 2016 resulted in three years of speculation before decisions were eventually made to not recommend prosecution on a number of charges (Cadwalladr, 2018; National Crime Agency, 2019).

The political disruption of anti-system politicians (and the machinery they have created) is driven by those with essentially Maoist tendencies, in the sense of wanting to rip down established institutions and ways of doing things. This Maoist meme—in the early days of the Conservative–Liberal Democrat coalition—even prompted the usually sober *Financial Times* to assess new Conservative policy initiatives on a Mao-meter (*Financial Times*, 2010). These rather jolly connotations were soon replaced with a more sombre tone as the extent to which Conservative ministers were determined to radically overhaul the size of the state (through many years' worth of severe austerity measures) became clear. Such a rolling back of the state was later connected to other developments in British politics, which saw the stretching of norms and conventions to breaking point, including the unlawful prorogation of parliament in 2019. These contemporary neo-Maoists believe in breaking down established political and social orders to create a chaos that will then see the strongest innovate and flourish. They believe the societal and political order will correct itself when faced with existential crisis. This ideology of disruption has a close relationship with technological disruption, of society-changing innovations in communication, travel and data collection. This ideology is closely related to the radical libertarian spirit that fuelled the emergence of the dot. com era in technology and these technologists find themselves in unhappy concert with those forcefully pushing largely illiberal political disruption. The disruptive technologists have had the vision of a form of participant capitalism, of sharing, of looser ties and social liberalism but in which—paradoxically—they have become kleptocrats. The political disruptors they have become entwined with have sought a variety of conservative outcomes from their projects, but all premised upon the most radical of transformations. The point at which intelligence officers—with their duty to uphold existing systems of parliamentary democracy—might feel moved to reflect and act is not clear, but the prorogation of the UK Parliament in 2019 and the storming of the US Congress in 2021 should have piqued the interest of those employed to protect the respective constitutions.

For anti-system politicians, those who are expert and those who maintain the status quo order are enemies of these changes because they actively work to avoid the chaos that the neo-Maoists believe will be the rescue of the nation state. This places government intelligence agencies and officers directly in their firing line, because they see the established order as one of managed decline. The anti-system movement aims to break free of this historical inevitability and to reassert a late nineteenth or early twentieth-century order on the world: one that does not constrain state activity, a key ill they have identified of the so-called liberal world order. The neat psychological trope here is that this is an existential fight, and so intelligence agencies are faced with the invidious situation of being made both partial and political by anti-system activists.

Modern political disruptors do not come from a unified or classic political perspective. They are neither resolutely neoliberal nor socialist, and it is partly the breaking of these traditional groupings that wrong-footed political opponents. The unifying characteristics of these disruptors across Europe and North America are:

(1) the existing system is broken;
(2) the existing system will see 'us' continue to lose influence and power in the global system;
(3) there is an identifiable cause of the dysfunction in the system, and this can be labelled as the establishment in various forms and outsiders who are undermining the nation;
(4) those establishment interests (be they political, media, academic, economic) and outsiders, who represent the cause of the dysfunction, should be subject to an immune system response from the new political order;
(5) nearly all means justify these ends;
(6) only a 'strong' government can return the nation back to the position it should have always been in.

The economic logic underpinning this vision is multi-fold. There are many neoliberal populists but also public-ownership populists.

Much as with the 'pragmatic' alliances with foreign powers, these classic working class and monied groupings with diametrically opposed economic models seem unprepared for the moment when they need to resolve their points of difference around rival economic visions. Such moments will be starker in the European countries, where there is a mixed history of economic models. The clash between 'hard'-Brexit supporting Labour cleavages, who favour public ownership and increased worker involvement in the economy, versus the 'hard'-Brexit supporting Conservative and UKIP right, who wanted a radical rewriting and thinning of labour and regulatory frameworks, are still working their way through the British political conscience. It is not yet clear how this contest will be resolved: the COVID-19 pandemic and the war in Ukraine have provided a great number of distractions and distortions that have prevented a clear line of sight onto the impacts of Brexit, despite some signals indicating the negative economic consequences and the problems in travelling across the EU with new passport rules in force. In the US there is a far more settled economic vision and so, whilst rhetorically stark positions are taken, a form of neoliberal economics essentially prevails unchallenged, albeit with different and contrasting emphases on how internationally connected economies should be.

For disrupters of the left and right there is an unresolvable tension when it comes to public finances. The neoliberal manifesto of radical corporate and personal tax cuts, of deregulation and diminution of the rights of workers, reduces the money available to central and local government for public goods, including those working for intelligence and law enforcement agencies. The neoliberal agenda has sought to reduce the role of government in the economic sphere whilst missing that there are some essential public goods that are necessary preconditions for trade to flourish. Core infrastructure such as roads and rail are two such examples, whilst the development of high-end defence and security technology is necessarily risky (in terms of the technology coming to fruition) and thus the reality is that it is only the state that can reasonably step in to underwrite these risks. The neoliberal right has no coherent answer to the problem of public goods, and the mechanisms it prefers for delivering these have been found to be considerably more expensive, inefficient or ineffective over time. This anti-system right, including Boris Johnson, has uneasily reconciled this tension by flooding ailing areas of economic life—spurred by the COVID-19 pandemic—with public money (Sawyer, 2021). The general reduction in the size of the state has included a reduction in law enforcement capability, which in turn has seen rises in offences against property and the person. This reduction in the size of the state has also impacted upon the work of the intelligence community, who are in part reliant upon law enforcement partners for some aspects of the counterterrorism and counter-radicalisation brief. The 2020 *Integrated Review of Security*, saw the UK's National Crime Agency, the nation's foremost intelligence-led law enforcement agency, fare very poorly in the new redistribution of security monies, with the key increases being seen in high-end cyber capabilities instead (Sweeney & Winn, 2021).

The British newspapers, and local social media feeds, are full of stories of car theft facilitated by the sophisticated interception of key-less entry device signals, or the burglary (whilst residents are asleep) of car keys, but often with no response from law enforcement agencies beyond noting a crime number that can be used for a car insurance claim. Similarly, cyber-crime (such as credit card fraud or the use of stolen identities to secure consumer credit), which is connected to terrorist logistic lines, and the funding of rogue states like North Korea, has grown exponentially but yet is often reported as a 'hidden crime' epidemic, particularly when the response of law enforcement has been largely to ignore it (Morgan-Bentley, 2021). These issues, which straddle the law enforcement and intelligence divide, have been strongly affected by the parallel developments of international criminals becoming more active in the UK and the cuts to policing numbers. These developments, along with significant advances to so-called 'deep-fake' technologies (the ability to make it appear that a person has said things that they have not), constitute a technological disruption arms race where the adversaries are a complex mix of public and private actors. The means by which to identify and counter these threats are—themselves—ever more expensive and complex, signalling a strong parallel with the Cold War arms race.

The Challenge of Globalisation

A challenge for intelligence services in the twenty-first century is how to deal with the consequences of globalisation. At a conference in Pisa in 2007, Richard Aldrich remarked (and probably does not thank me for remembering this) that 'intelligence agencies are the toilet cleaners of globalisation'. I interpreted his comments as meaning that intelligence agencies have been responsible for securing domestic economic interests abroad: for example, providing warning notice and protection for assets in volatile African and Middle Eastern locations. They have also performed counterintelligence and assurance services to protect intelligence property at home, and to guard against attacks on core national infrastructure that would have large economic impacts (Aldrich & Cormac, 2021; Stephens & Phillips, 2021). As I note elsewhere in this book, the concept of policing with consent applies as much to the intelligence services as it does to law enforcement agencies. There should be concern about the negative impact of alienation—and I mean the plain English understanding of the term, rather than the Marxist critique—of the working class from many layers of society that has caused wholesale political shifts on both sides of the Atlantic since 2008 (Øversveen, 2021). Being able to identify and understand these shifts is essential to the conservative role of state preservation that is core to the defensive proposition for intelligence: it provides insights into the motivations of adversaries and how to divide the hardcore from those who are participating but persuadable. In this respect, the contest between intelligence agencies and adversaries feels akin to some of the dynamics present in counterinsurgency, where it becomes an issue of undermining the morale of the adversary through disruption and making it harder to fight.

The societal alienation and dislocation is felt by the public day-to-day; it is felt locally and it is the lived experience of much of society (Harvey, 2012). This alienation is informed by communities of interest, by legacy and social media narratives, and it is premised upon observable unfairnesses (be they real or imagined moments of unfairness such as elites being unpunished for allegedly breaking the law, or in receiving contracts without proper process)

(Saddique, 2022). The core of the issue is not that the UK, much of the EU and the US have been unable to create wealth—they have done so with remarkable success—but more particularly that they have been unable to distribute that wealth in a way that maintained a social balance. The imbalances present in the system have led to the working class in the UK and the US voting against their core economic interests, partly because (unlike the liberal elite, I am undoubtedly also a part of) they do not see that their position could be made worse by their political choices: thus voting for Trump or Brexit was an acceptable risk for them to take (Mckenzie, 2017). For American agencies this choice immediately resulted in a dislocation with their Commander in Chief. Not only did he not want to read the Presidential Daily Brief, but he continuously suggested that they—and the 'deep state'—were working against him (Pfiffner, 2021). In the UK, the Brexit vote put at risk access to useful tools such as the European Arrest Warrant and the SIS II information system, which the UK was then accused of illegally copying prior to leaving the EU in January 2020.

There is a strong disconnect between the lived experiences of the citizen and how elites have shaped various economic and political debates: as with the debates around economics and redistribution, a significant percentage of the population experience these issues in a radically different way to the way they are told they should experience them, or the way that they are told they have experienced them. This disconnection has resulted—in time—in a significant fracture between those governing and the governed, placing a continued strain on the ability of the intelligence community to operate with the consent of their publics. On this issue, the impact of social media and the evolution of the news media publishing opinion as news has contributed to forms of collective action amongst 'ordinary folk' that we would have previously only expected from the far right. Mainstream populist movements, and then major parties responding to the shift in the centre ground of politics towards anti-immigration sentiment, have been 'from the ground up' movements in their formation and operation. In countries where the electoral system works against smaller parties, they (populist politicians) have been very successful in capturing the narrative, if not the electoral advantage (Dennison & Geddes, 2019). Some of their publicly held views are very close to the definition of subversion used by intelligence officers: itself a problem when these views become part of the mainstream.

The hollowing out of the state in providing services to place the population on a basic, but level platform has impacted upon the working and middle classes more significantly, and it is these people who feel they are the losers from globalisation (Teney, Lacewell & De Wilde, 2014). The evidence for whether they are objectively the losers from globalisation is not as clear cut. At the localised level it is possible to see why people feel that they are worse off. The traditional industrial jobs that were enjoyed by their parents and grandparents no longer exist, or exist sparsely; the public and social goods that were assumed during the 1970s, 1980s and 1990s, and which were engines of social change, such a public libraries, now barely exist; the local hospital no longer exists, and it is a struggle to secure timely appointments with medical doctors; and so not only do these people feel they are the losers of globalisation but we can provide tangible evidence of how that loss has occurred. The role of the intelligence agencies as a bulwark of defence for agents of globalisation—be it disarming anti-globalisation protests, or assuring protection for economic interests, even when those companies are not British, has placed the agencies on the wrong side of a growing cleavage of disaffected citizens alienated from this era of globalisation. That should be of concern to the agencies: the greater the disconnection the starker the resistance to their activities will be.

Government agencies have found themselves on the wrong side of another facet of political disruption, which has focused, in part, upon the notion of native vs 'alien' identities. Public policy issues such as immigration and integration have been weaponized by theocratic radicals, and also those of the far right and far left (Rubin, 2021). The response of governments in the 2000s—to tell the concerned public that they were being racist or ignorant—exacerbated, rather than ameliorated, these societal tensions, providing a vacuum for political disruptors to move into. One of the challenges for these disruptors is that some of them have wealthy foreign backers whose interests do not align with the UK. Some of these patrons are considered by the intelligence community to be actively hostile to the UK. The connection between these people of concern and political paymasters in government makes it more difficult for intelligence officers to investigate malfeasance in the political system. Similarly, the divestment—for example, from expertise in Russian government and security, as evidenced by the closure of the eminent internal research unit known as the Conflict Studies Research Centre, left the UK particularly vulnerable to the migration of security issues from the eastern bloc that occurred in the 1990s and 2000s (UK MoD, 2021). Former counterintelligence officers often vividly describe how they were overwhelmed by the influx of politically charged dissidents and foreign security officials and, whilst they baulk at this suggestion, it is clear to me that London has become a site for foreign political contests to be played out: be they between Russians, Saudis, Pakistanis or Bulgarians (Cheskin & Kachuyevski, 2019). The lack of control over these sometimes violent contests has done nothing to improve the reputation of our intelligence agencies in the eyes of a public, who at once marvel and recoil from the conspicuous wealth and lawless violence of these ex-patriots on British soil.

Despite the localised nature of identity politics, a similarly challenging dynamic has come from the surprising and paradoxical transnationality of populist politics. Whilst the public face of these movements has been grounded in domestic politics, and the evocation of domestic political myths, the organisation of these movements has been both local and transnational. The political and media management techniques, the data analysis and finance these movements have used, have been transnational, with some of the data analytics occurring off-shore, and with nodes of influence that have notably sat in the United States but which have also been felt in Scandinavia, Germany and France (Shaw, 2016). Consequently, it should not be a surprise that intelligence agencies and these movements have experienced friction between them. The complex, international interdependencies of these movements have seen intended and unintended overlaps between individuals, organisations and techniques that have been seen as problematic in security terms from time to time. The movement of personally identifiable and sensitive data across jurisdictions for analysis, and action, is of interest to parts of the intelligence community in as much as it would be an interesting target for signals intelligence and for counterintelligence and countersubversion purposes. Foreign interference in domestic politics has occasionally cut across the sensitive networks of parallel diplomacy enjoyed by intelligence agencies, and disrupted their lines of communication as a result. The geographical bounding of intelligence activity—of where agencies seek to defend, always contested when national interests are naturally also found abroad—is increasingly tested by the way that a heavily interconnected political community transmits techniques, data and analysis across international boundaries.

Controlling the Venn Diagram of the Establishment

There is a more sensitive and problematic dimension to the relationship between populists and intelligence agencies, and that is the question of security vetting (which crops up at several points in this book) and the protection of sensitive materials. Those reaching high office across all developed democracies become privy to the secrets collected by their own states, as well as sensitive information about allied and adversary states and information shared by allied and elements within adversary states. Part of the impact of any charges brought against high-ranking intelligence officials working within the Five Eyes nations (Australia, Canada, New Zealand, the United Kingdom and the United States) is that any unauthorised release of information might also include that of an allied nation, as it had done in the cases of Kim Philby, Guy Burgess, Donald Maclean, Anthony Blunt and John Cairncross (the Cambridge Five), and across the Atlantic in the case of Aldrich Ames. Information security has been rendered more complex because of the technologies involved, not because the business of information has fundamentally changed: the amount that can be stored on a drive no bigger than a finger nail would have required a van in the 1960s to physically move it. In absolute terms, the imperative to secrecy is strong within developed democracies, in part because intelligence product provides competitive advantage, but also because the unauthorised release of materials can jeopardise collection techniques, and because human sources are peculiarly vulnerable to unauthorised disclosures. In a persuasive piece of research Richard Aldrich and Chris Moran describe secrecy in the modern era as being akin to delayed disclosure, and the extent to which citizen journalism and strategic leaks by competitor agencies erode our traditional conception of state secrecy weighs heavily on intelligence agencies (Aldrich & Moran, 2018).

The erosion of investigative journalism has been connected to formal divestment from investigative journalists and towards opinion-based reporting. The cynical management of information in the run up to the 2003 Iraq War, which also helped to sour the British and American public's view of 'experts' in providing critical information, and which was further compounded by the financial crash of 2008, was an important antecedent. This mistrust of expertise (a sign of a preference for value or belief-based knowledge) has combined with the relative distance of ruling elites from the ruled, something that disrupters have catalysed in their campaigning.

The debate around personal security vetting and our politicians is a difficult one. The received and accepted perception is that intelligence agencies are accountable to elected officials, and, therefore, the public's choice of elected officials overrides the security imperative. This is only partly true. In the UK, intelligence agencies are accountable to the relevant secretary of state: MI5 to the Home Secretary, MI6 and GCHQ to the Foreign Secretary, although neither is a constituent part of the Foreign, Commonwealth & Development Office. In terms of parliamentary oversight, the intelligence agencies report to the parliamentary committee (which is distinct from a select committee), which is appointed by the prime minister directly, and all of whom are subjected to security vetting before appointment. This committee is able to view classified documents but not to publish them. Similarly, their reports are subject to prime ministerial approval, something that became highly controversial when their report into Russian interference in the British electoral process did not receive written assent from Prime Minister Johnson before the December 2019 general election, giving rise to strong speculation that it contained awkward revelations about Russian financing in British politics (Sabbagh & Harding, 2019).

That the agencies, the parliamentarians on the ISC and the report itself are all dependent upon Number 10, highlights the potential vulnerabilities of a political system governed by convention rather than, as compared to the US, by a system where the constitutional rules are clearly drawn out.

In a similar way, membership of the Privy Council—which is a committee of senior parliamentarians who become 'Right Honourable' when elevated to the council, and which advises the monarch on the discharge of her prerogative powers—is privy to highly sensitive information, including intelligence assessments, and is again subject to security vetting. The oath that Privy Counsellors take on joining the council makes clear why this is the case, as was disclosed in a written answer in parliament in 1998 (my emphasis in bold):

> *You do swear by Almighty God to be a true and faithful Servant unto the Queen's Majesty, as one of Her Majesty's Privy Council. You will not know or understand of any manner of thing to be attempted, done, or spoken against Her Majesty's Person, Honour, Crown, or Dignity Royal, but you will let and withstand the same to the uttermost of your Power, and either cause it to be revealed to Her Majesty Herself, or to such of Her Privy Council as shall advertise Her Majesty of the same. You will, in all things to be moved, treated, and debated in Council, faithfully and truly declare your Mind and Opinion, according to your Heart and Conscience; and will keep secret all Matters committed and revealed unto you, or that shall be treated of secretly in Council. And if any of the said Treaties or Counsels shall touch any of the Counsellors, you will not reveal it unto him, but will keep the same until such time as, by the Consent of Her Majesty, or of the Council, Publication shall be made thereof.* **You will to your uttermost bear Faith and Allegiance unto the Queen's Majesty; and will assist and defend all Jurisdictions, Pre-eminences, and Authorities, granted to Her Majesty, and annexed to the Crown by Acts of Parliament, or otherwise, against all Foreign Princes, Persons, Prelates, States, or Potentates. And generally, in all things you will do as a faithful and true Servant ought to do to Her Majesty.** *So, help you God.* (Beckett, 1998)

The possibility, therefore, of senior politicians attaining high office, who are vulnerable to the attentions of foreign powers or who have improper relationships with foreign powers, would place at risk intelligence secrets and foreign relations. We need only cast back to the accusations about Labour Prime Minister Harold Wilson— who was accused of being a KGB asset by the high-profile and well placed defector Anatoli Golitsyn and who became convinced that his offices at Number 10 Downing Street had been bugged by the security services—to see the negative impact of suggestions of high-level compromise. Wilson's suspicions were given credibility by ex-MI5 officer Peter Wright's highly controversial book *Spycatcher*, which details the alleged plot against Wilson, but which has also been refuted by an internal MI5 inquiry and a later government inquiry into the impartiality of the intelligence community towards Wilson (Wright, 1987). More recently, Jeremy Corbyn, the leader of the opposition (2015–20), has been perennially accused by the more right-wing press of being a security threat and having been in some way allied to foreign powers in the past (Day, Dixon & Sawyer, 2018). Against decades of precedent, Corbyn was denied a briefing on the US assassination of Iranian General Soleimani in January 2020, which he had sought on Privy Council terms (which denote that it has been given confidentially and with access to government intelligence product). The denial of this briefing gave rise to suspicions that Corbyn's historical connections to some controversial Middle Eastern groups, some of which Soleimani had been responsible for funding, had been the cause of this breach of precedent (Peston, 2020).

A Shifting International Order

Populist movements have cast the international liberal order, established in the wake of the Second World War, as being antithetical to their purposes. This international order aimed to provide a mesh of interdependencies that rendered conflicts between developed states expensive and logistically impossible. The earliest days of the European Union, the European Coal and Steel Community was fundamentally contrived to prevent France and Germany going to war again (Calleo, 2009). NATO was formed to provide a cohesive security bloc to dissuade the Soviet Union from attempting to invade western Europe and to tie the United States into the ongoing future of Europe. Similarly, the Five Eyes intelligence sharing organisation was conceived, in part to reinforce the hegemony of the Anglosphere—the English-speaking nations—but also to ensure the global coverage of Western intelligence assets and knowledge. The creation of these influential international organisations brought with it a broadly agreed set of political beliefs, which took hold— albeit with some resistance along the way, notably during '1968' and at flash points during the 1970s, 1980s and early 1990s—and formed what is widely considered to be a form of universalised beliefs (Fukuyama, 1992). Fukuyama's famous thesis attracted almost immediate criticism, whilst being more widely seen as representing something of the truth. Samuel Huntington wrote his essay-length and then book-length clash of civilisation pieces as direct responses to Fukuyama's *The End of History*; and others such as Benjamin Barber noted that those opposed to Western capitalist dominance were using the tools of capitalism to undermine it. The arguments made in Barber's *Jihad vs McWorld* are still relevant today as the attacks on Western democracies via so-called fake news, social media exploitation and cyber attacks are yet more evidence of the kinds of technological misappropriation Barber was discussing more than twenty years ago. Contemporary scholars like Patrick Porter have also questioned the extent to which an international order of this kind ever existed, and suggested that the evocation of the term is more symbolic than real. Whilst Porter's argument is persuasive, it remains—at the time of writing—still a relatively marginal view. I find it difficult to reconcile Porter's convincing argument with the strength of rhetoric from politicians and other interested parties advocating strongly for and against the presence of an international rules-based order. Similarly, the presence of a mainstream dialogue about the effectiveness and role of a rules-based order demonstrates that such an order exists in the imagination of international politics, and has real-world impacts upon it (Porter, 2018).

The presence of important intelligence partnerships and forums such as NATO and the Five Eyes group does provide some credence to the populist critique of there being a broadly international coalition (which is not quite as loaded a term as 'an order') that is seeking to maintain particular forms of politics and trade. Populists channel 'greed and grievance' politics. They make claims about who is taking a disproportionate share of the national wealth and how those identified as disadvantaged can wrest back control. Populist critiques meld identity politics, historical myths and partial reading of economic relationships to create a narrative around the international liberal order and neoliberal forms of globalisation. When former Prime Minister Theresa May evoked the idea of citizens of nowhere versus citizens of somewhere, she neatly summarised the gap between predominantly younger, university educated, metropolitan city dwellers and older, less educated, traditional town or northern city folk. Those feeling left behind by neoliberal economics moved from being marginalised anti-globalisation protestors (a small, vocal and consciously outsider group) in the early 2000s to 2010, to sufficient numbers of the population to see Boris Johnson elected to a majority government in 2019, via attempts by Prime Minister Tony Blair in his wealth distribution initiatives of Sure Start centres and Working Tax Credits and David Cameron's attempts to convince the public that 'we are all in it together' in his government's austerity measures. The public see little tangible and positive impact on their lives from these international organisations or these guiding political philosophies and so have sought to reject them. It is no surprise, then, that key actors in contemporary political disruption have campaigned against, and sought to undermine, the European Union, NATO and the United Nations.

Similarly, these disruptors—who, whilst establishment figures in the sense of having had successful business or media careers, also have a history of being rejected by the establishment—have been quick to 'pragmatically' accept the help of outsiders who also have an interest in undermining the cohesion of the post-industrial liberal order. For those accepting this help, questions remain about whether they see themselves as now beholden to these foreign patrons or advisors, or whether indeed they understand the implications of being potentially beholden to competitor nations. Irrespective of the truth of the claims, we can vividly imagine how difficult this could be for a political leader, if even a tenth of the accusations contained in the leaked Christopher Steele dossier around Russian interference in the 2016 US presidential election were proved to be accurate (Harding, 2017).

The security implications of these reported developments and accusations of foreign dependency can only be properly understood through counterintelligence logics. A key element of counterintelligence is assessing the vulnerability of the subject to blackmail or exploitation. For private individuals (including public figures), that vulnerability might centre upon the potential to fracture close personal relationships they enjoy, or their reputation. For high-ranking politicians, or those who might go on to be senior politicians, the vulnerability extends to providing continuing service and advantage to the state or organisations exploiting the vulnerability (be it directly or indirectly). The infamy of the Russian state's obsession with collecting compromising material (*kompromat*) on all figures of potential use, has been linked to idiosyncratic decisions made by some political figures. Given that representative democracy trumps security concerns, if the public place a compromised figure in a position of high responsibility, then that vulnerability will invariably persist until such time as that individual is no longer in office. Whether intelligence agencies can disrupt the career trajectory of an unknown or lightly known but compromised politician early in their career before they gain real traction or position will be a question of resource and inclination but also appropriateness. High office is vetted by party members and the electorate, and that position seems set to stay.

Conclusion: The Deep State? Or the Place of the Security State (and Security Industrial Complex) in Our Modern Politics

There is an interesting set of paradoxes in the contemporary narrative around security: paradoxes that highlight the contest between framing visions of the way the world works and the foundational logics underpinning these. Invasive security is good. Unless it is directed at 'us'. It is good when it is directed at 'them'. And 'they' would have nothing to fear if they were not doing anything wrong. Intelligence and policing levels should be reduced because they represent bad value for money, and they do not investigate the right things, but security vulnerabilities and crime are increasing because 'they are revolting' and that is intolerable. The core problems in these narratives centre on the questions of 'them' and 'us', and indeed on what underlying state activity is permissible. These are questions of individual judgment and taste, but also of collective identity.

Similarly, international collective security jars with contemporary political disrupters, whilst being the mainstay of our contemporary security, because it is part of the rules-based system that opposes them. But, equally paradoxically, most populist disruptors are very keen on national defence and security (of which no nation bar the Americans can truly afford). Reductions in the tax base and reduction in state involvement in private enterprise are also popular: something that has to underpin defence and security research due to the percentage chance of failure in very high-end technologies and the sheer size of the investment required.

The politicisation of security and surveillance comes through in the advanced uses of data analytics and data driven political marketing, but also in the constant prompting for investigations and prosecution of opponents. Security is—therefore—not subject to logically consistent narratives. There is also a set of constitutional questions around the positioning of intelligence and security actors guarding our democracies and our democratic institutions that are becoming more real than they have previously and which would be valuable to air. The disruption of our politics is as much about the hidden wiring of the state (the security and intelligence services) as it about conspiracies around the activities of the 'deep state', which is the pejorative term, a form of alienating coda for the same actors. The 'deep state' is a useful trope for suggesting frustration and resistance to the popular will. Populism, political fracture and the form of uneven transnationality we have seen in these new forms of politics, have placed considerable burdens upon intelligence agencies. In several cases, arguments can be made (and countered) that these burdens have forced intelligence officers and strategic level intelligence officials into, or very near to, the overtly political realm.

The debates around former FBI Director James Comey's actions in the 2016 presidential election are fierce and will only be resolved historically, beyond the lifetime of the participants. The same is true for the investigations into the 2016 EU Referendum in the UK, where despite the National Crime Agency determining there was no file to pass to the prosecutors, many of those supporting the 'remain' camp mutter darkly about malfeasance.

This proximity to overt politics does not help intelligence agencies maintain their position of being above mainstream party or issue politics: their political scope is the maintenance of this democratic system of representative government. This chapter has argued that this defence and maintenance of representative government is a political role because it makes key assumptions about optimum or desirable forms of governance and of particular and well established forms of political, social and economic choices that are reflected in the contest for ideas and ideologies that is waged between the Euro–Atlantic area and its competitors. In this sense, intelligence agencies are grappling with the challenge that comes from ongoing attempts to adapt to the radical changes to technology, adversaries and politics, and also from those who seek to disrupt the political certainty, which suggests a situation closer to unsettled steady state, rather than deep state.

References

Aldrich, R. J. and Cormac, R. (2021) 'From circumspection to centrality: Prime ministers and the growth of analysis, co-ordination, management in the UK intelligence community'. *Journal of Intelligence History* 20 (1), 7–24.

Aldrich, Richard and Moran, Christopher. (2018) 'Delayed disclosure: National security, whistle-blowers and the nature of secrecy'. *Political Studies* 67 (2), 91–306.

Anderson, J. and Rainie, L. (2021) 'Many tech experts say digital disruption will hurt democracy'. Washington, DC: Pew Research Center. Internet & Technology.

Atkinson, J. D., Ingman, K., Pierandozzi, J. P. J. and Stump, P. (2020) 'At the intersection of mainstream & alternative media: Spygate & the Hannity rant'. *Journal of Communication Inquiry* 45 (3), 1–18.

Beam, M. A., Hutchens, M. J. and Hmielowski, J. D. (2016) 'Clicking vs. sharing: The relationship between online news behaviors and political knowledge'. *Computers in Human Behavior* 59 (C), 215–220.

Beckett, Margaret (1998) 'Privy Counsellors'. *Hansard.* 28 July. Accessed 4 December 2019. https://publications.parliament.uk/pa/cm199798/cmhansrd/vo980728/text/80728w22.htm#80728w22.html_sbhd8

Cadwalladr, Carole (2018) 'Why Britain needs its own Mueller'. *New York Review of Books.* 16 November. Accessed 9 January 2020. https://www.nybooks.com/daily/2018/11/16/why-britain-needs-its-own-mueller/

Calleo, David (2009) *The German Problem Reconsidered: Germany and the World Order, 1870 to the Present.* Cambridge: Cambridge University Press.

Cheskin, A. and Kachuyevski, A. (2019) 'The Russian-speaking populations in the post-Soviet space: Language, politics and identity'. *Europe-Asia Studies* 71 (1), 1–23.

Clulow, A. (2021) *IHS Podcast–Episode 1: Faith in Science? COVID, Antivaxxers, the State, and Epistemological Power.* Not Even Past: IHS & Public History Collection. History Department, University of Texas at Austin, 25 August.

Coletta, G. (2018) 'Politicising intelligence: What went wrong with the UK and US assessments on Iraqi WMD in 2002'. *Journal of Intelligence History* 17 (1), 65–78.

Davis, A. (2021) *Reckless Opportunists: Elites at the End of the Establishment.* Manchester: Manchester University Press.

Day, Matthew, Dixon, Hayleynd and Sawyer, Patrick (2018) 'Jeremy Corbyn knew I was a spy and was a Cold War source, says Czech "diplomat"'. *The Daily Telegraph*, 16 February.

Dennison, J. and Geddes, A. (2019) 'A rising tide? The salience of immigration and the rise of anti-immigration political parties in Western Europe'. *The Political Quarterly* 90 (1), 107–116.

Dover, R. (2022) 'The deep state'. In R. Dover, H. Dylan and M. Goodman (eds), *A Research Agenda for Intelligence Studies* (pp. 148–157). London: Edward Elgar Publishing.

Eurobarometer Survey. (2018, February) Details to come at proof stage. February 2018.

———. (2018, October) Details to come at proof stage. October 2018.

Financial Times. (2010) 'How policies score on the FT's "Mao rating"'. *Financial Times*, 22 December.

Foster, R. and Feldman, M. (2021) 'From "Brexhaustion" to "Covidiots": The UK United Kingdom and the Populist Future'. *Journal of Contemporary European Research* 17 (2), 1–12.

Fukuyama, Francis (1992) *The End of History and the Last Man*. New York, NY: Free Press.

Harding, Luke (2017) *Collusion: How Russia Helped Trump Win the White House*. London: Faber & Faber.

Harvey, David (2012) *Rebel Cities: From the Right to the City to the Urban Revolution*. London: Verso.

Hellinger, D. C. (2019) 'Trumpism, fake news and the "new normal"'. In D. C. Hellinger, *Conspiracies and Conspiracy Theories in the Age of Trump* (pp. 79–103). Berlin: Springer.

Hopkin, Jonathan (2020) *Anti-System Politics: The Crisis of Market Liberalism in Rich Democracies*. Oxford: Oxford University Press.

Mckenzie, L. (2017) 'The class politics of prejudice: Brexit and the land of no-hope and glory'. *British Journal of Sociology* 68 (Supp. 1), 265–280.

Moran, J. (2014) 'Conspiracy and contemporary history: Revisiting MI5 and the Wilson plot [s]'. *Journal of Intelligence History* 113 (2), 61–175.

Morgan-Bentley, P. (2021) 'Action fraud scrapped after Times exposé'. *The Times*, 28 July. https://www.thetimes.co.uk/article/fraud-line-scrapped-after-times-expose-n2tlkbmrv

Muller, E. (2020) 'Delimiting disruption: Why Uber is disruptive, but Airbnb is not'. *International Journal of Research in Marketing* 37 (1), 43–55.

National Crime Agency (2019) 'Public statement on NCA investigation into suspected EU referendum offences'. National Crime Agency, 24 September. Accessed 9 January 2020. https://nationalcrimeagency.gov.uk/news/public-statement-on-nca-investigation-into-suspected-eu-referendum-offences

Øversveen, E. (2021) 'Capitalism and alienation: Towards a Marxist theory of alienation for the 21st century'. *European Journal of Social Theory* 1–18.

Peston, Robert (2020) 'PM's refusal to hold Privy Council briefing about US assassination of Qassem Soleimani raises questions over legality'. ITV News, 7 January. Accessed 10 January 2020. https://www.itv.com/news/2020-01-07/pm-s-refusal-to-hold-privy-council-briefing-about-us-assassination-of-qassem-soleimani-raises-questions-over-legality/

Pfiffner, J. P. (2021) 'Donald Trump and the norms of the presidency'. *Presidential Studies Quarterly* 51 (1), 96–124.

Porter, Patrick (2018) *A World Imagined: Nostalgia and Liberal Order*. CATO Intitute Policy Paper No. 843 [online], Washington: CATO.

Rubin, G. (2021) 'Flattening the radicalization curve: How to reduce host and migrant radicalization'. In G. Rubin, *Migration and Radicalization* (pp. 119–136). London: Palgrave Pivot.

Sabbagh, Dan, and Harding, Luke (2019) 'PM accused of cover-up over report on Russian meddling in UK politics'. *The Guardian*, 4 November.

Saddique, H. (2022) 'Use of 'VIP lane' to award Covid PPE contracts unlawful, high court rules'. *The Guardian*, 12 January.

Sawyer, M. (2021) 'Economic policies and the coronavirus crisis in the UK'. *Review of Political Economy* 33 (3), 414–431.

Schleiter, P. and Fleming, T. G. (2020) 'Parliamentary prorogation in comparative context'. *The Political Quarterly* 91 (3), 641–648.

Shaw, Tamsin (2016) 'The new military–industrial complex of big data psy-ops'. *New York Review of Books.* 21 March. Accessed 9 January 2020. https://www.nybooks.com/daily/2018/03/21/the-digital-military-industrial-complex/

Si, S. and Chen, H. (2020) 'A literature review of disruptive innovation: What it is, how it works and where it goes'. *Journal of Engineering and Technology Management* 56, 101568.

Stephens, M. and Phillips, C. (2021) *What Next for Britain in the Middle East?: Security, Trade and Foreign Policy After Brexit.* London: Bloomsbury.

Sweeney, S. and Winn, N. (2021) 'Do or die? The UK, the EU, and internal/external security cooperation after Brexit'. *European Political Science* 1–18.

Teney, C., Lacewell, O. P. and De Wilde, P. (2014) 'Winners and losers of globalization in Europe: Attitudes and ideologies'. *European Political Science Review* 6 (4), 575–595.

Tusk, Donald (2005) *Solidarnosc I duma.* Warsaw: Slowo.

UK MoD (2021) 'Conflict Studies Research Centre. UK Defence Academy'. 30 May. https://webarchive.nationalarchives.gov.uk/ukgwa/20080603101657/http%3A//www.da.mod.uk/colleges/csrc

White, J. (2019) 'Performative prorogation: What Johnson, Cummings and Co are trying to teach the public'. British Policy and Politics at LSE [Blog]. London: LSE.

Williamson, P. J., Wan, F., Eden, Y. and Linan, L. (2020) 'Is disruptive innovation in emerging economies different? Evidence from China'. *Journal of Engineering and Technology Management* 57, 1–15.

Wright, Peter (1987) *Spycatcher.* New York, NY: Viking Press.

2

CULTURE AND INTELLIGENCE
THE IMPORTANCE OF CULTURAL DIVERSITY IN THE WORK OF INTELLIGENCE AND SECURITY AGENCIES

What You Need to Know...

Culture is at the heart of understanding any conflict, from the interpersonal through to international conflicts. Questions of culture are vital to the interpretation of hostility and to mediating cultural cues. The ancient lessons from Sun Tzu are as well drawn now as they were at the time of his first telling. From the outside, Western intelligence agencies seem to be relatively underdeveloped when it comes to their understanding of outsider cultures and how to encounter them; and, indeed, underdeveloped when it comes to their own cultural diversity. There are strong structural limitations on agencies in terms of recruitment, organisational culture and the form and use of their products: even when trying to diversify, agencies are hamstrung by the cultural homogeneity that their recruitment processes lend themselves to. At the heart of the debate around intelligence cultures is the paradox of globalisation: information about all manner of cultures is readily available, but increased levels of insecurity have driven us to access this information in a way that prevents us from gaining deeper cultural understandings. Digital globalisation and the policing of alternative cultures has served to homogenise Western cultures and to embed Euro- and US-centric cultural dominance: the space for alternative cultures is both limited and framed in terms of threat and anxiety. The way that intelligence analysts learn, and filter, information is generating vulnerabilities for Western analysts, leaving them unable to filter for programmatic bias or deeper learning. This chapter suggests some public policy proposals to enlarge the intelligence estate and the number of intelligence tasks that are placed in organisation stovepipes, to facilitate a greater diversity of lightly cleared intelligence officers to work on open source tasks.

***

Intelligence agencies are organisations like any other. But these are organisations that happen to work on subjects that are widely recognised to be important for their potential impact upon life and limb, in guarding our political system, and protecting our core national infrastructure and interests. It is the subject matter that sets them apart from other organisations, but so does the way they gather and treat their material, and the way they disseminate their products. It is the process of intelligence that has historically led to the presence of monocultures, and the way in which the security imperative has led to reinforcing patterns of recruitment, in varying intensities across often highly distinct organisations. Such patterns serve to reinforce and embed political and ideational preferences and assumptions, so that what is perceived to be diverse—a head count of those from different genders, religions, ethnic backgrounds, socio-economic class—is actually just self-deluding and a more comfortable version of homogeneity. So, these two versions of diversity are important, and can be dealt with as separate lines of inquiry.

In his book, *Rebel Ideas,* Matthew Syed has provided a compelling discussion around the business of intelligence needs and his evidenced assessment that cultural diversity and cultural reflexivity will continue to help the intelligence community improve the way it identifies, contains and rolls back these threats. Syed argues that cultural blindness removes access to the full threat picture (Syed, 2019). Intelligence provides the setting for just one of Syed's case studies, and I argue that his general thesis is more effective for organisations outside the secret space, as I will explain throughout this chapter. The significant headwind against cultural dynamism in intelligence are the structural constraints of government intelligence: this sort of cultural blindness is sometimes an absolutely core part of intelligence analysis, national strategy and security vetting, which has placed significant additional constraints on the agencies' willingness or freedom to be culturally sensitive.

Diversity in Human Resource

Recruitment into intelligence agencies is no longer conducted by the famous 'tap on the shoulder', although anecdotally this remains a possible route into intelligence careers in order to capture niche skills and experiences (*The Daily Telegraph*, 2017). This shoulder-tapping method was ripe for replicating class, colour and cultural biases, because it is a well-established principle that recruiters consciously or unconsciously tend towards people they identify as being like them (Fernandez & Fernandez-Mateo, 2006; Fernandez, Castilla, & Moore, 2000; McPherson, Smith-Lovin, & Cook, 2001). The vulnerabilities of the social network or tap-on-the-shoulder method was part of the mix of blame for the Cambridge Five spy ring that undermined the UK–US intelligence relationship in the 1950s and 1960s, and which cost the lives of dozens of Western intelligence assets in the Soviet Union over that time (Pincher, 2014). Ironically, the 'tap on the shoulder' is now being used as a means to widen the cultural mix in intelligence, by targeting those with the appropriate skills to come and work for the intelligence agencies in salaried or voluntary roles. The expert volunteers have been described by Basham and Catignani in a military context as people engaging in 'serious leisure' (Catignani & Basham, 2020).

More generally, recruitment into intelligence careers occurs through open direct recruitment and by transfers in from cognate employment, such as law enforcement, the armed forces, technology providers, and so on. This open recruitment has placed process in between recruiters and candidates, and, along with a raft of mandatory courses, has provided for a partial rebalancing of cultural, racial and social profiles in the intelligence world. If intelligence agencies are to reflect the societies they serve, and this is key to any form of policing by consent, then clearly the gender, religious and racial mix needed to change. My argument is that responding to these identifiers as targets in and of themselves has not generated a cultural transformation. Focusing in on identifiable and measurable characteristics has seen aspirational goals set, to reach x or y percentage of any given characteristic, without necessarily improving the cultural diversity or range of perspectives in an intelligence setting. The utility of diversification is in the different angles on a particular subject it produces and the ability to understand and decode different cultural signals and inputs. Diversifying to meet targets is useful in being legally and ethically compliant, and also in being able to authentically note that agencies are broadly representative of society.

If we think back to the August 2011 riots that began in Tottenham in London and quickly generated copy-cat violence in other British cities, what advantage would there be between a middle-class white Russell Group graduate and a middle-class Asian Russell Group graduate in an analytical role? We might reason that the latter is likely to have had more experience of discrimination and therefore a greater facility to understand alienation, but neither is likely to have a ready access to the daily experience of poverty, gang activity and violence that coalesced so readily that summer (Tyler, 2013). So, we might want an intelligence officer who could operate in those environments without attracting undue attention, who was able to report back what he or she was seeing and hearing in a way that was translatable into the concepts used in the agency, coupled with an analyst with the skills to make an assessment of that intelligence that can be translated into action. Our intelligence officer would need to look right, sound right, and be able to adopt behaviours to blend in without arising undue suspicion. The same conundrum occurs repeatedly in the counterterrorism world, where the balance between the prohibition on communicating with adversaries and being able to converse authentically with potential Jihadists or Far Right activists is a pre-requisite to being able to identify, contain and roll back these threats. Such officers require the crucial skill of empathy—being able to understand where particular actions should be interpreted as hostile, or where hostile acts are actually symbolic rather than a trigger point for violence, albeit with controversies when applied in Iraq and Afghanistan (Forte, 2011). Our analyst wouldn't need to look or sound right for this context, but they would need to be able to place themselves in the shoes of the adversary, which is where pressures on the intelligence agencies brings us back to the need for cultural diversity, and beyond the niceties of the standard training packages on unconscious bias and cultural awareness.

These essentially cultural problems are also present in the disciplining of dissent and subversion. My research into the use of government intelligence in the arms trade revealed what I saw as a sub-genre of intelligence activity that seemed counter-intuitive to me (Dover, 2007). Whilst there were significant private and government intelligence efforts being made to counter anti-arms trade activists, what I could observe were nearly entirely law-abiding, non-violent, and nearly entirely ineffective peace campaigners who objected to the manufacture and sale of military equipment on ethical grounds. The investigative reporter turned academic Eveline Lubbers has done extensive research into these questions, and her work is to be commended (Lubbers, 2015). Very few engaged in direct action, and even this direct action was highly capable of being disregarded as a nuisance: even at the extreme of this, which could be seen at the Brighton-based site of the military equipment manufacturer EDO, where campaigners kept a constant and noisy vigil, the protests and police action had a performative quality to it. The activism around EDO—by a group calling itself Smash EDO—resulted in an injunction against the activists, a court case in which the Attorney General provided advice to the EDO counsel and which resulted in an out of court settlement and undertakings by the activists not to do certain things at the EDO factory site (EDO MBM Technology Ltd *v.* Campaign to Smash EDO, 2005).

Most anti-arms trade activists were people who should have been seen by manufacturers as more an irritation than a threat and yet there is really good evidence that significant surveillance efforts were made against these groups, including systematic online surveillance, the insertion of undercover officers and the covert collection of materials (Lubbers, 2012; Uldam, 2017). Against environmental campaigners, and the parents of the murdered London school boy Stephen Lawrence, far greater police intrusions were authorised and conducted and which are now subject to what is known as the Pitchford Inquiry (Evans & Lewis, 2013; Griffin, 2020). The missing cultural dimension in these examples is in the interpretation of these groups and their activities. Does the excitable rhetoric of a peace campaigner, talking of the evils of imperialism and evoking comradeship with fellow campaigners, indicate a fifth columnist with ambitions to undermine parliamentary democracy or someone using the lingua franca of these sorts of ethically driven communities? Why have law enforcement intelligence officers been unable to distinguish adequately between organised football violence (which presents a number of real and present threats, including links to far-right terrorism) and other types of activism, such as campaigning for racial equality in criminal justice (per the Stephen Lawrence campaign)? We might reasonably suspect this is down to a form of organisational culture that understands those campaigning in a way that might impinge on security and law enforcement intelligence as being a threat, and certainly not according with intelligence organisational cultures. Similarly, the notion of activism runs entirely contrary to the mindset required to work in government intelligence, and engagement with (or close proximity to) acts considered to be subversion, are excluding factors in security vetting (Scott, 2020). The GCHQ translator and then whistleblower Katharine Gun was only loosely activist in her disposition, but her morally driven outrage at reading a memorandum that made it clear that the US–UK coalition had been using electronic listening devices in the United Nations prior to votes on the then prospective Iraq War was enough to create an intelligence scandal, and awkward diplomacy for both the UK and the US with their international partners.

So, the notion of cultural plurality and the added value that might be driven by improving cultural difference within the intelligence community has to be tempered by the structural constraints that recruitment into the agencies provides. Psychometric testing and extensive background checks, aligned to the self-selection of candidates, results in a reduction in the diversity of candidates being employed by the agencies: there is no equivalent of the Dominic

Cummings' New Year 2020 call for 'misfits and weirdos' to join the agencies, for all good and historically grounded security reasons (Cummings, 2020). But whilst Cummings remains a politically controversial character in the UK, even after he left his post in Downing Street, the blogpost in which he advanced his 'misfits and weirdos' call was absolutely right in looking to seek alternative angles on classic problems of government, and sits in the traditions of people like Buckminster Fuller. On this, the British communications intelligence community is ahead of other industries, including academia, in recognising the added value of neurodiversity, and publicly campaigned on autism awareness (GCHQ, 2019; Williams, 2018).

Culture in the Mechanics of Intelligence

The difference between intelligence—as it is taught in universities—and intelligence practice is often stark, and we spend a good deal of time trying to accurately portray the business of intelligence to our students. Academic courses mostly teach the politics of intelligence, intelligence history, and some form of intelligence analysis, be it tactical or strategic. The politics of intelligence can contextualise intelligence activity in a wider international setting, intelligence history can focus upon historically noted successes or—more likely—historically noted failures and scandals. Intelligence analysis sits closest to academic practice, in the production of knowledge, with constraints. Consequently, academics tend to focus on the intelligence cycle (and its critics) as a convenient description of a set of discreet processes that start with a question from a government customer, moves round to collection, onto analysis, and then a final product is disseminated to the customer. It is a cycle because the customer invariably asks for further work and so the process continues to turn. In reality, the discrete elements of collection and analysis are often collapsed into each other, and the process is more a continuous conversation between the end recipient and the officer, who is both collector and analyst (Hulnick, 2006). This system exists because the increased number of threats and reductions in budgets mean that officers have larger caseloads; but it also means that the officer is a point of vulnerability and is responsible for validating the data they then use in their assessments. My fictitious culturally appropriate officer in the 2011 riots, matched to my equally fictitious empathetic analyst, provided some reassurance that culture did not matter as much as we might think it does in intelligence. Conflate the two roles into one and, suddenly, culture might be the most important determinant of whether the intelligence product that is disseminated to government is useful or useless.

But my fictionalised August 2011 example is a bit of a straw person, because it is based around events of just a few evenings, and therefore not emblematic of the reality of much intelligence work, which is ongoing, enduring and—crucially—comprised of intelligence data that flows in from multiple agencies, in multiple formats and often from multiple countries. And so, one of the largest cultural vulnerabilities to intelligence agencies is misunderstanding the multiple lines of information they are receiving, from all these individual actors and organisations. The inquiries into the 2003 Iraq War highlighted how American and British intelligence officers understood the words 'might', 'possible' and 'likely'. In their respective contexts 'might' meant unlikely to some, whilst quite likely to others. 'Likely' meant a fifty-fifty chance to some, whilst nearly certain to others. These differences in language have a similar impact as me walking into a Hull supermarket and trying to order in Danish. So, each British agency has its own institutional memory and culture. Each uses its own jargon, and terms of reference to create insider and outsider groups: again, something we would see in all businesses and organisations. The same is true in the United States. But, in a crisis, having to get over these cultural hurdles is a barrier to effectiveness: it might cost lives. The situation becomes more complicated and difficult to overcome if we add non-Anglophone targets or countries. For example, in my fictional crisis there is now a helpful input from the DGSE in France, the equivalent of MI6. Now, the barriers are linguistic, cultural and organisational, and producing a common understanding can be both mission critical and devilishly difficult for the analyst sat at their desk: it is more a question of judgment than of science.

The same, of course, applies to security challenges that require translation and a working knowledge of what the words mean in their cultural context. The US military attempted to overcome this problem in Afghanistan between 2007 and 2015 with a programme that employed 500 social scientists, including anthropologists, ethnographers and political scientists, which they called the Human Terrain System (Gonzalez, 2018). In this programme the academics were embedded in with frontline combat units to reduce uncertainty through more advanced understandings of social context and social relations (Medina, 2014). The programme was well funded and attracted a large number of participants, but it was also highly controversial, with the American Anthropological Association declaring in 2007 that it was unethical (American Anthropological Association Executive Board, 2007). There were also several notable incidents where the embedded academics discharged firearms, thus creating further complicating scenarios. The underpinning rationale for the programme was to improve the cultural reflexivity of the armed forces, and thus to help limit military activity. The Human Terrain System still involved an engagement that many felt was beyond the acceptable boundaries for academics, and there remained a suspicion that the effect of the programme was to make for smarter killing, not necessarily to reduce killing. There is a less vocal, but similar, critique made of non-governmental organisations and their ability to operate in the hazardous spaces in which intelligence officers cannot operate and the formal or informal intelligence they are able to pass on to government intelligence officers (DemMars, 2010). Any sense that NGOs are collecting intelligence places them at considerable reputational and physical risk in a conflict zone, again demonstrating the boundaries within which both intelligence agencies and outsiders operate, and the limitations faced by intelligence agencies in widening their cultural feeds.

In the counterterrorism sphere, attempts to use third-party organisations to engage in deradicalisation have similarly resulted in controversy and claims of organisations being government sock-puppets and similar. The labelling of these organisations in this way has almost always been unfair, and sometimes this labelling has been done to disrupt the activities of third-party or charitable organisations. This disruption has become far simpler to achieve in the era of plentiful digital connections and the reputational risks of social media (Baccarella *et al.*, 2018). A stark example of the effect of reputational damage can be seen in the aftermath of the sex exploitation allegations made against Oxfam staff in Haiti, where the charity saw a marked drop in donations and its public standing, principally due to the 'Twitter storm' that was generated against it (Dudman, 2019; Scurlock, Dolsak & Prakash, 2019). Willingness to engage with intelligence agencies is not straightforward, regardless of the perceived good that doing so might create.

Intelligence agencies have attempted to overcome their own domestic and international organisational–cultural barriers through extensive 'liaison relationships', which are bilateral relationships between intelligence agencies that might be closer than the official diplomatic relationship between nations. Agencies have also—domestically and internationally—constructed 'fusion centres', which are staffed by officers from across organisations and are often co-located in one building (Catano & Gauger, 2017; Monahan & Palmer, 2009). In the UK, the Joint Terrorism Analysis Centre (JTAC), which is best known for producing the official threat levels, draws together officers from MI5, MI6, GCHQ and the law enforcement community to break down institutional barriers and to create more efficient pathways to combat the threat from terrorism. International security organisations like INTERPOL, EUROPOL and NATO have created their own intelligence fusion centres to bring in analysts from across their international areas to work on thematically driven security problems, such as cybersecurity, terrorism and threats from specific regions of the world (Deni, 2015). These centres provide an opportunity to overcome linguistic and cultural barriers to intelligence, to draw upon different operational and life experiences and to adopt more inclusive analytical practices to work towards more effective assessments. Such initiatives are steps in the right direction and they do address some stark vulnerabilities but, much as my two fictional graduate intelligence officers in the August 2011 riots were much of a muchness because of their shared experiences, these fusion centres call upon a transnational community of security officers—they have more in common than they do in difference, because these communities train in similar ways, have similar value sets and belief systems, and all have a requirement to achieve security clearance, which serves to homogenise the officer class.

The Two Faces of Digital Globalisation

Digital globalisation has brought the world closer together but it has—paradoxically—created a greater number of hindrances to our understanding of foreign or alternative cultures. A failure to understand the cultures that agencies are operating with or against is a key reason for intelligence or strategic failure (Porter, 2009). In terms of the opportunities that digitisation has produced—for 15 pounds sterling, or around 20 US dollars, consumers can purchase a basic virtual reality (VR) headset (such as Google's Cardboard), insert their mobile telephone with the correct fee to acquire programmes, and can then virtually walk around parts of urban or rural China, wander around Greek monuments, or visit the streets of Nairobi. Consumers can be in these places without actually being. That is the promise and mostly delivered reality of VR.

Using Google's Street View service, I have pre-loaded routes for cycle and road running races I have competed in, and have been able to visualise them prior to undertaking them. And I have done the same for some global cities I have been interested in. In doing so I feel I get the flavour of those places to a better degree than if I had looked at a traditional overhead street map, or even at satellite imagery (again available via Google Maps). But the flavour one gets from these services can be compared to aspartame over sugar, or vegetarian burgers over meat products: it hints towards the real thing but never quite achieves it. The most astute area studies scholars I know are people who actually speak the native language, and who frequently travel to the country or region they study. Whilst machine translation and video calls allow a researcher or analyst to get a flavour of the target country, they do not provide the authentic feel or the necessary authentic cues that you get from being there, speaking to locals, using native shops and restaurants and so on. The difference in quality of assessed output from area studies scholars who are desk-based and from those who do not speak the native language, compared with that from those who both travel to those countries and who speak the native languages, is marked and there is a notable snobbery between those who do and do not travel. The second part of Patrick Porter's 'Military Orientalism' thesis pointed out that there were considerable dangers for analysts in becoming too preoccupied by the mystique of 'the other', which is just as beguiling and misleading as being culturally unaware (Porter, 2009). This is a well observed point, and obsessions about the centrality of Putin to any and all Russian activities, much as of the centrality of Erdogan to Turkey or Assad to Syria, is over-read in a way that would be unsustainable if we saw it run against the UK or US by researchers.

Digital globalisation has made acquiring information cheaper, quicker and more convenient. It has not made the acquisition of quality information simpler, because the effort required to filter data and to validate it is now more pronounced and problematic. The sheer quantity of data that is available to analysts means that there is a far greater presence of machine-based filtering and sorting, and as has been seen with the analysis done on Facebook and Google as mediators of information, the feed of information can be readily skewed in the attempt to generate a greater number of views (Kulshres *et al.*, 2019; Weidmann, 2016). Anecdotally, it is said that some international intelligence agencies have barred their analysts from seeking contextual information online, as a means to avoid the skewing of their views by search algorithms and—presumably—the possibility of being fed mis- or disinformation by adversaries. Such prohibition does not seem to be widespread, but a strong argument can be made for it, given the research suggesting systemic bias in search and automated news feeds currently.

Digital globalisation has also seen the cultural gap between societies close. The impact of US cultural icons and outputs on the rest of the globe was well drawn through the Cold War and its aftermath. The homogenisation of culture in the internet age has its antecedents in Immanuel Wallerstein's World Systems Theory, but with the dominance of the US in administering the internet, and the dominance of US-based search and social media platforms, there has been an observable degradation of local cultural difference, and so those studying cultural difference will be faced with the challenge of local cultural inflections upon a homogenised foundation (Holton, 2017).

In the economic sphere there has been adaptation of US free market economics into forms of heavily controlled capitalist economies, which now present significant challenges to the American model. It can be reasonably assumed that the forms of cultural homogenisation that we can currently observe will not always be in the control of the Global North, and may quite quickly start to present significant challenges to us. The way that Russian, Iranian, Chinese and North Korean sponsored individuals and agencies have leveraged the internet and social media provides the Global North with a warning notice about what might be possible in the short to medium term from these nations, and those who seek to emulate them.

Cultural Movement but Two Clear Challenges

So, whilst we can see the clear advantages to cultural diversity for intelligence, and the laudable efforts that have been taken to mitigate cultural difference, there remain two largely insurmountable cultural issues for intelligence communities to tackle: the first exists around security clearances for staff and contractors, commonly known as vetting, and the second is the reliance upon computer systems driven by algorithms to do more of the heavy lifting for agencies in sifting, sorting and pre-assessment work.

Given that one of the core tasks for intelligence agencies is keeping secrets, as opposed to just discovering them, ensuring that the staff and contractors of the agencies are trustworthy, that they keep secrets, and that they do not demonstrate risky behaviours that will expose the agencies to risks of interference from adversaries, is essential. Through history there have been very high-profile cases where officials have sought to share secrets with hostile nations or investigative journalists for money, for ideology, for infamy or as a form of whistleblowing. In the Cold War, the Cambridge Five were eventually revealed to have been passing secrets to the Soviet Union for mostly ideological reasons. Whilst holed up in Moscow, Kim Philby rejected the idea that he was a double agent, noting— rather awkwardly for the UK security services—that he only ever considered himself to be an agent of the Soviet state (Macintyre, 2014). The discovery of the Cambridge Spy Ring, something that had initially been revealed by the Soviet defector Konstantin Volkov in 1945, and then with a greater evidence base by the more notable KGB defector to the United States Anatoli Golitsyn, had a profound impact and is said to have placed a serious brake on the liaison relationship between the UK and US for more than a year, something that was—and is—unprecedented in the post-war history of the two nations (Ennis, 2006). The nearest we have to such a brake in the modern era is limited to hearsay evidence of a very temporary throttling of intelligence sharing around critical incidents after President Trump tweeted out British intelligence assessments around the 2017 bombing of the Ariana Grande concert in Manchester.

During the Cold War and post-Cold War era there were other examples of intelligence officers demonstrating the damage that can be caused by unauthorised releases of information, including the CIA officer Aldrich Ames and FBI officer Robert Hanssen who were convicted respectively of passing details of US intelligence assets to the Russian KGB and Russian Embassy, which cost the lives of these assets, and of having passed strategically sensitive documents to the GRU, both of whom did so for financial motivation. More contemporaneously, there has been Katharine Gun—as mentioned above—and her decision to leak papers based on what has been described as her moral outrage, whilst Edward Snowden famously passed classified presentations and materials to the journalists Glenn Greenwald, Laura Poitras and Ewen MacAskill, revealing or—more precisely—confirming details of a global surveillance network operated by the US National Security Agency (Greenwald, 2014). Both Gun and Snowden acted, so it seems, on the basis of individual conscience and political belief. Contrary to the general coverage, and the strong condemnation from intelligence agencies, Snowden's revelations did not reveal anything particularly new or unheard of but, in providing the internal PowerPoint presentations, this pattern of official behaviour could not now be avoided. The follow-on revelations around the NSA's alleged interception of the communications of heads of state made for some awkward diplomatic moments in the aftermath, particularly for President Obama and German Chancellor Merkel (Dearden, 2017). More importantly, the Snowden revelations sparked off a general cultural moment around more careful consideration of the balance between privacy and security, and the citizens' relationship with the security state.

Having security-cleared staff is essential to intelligence agencies. The work of these agencies is as much about protecting secrets as it is acquiring them. The scarring experience of the havoc created by the Cambridge Five still weighs heavily on intelligence recruiters keen to avoid employing the next big security leak. Achieving security clearances to work in the intelligence community is time-consuming, and invasive (Scott, 2020). If you have ever wanted to tell someone about your most intimate private desires and 'achievements', your browsing history, and how you are not terribly good with alcohol or money, a vetting interview is the chance you have been looking for. Whilst the agencies have liberalised their views on sexuality (being openly gay is no longer considered a blackmail risk and therefore not a vetting risk), the standard test is whether an individual has anything in their life or past that would put them at risk of being compromised. That is as much an objective question of whether a person has particular characteristics or risk profile elements, as it is about an individual's particular state of mind or disposition to exposure of certain personal things. In the age of social media, internet dating and online commenting, the likely exposure of personal details is far higher than it was twenty years ago, and so this is likely to exclude a good number of people. But the exclusion of large parts of society for this kind of work removes cultural representation. It is likely to be more useful—in terms of tradecraft—to have officers who have a strong connection to how the world actually works than those who have safe profiles. It is impossible for any agency to have no exposure to risk from its staff, so it may as well accept a little more risk to ensure a strong cultural and experiential blend amongst its human resources.

The cognitive skills required to be an intelligence officer, or an analyst, are also specific and relatively niche, which also serves to exclude many applicants. Notable amongst these skills is the ability to retain confidences, and the will to public service. Our digital and post-Thatcher age systematically mitigates against both these things: the imperative to share is currently nearly pathological amongst the younger generations (Fulton & Kibby, 2017); and the reduction of everything to the needs of the individual is again almost entirely accepted save for, in the UK context, the so-called Corbynistas of the left-wing Momentum faction of the Labour Party, and, in the US, those who ideologically align to Bernie Sanders and 'the squad' in Congress (Perryman, 2019). If we focus on the essential skill set needed by the intelligence community, and upon achieving a cultural blend with that skill set, we can equally surmise that this will depend upon a wider range of schools and non-elite universities providing the right skills to their students, and also government recruiters recognising unconventional presentation of skills. I think we should note that, even within this diversity, we are still likely to see the replication of core ideological and political values. In a limited way this might be acceptable, because that is the structural role of intelligence but we might also wonder whether there are different ways of doing intelligence, ways of including a wider array of people in intelligence tasks without requiring full security clearance. This broadening could be achieved by having a larger intelligence estate, and focusing that wider estate on heavily stovepiped open source intelligence endeavours, for example.

The second major cultural challenge comes from the dependence on algorithms. We collectively assume that a computer neutrally processes information and therefore produces objective answers. The 'we' is instructive here: *we* can be defined here as both everyday citizen consumers, and security officials. I have assumed that those engaged in the highest levels of data interrogation in the security community are aware of and try to mitigate or contextualise these inbuilt biases, but, from conversations I have had with strategic level security officials, the impact of this systemic frailty is poorly understood both in terms of its intellectual antecedents and its practical consequences. So, citizens and officials are more likely to trust a computer judgment than a human one and are happy to disregard that the fact that the algorithms are programmed by humans and therefore bake in the conscious or unconscious biases of these programmers. There are already examples of where AI security systems have been judged to discriminate on the basis of race, something that only helps to further alienate marginalised groups (Buolamwini, 2019; Cossins, 2018). A culturally aware ethical compact for computer security programming would be a reasonable first step to address this large vulnerability in our intelligence machinery (Martin, 2019).

We are a long way from understanding the full impact that cultural diversity—or more particularly cultural homogeneity—has on the business of intelligence, but it is possible to begin to craft a strong appreciation of what this space might look like. To do so requires high-profile interventions, such as Matthew Syed has made, but also funding the work of multi-disciplinary teams to capture the cross-cutting impacts of culture, race, gender, socio-economics, linguistics and organisational cultures on the production of usable intelligence for government. Whilst it is always difficult to prove cause and effect in intelligence, certainly from outside the intelligence community and using open source material, historical examples show us that a failure to properly account for cultural difference has resulted in costly and embarrassing intelligence mistakes. We only need to think of the way that Western intelligence agencies misread the likely reception of their militaries in Iraq in 2003, and the ongoing problems of community policing and intelligence in major European cities, to understand the damage that failing to understand the cultural dimension can mean. Academics can use the various approaches of cultural, anthropological and ethnographic study to reveal strengths and weaknesses in the approach of the security agencies, but they can only do this work currently from the position of outsiders utilising open source materials, with very few exceptions (Stalcup, 2009). It is for the senior officials to recognise the potential added value of engaging with the issue of the impact of culture and to rise to the challenge of opening up the community, in a safe way, to reveal the cultural nuance of 'the hidden wiring of the state'.

References

American Anthropological Association Executive Board (2007) *Statement on the Human Terrain System*. 6 November. Retrieved from American

Anthropological Association: http://s3.amazonaws.com/rdcms-aaa/files/production/public/FileDownloads/pdfs/pdf/EB_Resolution_110807.pdf, accessed 10 December 2021.

Baccarella, C., Wagner, T., Kietzmann, C. and McCarthy, P. (2018) 'Social media? It's serious! Understanding the dark side of social media'. *European Management Journal* 36 (4), 431–438.

Buolamwini, J. (2019) 'Artificial Intelligence has a problem with gender and racial bias. Here's how to solve it'. *Time Magazine*, 7 February.

Catano, V. and Gauger, J. (2017) 'Information fusion: Intelligence centers and intelligence analysis'. In I. Goldenberg, J. Soeters and W. Dean (eds) *Information Sharing in Military Operations* (pp. 17–34). Geneva: Springer.

Catignani, S. and Basham, V. (2020) 'Reproducing the military and heteropatriarchal normal: Army Reserve service as serious leisure'. *Security Dialogue* 52 (2), 1–19.

Cossins, D. (2018) 'Discriminating algorithms: 5 times AI showed prejudice'. *New Scientist*, 27 April.

Cummings, D. (2020) '"Two hands are a lot"—we're hiring data scientists, project managers, policy experts, assorted weirdos…. 2 January'. Retrieved from Dominic Cumming's blog: https://dominiccummings.com/2020/01/02/two-hands-are-a-lot-were-hiring-data-scientists-project-managers-policy-experts-assorted-weirdos/, accessed 6 January 2021.

Dearden, L. (2017) 'US and UK intelligence agencies did not spy on Germans, investigation into Snowden files suggests'. *The Independent*, 15 October.

DemMars, W. (2010) 'Hazardous partnership: NGOs and United States intelligence in small wars'. *International Journal of Intelligence and Counterintelligence* 14 (2), 193–222.

Deni, J. (2015) 'Beyond information sharing: NATO and the foreign fighter threat'. *Parameters* 45 (2), 47–60.

Dover, R. (2007) 'For Queen and company: The role of intelligence in the UK's arms trade'. *Political Studies* 55 (4), 683–708.

Dudman, J. (2019) '"We think we're the good guy": How abuse still stalks the charity world'. *The Guardian*, 26 July.

EDO MBM Technology Ltd *v.* Campaign to Smash EDO & Others, EWHC 837 (Queen's Bench, April 2005).

Ennis, J. (2006) 'Anatoli Golitsyn: Long-time CIA agent?' *Intelligence and National Security* 21 (1), 26–45.

Evans, R. and Lewis, P. (2013) 'Police "smear" campaign targeted Stephen Lawrence's friends and family'. *The Guardian*, 23 June.

Fernandez, R. and Fernandez-Mateo, I. (2006) 'Networks, race and hiring'. *American Sociological Review* 71 (1), 42–71.

Fernandez, R., Castilla, E. and Moore, P. (2000) 'Social capital at work: Networks and employment at a phone center'. *American Journal of Sociology* 105 (5), 1288–1356.

Forte, M. (2011) 'The human terrain system and anthropology: A review of ongoing public debates'. *American Anthropologist* 113 (1), 149–153.

Fulton, J. and Kibby, M. D. (2017) 'Millennials and the normalization of surveillance on Facebook'. *Continuum* 31 (2), 189–199.

GCHQ (April 1, 2019) 'Daring to think differently and be different. Why supporting neurodiverse staff is crucial to our work'. Retrieved from Government Communications Headquarters: https://www.gchq.gov.uk/information/daring-to-think-differently-and-be-different, accessed 10 December 2021.

Gonzalez, R. (2018) 'Beyond the human terrain system: A brief critical history (and a look ahead)'. *Contemporary Social Science* 15 (2), 227–240.

Greenwald, G. (2014) *No Place to Hide: Edward Snowden, the NSA, and the U.S. Surveillance State.* New York, NY: Metropolitan Books.

Griffin, N. S. (2020) '#Notallcops: Exploring "rotten apple" narratives in media reporting of Lush's 2018 'Spycops' undercover policing campaign'. *International Journal for Crime, Justice and Social Democracy* 9 (4), 177–194.

Holton, R. (2017) 'Globalization's cultural consequences revisited'. In R. Robertson and D. Buhari-Gulmez (eds), *Global Culture: Consciousness and Connectivity* (pp. 55–74). London: Routledge.

Hulnick, A. (2006) 'What's wrong with the intelligence cycle'. *Intelligence and National Security*, 959–979.

Kulshres, J., Eslami, M., Messias, J., Zafar, M., Ghosh, S., Gummadi, K. and Karahalios, K. (2019) 'Search bias quantification: Investigating political bias in social media and web search'. *Information Retrieval Journal* 22, 188–227.

Lubbers, E. (2012) *Secret Manoeuvres in the Dark: Corporate and Police Spying on Activists.* London: Pluto.

———. (2015) 'Undercover research: Corporate and police spying on activists. An introduction to activist intelligence as a new field of surveillance'. *Surveillance & Society* 13 (3–4), 338–353.

Macintyre, B. (2014) *A Spy Among Friends: Kim Philby and the Great Betrayal.* London: Bloomsbury.

Martin, K. (2019) 'Ethical implications and accountability of algorithms'. *Journal of Business Ethics*, 160 (4), 835–850.

McPherson, M., Smith-Lovin, L. and Cook, J. (2001) 'Birds of a feather: Homophily in social networks'. *Annual Review of Sociology* 27, 415–444.

Medina, R. (2014) 'From anthropology to human geography: Human terrain and the evolution of operational sociocultural understanding'. *Intelligence and National Security* 31 (2), 137–153.

Monahan, T. and Palmer, N. (2009) 'The emerging politics of DHS fusion centers'. *Security Dialogue* 40 (6), 617–636.

Perryman, M. (2019) *Corbynism from Below.* London: Lawrence & Wishart.

Pincher, H. (2014) *Their Trade is Treachery: The Full, Unexpurgated Truth about the Russian Penetration of the World's Secret Defences.* London: Biteback Publishing.

Porter, P. (2009) *Military Orientalism: Eastern War Through Western Eyes.* London: Hurst.

Scott, P. (2020) 'The contemporary security vetting landscape'. *Intelligence and National Security* 35 (1), 54–71.

Scurlock, R., Dolsak, N. and Prakash, A. (2019) 'Recovering from scandals: Twitter coverage of Oxfam and Save the Children scandals'. *VOLUNTAS: International Journal of Voluntary and Nonprofit Organizations*.

Stalcup, M. (2009) 'Connecting the dots. Intelligence and law enforcement since 9/11'. Doctoral dissertation, San Francisco & Berkeley, University of California.

Syed, M. (2019) *Rebel Ideas: The Power of Diverse Thinking.* London: John Murray.

The Daily Telegraph (2017) 'Spy agencies return to "tap on back" method to avoid James Bond wannabes, says MI6 chief Alex Younger'. *The Daily Telegraph*, 3 March.

Tyler, I. (2013) 'The riots of the underclass? Stigmatisation, mediation and the government of poverty and disadvantage in neoliberal Britain'. *Sociological Research Online* 18 (4), 25–35.

Uldam, J. (2017) 'Social media visibility: Challenges to activism'. *Media, Culture and Society* 40 (1), 41–58.

Weidmann, N. (2016) 'A closer look at reporting bias in conflict event data'. *American Journal of Political Science* 60 (1), 206–218.

Williams, O. (2018) 'Is autism an asset to UK cyber security?' *New Statesman*, 18 October.

3

INTELLIGENCE AGENCIES AND
THEIR OUTSIDERS[1]

What You Need to Know...

After the 2003 Iraq War, inquiries on both sides of the Atlantic recommended that government intelligence services make more use of external expertise, including that provided by academics. Humanities and social science academics have made individual contributions in engaging with government analysts, and there have also been some fledgling attempts to place some systems and processes around this. In the US, there is a far stronger tradition of academics moving in and out of secondments with the agencies, whereas in the UK the relationships have occurred on a piecemeal basis or through funded research projects. This chapter argues that external experts can add value to the intelligence community but that there are considerable cultural and practical barriers to be overcome if these engagements are to work for both sides. Expectations are often misaligned between academics and intelligence professionals, and particularly between academics and their employers. Consequently, far from arguing for more embedded forms of engagement, this chapter argues for a reversion to treating external experts as unembedded sources or community contacts, which allows both communities not to have to compromise their key operating cultures. It should be noted, however, that the external experts merely help to improve the function of intelligence agencies within the pre-existing framework of understanding. This helps to reinforce these existing models, rather than challenging them or allowing for more fundamental changes: such things ensure that it is business as usual.

***

As a field of study, intelligence has continued to grow from the turn of the century in line with the dominance of security threats in the news media and across the social media, and—as shown in the chapters covering cultural representations—with the growing number of spying, espionage and covert action books, films, programmes and games available to consumers. The academic discipline has seen its numbers grow as students, as I was, were inspired by academics like Richard Aldrich, Christopher Andrew and Mark Phythian and then went on to try out careers in related fields, or to pursue research in this area (Phythian, 2018). And this in turn provided the space for universities to begin to recruit academics into named intelligence posts, rather than—as was the case when I began my career in 2003—into general international relations, history or politics posts in which we had to just shape our environment to allow the intelligence research and teaching to grow. The causal relationship between intelligence studies as a mostly uncritical field and being a marginal concern of many university departments is uncertain but, as a reflection of my professional experience, I think there is traction here. The first substantive contribution to 'critical intelligence studies' arose in 2021, in the journal *Intelligence and National Security*, the most influential intelligence journal in the academic realm (Bean, de Werd & Ivan, 2021). These academics noted that their criticality did not exist from decrying intelligence but in examining the normative commitments made in its study. Sophisticated theoretical treatments had been provided by Andrew Rathmell and James Der Derian, but the *INS* Special Section attempted to set an agenda (Der Derian, 1993; Rathmell, 2002). There is a good chance this book might be labelled by others as fitting in with this fledgling sub-discipline. I have no strong views about this: my commitment is to understanding the why of how intelligence operates as it does.

In the UK, the academic field is still relatively small: I think we would mostly know each other well enough to say hello to. In continental Europe the field is tiny, and the short-lived intelligence section of the European Consortium for Political Research (ECPR), the largest political studies association in Europe and its conferences gave several snapshots of a community beyond the confines of the Anglosphere. There are enclaves of intelligence studies in most European states, but many academics are co-badged as working on criminology, communications or some form of cyber research. There have also been some locations in Europe—notably in France—where research into intelligence matters has resulted in prosecutions. America has a large intelligence studies community, and the International Studies Association (ISA) conference hosts over 50 intelligence panels each year, which equates to around 200 academics (ISA Intelligence Studies Section, 2020). For their size Australia and Canada also have good-sized communities of scholars. America and Australia have a more established pattern of structured interactions between its scholars and its practitioners, with the American system being frequently described as having a revolving door between the communities, something that historically has been highlighted for the ethical challenges it generates (Mundheim, 1980). For its part, the UK has a modest revolving door with the predominant direction of travel being those in the intelligence community (and mostly analysts at that) moving into academia. Very few academics have enjoyed sustained relationships with the intelligence community, although some notable exceptions are discussed later.

The gaps in academic knowledge and practitioner understanding of the academic field often exist for the very good and necessary reasons around secrecy: protecting sensitive information and tradecraft. The layers of secrecy have historically ensured that the intelligence community is insulated from and denied (intentionally or otherwise) access to the world of academia and all the research resources and findings present within it. The paywalls erected around academic journals and university libraries mean that analysts often face insurmountable cash barriers to accessing university level research. From the academic side, this gap has also meant that academics have had to learn new and advanced techniques for discovering helpful pieces of information and bridging analytical gaps to piece together the architecture of intelligence or notable phases or incidents in intelligence history. Richard Aldrich and Philip Davies have been notably adept at achieving these things in their significant works (Aldrich, 2010; Davies, 2012).

Because of the firewall between the communities, we would naturally expect there to be very limited prospects for research impact in this field of government activity (particularly for those who study it) and yet there is good evidence that the opposite is true. In earlier treatments of this subject, I suggested and argued that the US system offered the greatest potential for practitioners and academics to learn from each other in productive ways (Dover & Goodman, 2019). In this chapter I revise this assessment, concluding that processes that allow for unclassified exchange and cooperation provide the most authentic means by which academics and practitioners can derive value from each other in the existing model of intelligence: they also offer the best chance for knowledge exchange that does not necessarily include the replication of political defaults.

Intelligence, in the context of this chapter, refers to intelligence analysis, rather than anything related to espionage, intelligence fieldwork or informing. Within the academic field it would be assumed that this was the case but, while listening to various Student Union speakers decrying the government's counter-radicalisation programme known as PREVENT and the online accusations made against impactful scholars that they are spies, this definitional precision needs to be spelled out (National Union of Students, 2021). In looking at intelligence analysis and assessments, I am also drawing in researchers who come from primarily arts, humanities and social scientific backgrounds, as these sit most closely with the government's own vocational definition of intelligence analysis (UK Civil Service, 2016). There is a lengthy history of engineers and related specialisms being employed by intelligence agencies to help with issues such as cryptography, and whilst there is a case to be made that engaging in these activities is political, that falls outside of what I want to discuss here.

In UK academia there is now a continual pressure to being doing research that is 'impactful' (Bandola-Gill, Flinders & Anderson, 2021). Academics have attempted to interpret impact in many ways, from working as committee clerks or scientific advisors in parliaments, to advising political parties on policy, participating in television and radio documentaries, inspiring theatre productions, through to working inside third-sector organisations or government for periods of time. Of course, to secure these opportunities requires some sense of aligning to the agenda, value and mission of the practitioner organisation: essentially aligning to the guiding framework and underpinning logic. Ultimately, however, research impact is about the effect that the research has on the non-academic world, be it on public understanding, on practitioners, the policy realm, or in changes to laws and regulations. In the intelligence realm research impact is likely to be generated through changes to techniques, policy, procedures or through a better understanding of the policy or historical context of current and wicked problems. It is very unlikely—by which I mean not impossible, but I have never heard of it—to be defined as participating in operations.

Mike Goodman (of King's College London) and I generated some of our research impact via a series of UK research council funded projects, collectively known as 'Lessons Learned' (Dover & Goodman, 2011). In this series of four projects we sat between the UK government's analytical community and academia. We conceptualised it as standing on a bridge with practitioners and academics on the land at either end of the bridge. We were able to take government requirements (the term used for expressing an actionable interest in a subject) and interpret them for an academic community, whilst locating an academic to provide their open source analysis on the question we had set. For each question set, the result was a closed source paper for government, an open source paper lodged on the Arts and Humanities Research Council website, and in our book *Learning from the Secret Past* (Dover & Goodman, 2011). We refer to these four iterations collectively as 'Lessons Learned' because they retained the core concepts of: (1) matching government analysts with appropriate academic expertise; (2) providing open source challenge to government; and (3) promoting interchange between the two communities that ensured the relationship incorporates sufficient elements of uploading as well as downloading to and from the academic community.

By the time of the fourth and final iteration, which took the project into its seventh year, we had gained the right of initiative over some of the subject areas. Consequently, we were able to scan the horizon of our own disciplines and push subjects we thought government analysts ought to be interested in. Having this wider prospectus also allowed us to widen the pool of academics that we drew into the project, including those whom we reasonably suspected would not normally be consulted by officials. Whilst I think we did achieve in this area, I would reflect now that I certainly self-policed those suggestions, imputing what and whom I thought would and would not be acceptable to officials. The current logics that frame government intelligence are—therefore—not a simple matter of what government officials push and shape but also how a panopticon effect of self-policing helps to reinforce these framing logics. In this instance, I was as big a problem as the officials in reproducing these logics.

The secrecy involved in some government work creates additional challenges to recording research impact: even if an academic knows the impact they have had, are they—for example—able to acknowledge it publicly? If they are not—and it is reasonable to expect that they are not—then what incentive does the employing university have for allowing their member of staff to engage in this work? Similarly, if the engaging academic is prohibited, by their agreement with the agency and by the Official Secrets Act, from sharing what they have learned in their research and teaching, what value are they adding to their university? Recording and understanding impact here, then, is more complicated than might otherwise be the case with less security-focussed parts of government. Historically there has been a measure of ad-hoc interaction between the UK government's analytical community and individual academics. There have also been interactions between those in privileged or knowledgeable positions outside the community. Prior to 2012 and the development of an imperative in universities to acknowledge knowledge transfer, there was no instrumental necessity to declare or reveal that interactions between academics and intelligence officers were occurring. The arrival of the knowledge transfer agenda and the imperative provided by the Butler and Blackett Inquiries that recommended a greater role for outside expertise has begun to transform the relationship between intelligence agencies and outside expertise. The need for universities, as public institutions, albeit funded in an increasingly private way, to be more visible as key sources of knowledge and innovation for the country has grown in line with the accountability to students, and parents, that high student fees has brought. Even in areas like intelligence and national security, it is not novel to suggest that there are untapped synergies between the two, but the expectation that these will be acted upon certainly has a new impetus.

The question of who is suited to doing impactful work with the security community is relevant here. During the early 2000s it was my experience, at academic conferences and during the lectures given by invited speakers, that some of the most interesting work was being done by scholars who described themselves as 'critical'. Often these hailed from universities with strong traditions of sitting outside the mainstream. In discussing the issue of impact with some of these scholars at conference dinners, (as it was becoming an issue at that time), it became clear that they viewed the act of working with government, and tangentially or directly assisting government, as heretical. It was the academic equivalent of being a musical artist who has 'sold out', much as my father's generation view the punk rock star Jonny Rotten advertising synthetic butter in the early noughties.

Some of the academics I talked to thought that engagement was only justified as a means by which to generate revelatory content, that holding the state to account was the purpose of academia. Others felt that academics have a duty to provide good advice to the state to improve its function, to bring it ethical context, and more experienced counsel gave me many examples of where academics had assisted government during the early years of the Cold War, and that they had watched the social sciences becoming progressively less engaged in practical matters and deliberately less helpful to the state. Others—in turn—countered that this insider-advocacy model had been a proven failure over many years. My assessment, as will become clear during the rest of this chapter, is that the insider-advocate model offers many tangible benefits to both communities, but that this model contains so many challenges and costs that its utility is overwhelmed by its negatives. Moreover, if the insider-advocate model dissuades practitioners from engaging with a wider community of scholars then it has constrained rather than liberated government's access to quality information and advice. Most importantly it is serving to perpetuate, rather than challenge, underpinning logics and understanding: it is merely providing the means to reproduce existing global power structures. Universities have helped to perpetuate these power structures in educating new generations of political and business leaders from the Global South in Euro–Atlantic educational norms and realities: something they then take back to their home nations.

Do External Experts Add Value?

When Mike Goodman, Martha White and I examined this a few years ago, we created a four-part taxonomy of value to try and draw out what was useful and what was of marginal utility. The first area we considered was whether official engagement with academics who have conducted research on similar topics to those being investigated by intelligence analysts using open source data could create value through critical checks and balances, as well as making increased sense of or enhancing the fragmentary datasets used by intelligence agencies. Secondly, we examined whether the engagement between academia and government analysts provided a forum for challenging conventional wisdom and assessments. We also wondered whether this would mirror imaging and groupthink in a unique forum. Thirdly, we considered whether engagement with academia provided a valuable analytical resource as it could provide trends analysis based on statistical data capture applicable to a range of thematic topics using both random and structured sampling. Lastly, we asked whether engagement with the academic community serves to enrich knowledge and the intelligence picture, providing information and knowledge left gapped by the government's intelligence coverage.

What we found was that most of the intellectual underpinnings of intelligence and university research were shared, particularly if you followed the line of argument that intelligence is knowledge production. Sherman Kent's iconic definition of intelligence was that 'intelligence as knowledge, intelligence as an organisation and intelligence as an activity' helps us to understand this, albeit we should note the different instrumental ends (Kent, 1949). The weight of the natural synergy between the two communities suggests that the major challenges are purely organisational. This natural synergy also suggests that university research, in particular, helps to shape the framing logics—the means by which we understand the world—that are pushed and policed by intelligence agencies.

For the less sensitive areas of government, interaction with the UK's academic community has been widely encouraged, and schemes have been put in place to facilitate it. There have been successive moves in central government to encourage civil servants not only to seek outside expert views, but to have the implementation of policies tested by expert outsiders. In 2013, the UK government established a network of seven independent centres to inform government decision-making through the provision of independently assessed evidence. The What Works Network covers a range of policy areas, including crime, health care, social care and education. Amongst others, the London School of Economics acts as a host for the What Works Centre dedicated to looking at local economic growth (UK Government, August 2015). In 2015, the What Works initiative expanded further in its outreach to academia by establishing a Cross-Government Trial Advice Panel, funded by the Economic and Social Research Council (ESRC).[2] The panel, comprising 25 academics, was established to educate civil servants in the use of experimental and quasi-experimental research methods (Cabinet Office, 2015). By 2015, a considerable infrastructure had been put in place by the Cabinet Office to encourage civil servants to seek external expertise, including academia, to inform a wide range of policy-making areas under the Open Policy Making initiative, using the 'latest analytical techniques, and taking an agile, iterative approach to implementation' (UK Government, 2015).

The Open Policy Making Initiative and What Works methodologies demonstrate a significant effort by the UK Government to utilise external expertise from, amongst others, the academic community.

However, engagement between the spheres of policy making and the academic community is unlikely to be replicated at an equal scale between academia (and particularly those parts which study intelligence) and the national security community due to the obvious requirement for secrecy and the protection of sensitive information, and the extent to which intelligence staff have been seriously overstretched over the last ten years. In the open source intelligence chapter (Chapter 4), I also recommend reforms to the way intelligence is considered and operationalised that would diminish the need to draw distinct contributions from outside experts and internal officials.

As noted earlier in this chapter, there have been two major reviews that have touched upon national security, which recommended greater links between academia and intelligence. In 2004, the first major review into the intelligence underpinnings of the Iraq War (*Review of Intelligence on Weapons of Mass Destruction,* more commonly known as the Butler Report) made several recommendations encouraging the value of engagement between the national security community and academia. The first recommendation was to provide an outlet for analysts within a closed national security community to challenge conventional wisdom, received options and assessments based largely on actively gathered intelligence. It was from this recommendation that the 'lessons learned' project sprang, and it was the initial benchmark against which we measured the project.[3]

The potential benefit of academic engagement is in the anticipated reduction of the cognitive biases of 'mirror-imaging' and 'group-think', allowing analysts to discuss assessments and theories with subject matter experts from universities who may provide a different perspective based on a different body of source material. This activity stretches into the education and training environment as well, where the King's College London Intelligence Studies Programme (known as KISP) and the University of Leicester's Strategic Intelligence Programme (which was a closed programme) and the MA in Intelligence and Security are good examples of higher education platforms where government analysts are encouraged to move beyond the tunnel vision of their specific day jobs to reflect upon their activity in a wider academic context (Dexter, Phythian & Strachan-Morris, 2017; Goodman & Omand, 2008).

Engagement with academia for the purpose of challenge analysis may benefit a closed national security community by providing an additional avenue for systematic and structured challenges. Whilst there are widely different research methodologies across different areas of academia, it can be broadly said that professional academics will have achieved a high degree of proficiency in terms of research practices, critiquing evidence and argument through doctoral training, peer review and professional engagement within the academic community. But, as noted in Chapter 2, the academic community doing the engagement is likely to be both selective and largely culturally homogenous, some of which is driven by the necessities of security and some of which will be driven by the desire to fit within acceptable normative or ideological boundaries.

Certainty in the quality of academic input into the intelligence realm is partly delivered by the *de minimis* standards for UK PhD students in research-intensive universities—that is driven by research council recognition—around research training. Similarly, the rigours of peer review enforce these standards for career academics. Lord Butler recommended that challenge analysis should be a systematic function of the UK's intelligence assessments: 'Challenge should be an accepted and routine part of the assessment process as well as an occasional formal exercise, built into the system' (Butler, 2004, p. 146). The intelligence community has taken some modest steps towards achieving this, and the UK Cabinet Office's creation of an Intelligence Academy in 2021 has set a more appropriate ambition for this form of challenge and training effort (Devanny *et al.*, 2018). The challenge that Butler outlined was not—it should be remembered—a challenge to fundamental conceptions of what intelligence is for, or what it in effect protects and projects. Rather, this was a tightly defined notion of challenge on intelligence as it is already defined on issues and from perspectives that are equally tightly defined.

The second key benefit outlined by Butler is the potential for widening the range of information available to analysts within the closed national security community: 'We emphasise the importance of the Assessments Staff and the JIC [Joint Intelligence Committee] having access to a wide range of information, especially in circumstances where information on political and social issues will be vital' (Butler, 2004, p. 153). Academics within research-intensive universities are likely—within reason—to have more time in which to produce in-depth assessments and to have the freedom to conduct structured fieldwork. Furthermore, the range of sources of information available to academics, unencumbered by any restrictions of official secrecy, is potentially wider than that of a closed national security community. Those whom Goodman and I dealt with in the Whitehall and law enforcement intelligence communities often cited the significant challenges they have getting hold of research materials that academics think of as their bedrock, such as electronic journal holdings (JSTOR and similar), which are blocked by financial and structural considerations; and when access is granted, the size of these research databases and holdings are often overwhelming for the analyst fresh to them.

Following extensive consultation within the intelligence community and with external subject matter experts, the *Blackett Review of High Impact Low Probability Risks* (2011) identified several recommendations to strengthen the government's approach to assessing strategic shocks which could, in turn, be applied more widely across government. While the recommendations of the Blackett Review built upon the practices that existed within the community, one of the key factors in the review was the need for the UK government to include a greater measure of external expertise in their assessment processes. Of the 11 recommendations identified by the Blackett Review, 6 concern engagement between closed intelligence communities and academia, 3 of which were specifically addressed to the Cabinet Office, where the central analytical function of the community sits. The Blackett Review highlighted many benefits for the intelligence community of engaging more fully with the academic community: to inform key risk assumptions; to inform judgments and analysis; to better detect early signs of strategic shock or surprise; to inform the development of internal and external risk communication strategies; and to strengthen the scrutiny of the National Risk Assessment. Although these recommendations were identified in the context of specific types of risk assessment, the recommendations are widely applicable to other areas of assessment and analysis across the UK government, and are most usefully seen in this widest context.[4]

The range of possible benefits that can be drawn out from the Butler and Blackett reviews should be sufficient to warrant a deeper investigation into how external experts can add more value to the operational aspects of academic–practitioner engagement. This has been done academically (Dover, Goodman & White, 2017), and it has been done, somewhat fitfully, by the Joint Terrorism Analysis Centre in 2005–6, and then across Whitehall from 2016 to the present day, culminating in the plans for the Intelligence Academy. Ultimately, all these initiatives serve to bolster and improve the status quo.

Producing Marginal Gains

Academia and academics—if they are organised appropriately and effectively—can provide the intelligence community with a form of additional high-quality, open source capability that is created within public institutions, which are—after all—organised to provide forms of all-source analysis. We do see, however, that there are debates raging within universities about what are acceptable fields of study and approach. Just as critical management studies, or more particularly those business studies scholars who are critical of American management sciences, have become increasingly scarce in universities, those who have adopted non-confrontational perspectives towards law enforcement or government secrecy have found difficulties in securing publication slots in mainstream journals. The subtle gatekeeping of disciplines has a significant and long-term impact over the direction of these fields and therefore their utility to practitioners.

On a more positive note, whilst acknowledging that this merely refines the operation of existing practices, systematic arrangements with cleared academics still do provide the opportunity for a form of external peer review facility. This is particularly true when it comes to technical aspects, such as cyber security or other forms of data analytical techniques. To embed this sort of work, a workshop of the

Oxford Intelligence Group in 2008 suggested to the Cabinet Office's Professional Head of Intelligence Assessments that she establish an intelligence version of the UK Defence Academy. This idea was then reworked and appeared in the International Institute for Strategic Studies' *Strategic Balance* publication that winter, as a means by which to create organisation and administration around these activities (International Institute for Strategic Studies, 2008). This initial plan involved academics providing open source challenges to analysts, something that was resource intensive in managing the security challenges of the original questions and the academics working on the questions, and it took some twelve years for this idea to gain a full head of steam. A collection of us argued that this idea needed to be revised, as it has been in Germany, and we were pleased to see the Cabinet Office responding quickly with plans for a UK intelligence academy and professionalised training programmes (Devanny *et al.*, 2018).

Whilst we focussed our suggestion of an intelligence academy on professional skills training and education, we also viewed that a key benefit of a maturing academy might be in providing additional corroboration and validation to intelligence analysts, in widening out further the context in which they are preparing their assessments. We judged that this extension could be provided through the following:

- Trends analysis based on statistical data capture applicable to a range of thematic topics using both random and structured sampling. Similarly, with qualitative research methods, of historical trends and essential context.
- Corroboration or validation from academic research that has undergone more rigorous testing and research techniques.
- Corroboration or validation from academic research conducted at a more granular level in terms of topic matter.
- Corroboration or validation analysis from academic research derived from a wider or alternative pool of information (Dover & Goodman, 2019).

Another marginal gain offered by academics is the ability to enrich the assessment staffs' knowledge and intelligence picture. Government analysts are preoccupied with responding to short-term customer-placed requirements that leave them unable to keep up with a wider pool of knowledge and context that is the domain of academia. So, a key marginal gain of the interaction between the two communities should be the analyst's ability to dip into the academic's larger pool of contextual knowledge, something that is important to the task of correctly interpreting information about other regions and cultures and the intentions of target nations. The tension with all these initiatives is the balance between improving pre-existing methods, logics and patterns of power, and working outside the existing paradigms to enact meaningful changes. The challenge of engaging dispossessed or lost academic voices is the most important work that can be done here: merely replicating and reinforcing existing assumptions does not advance the state's understanding of threat, or opportunity for that matter.

The government's national security community could quite feasibly increase its contacts across a wide range of disciplines, research organisations, universities and think tanks both in the UK and abroad. In doing so, it may be able to leverage or influence the direction of researchers without necessarily having to provide funding, although the reciprocity of the relationship is likely to have to be proved over the medium term to sustain such an arrangement. Access to the views of the national security community on mutual topics of interest, and the chance to use academic research to inform and impact upon decision-making on issues of national security, are likely to be incentive enough for those academics who are already predisposed towards the public service element of engaging with practitioners and who are keen to do so.

If the relationships are organised well, the benefits of practitioner–academic engagement should not just fall on the side of the national security community. There is potential for academia and academics to also benefit through a closer interaction between these two worlds—but a health warning has to apply that there is little evidence for this benefit at the time of writing. Indeed, I have some professional experience that suggests that the current expectations of practitioners are that this engagement is something that academics should want to do for government and want to do at the partial expense of other duties. This is not as unreasonable as it sounds. Motivation has always been an important factor for intelligence officers measuring the potential reliability of human sources, and my sense is that the intelligence community's attitude towards academics is well suited to thinking of them as human or confidential sources.

So, much as the benefit for the security community is corroboration and challenge analysis, the same applies for academics. Engaging with intelligence officers or analysts who are analysing similar topics using classified data has the benefit of providing them with informal measures of quality control, corroboration or confirmation of academic hypotheses and judgments, providing the officer feels so moved to express a helpful opinion. An external review function from a practising analyst can be very helpful to academics, helping them avoid erroneous conclusions and maintaining their reputation in the practitioner field, opening up a hard-to-reach form of peer review. The benefits to academics is heavily contingent on the ability and willingness of a closed analytical community to communicate their views in confidence or at an unclassified and non-compromising level. Such willingness is very closely aligned with issues of trust. This will be dependent on the internal risk versus benefits assessment of the closed analytical community, and places the academic in a supplicant position as regards knowing or understanding the quality of information they are receiving.

The other benefit to academics comes from the potential for the enrichment of their academic knowledge. Where a closed national security community could benefit from being able to close information and knowledge gaps by steering or influencing academic research, the academic community can equally gain from this process by being given a unique insight into decision making processes, organisational structure, organisational cultures and areas of research that would have an impact and benefit for national security and official policy. This could provide a high impact for future academic research commissioned or approved by academic funding bodies and higher education institutions. There is a pressure within academic departments to be connected more with external stakeholders, and thus, for most academics, whilst the intellectual advantages of engaging with the national security community will be very real, the necessity and demand to make an impact on the practitioner community will also play a part in driving engagement with the national security community.

Prolonged exposure to practitioners does, however, create a jarring experience for engaged academics when they read some academic journals or sit through conference panels where the mismatch between the open source presentation of security issues and challenges and the lived experiences of intelligence agencies is all too apparent. It also brings the academics who are frequently engaging with practitioners closer to a position of 'having gone native': that is, to having internalised the agendas and preoccupations of officials and departments. This is not unique to intelligence studies scholars: it is the same for academics working on finance, or with third-sector organisations, and is similarly true for specialist journalists, particularly political journalists, and should be put down to being part of the rich tapestry of life.

Academics and Spooks: Crossing the Divide?

The crossover of the two communities is not without fundamental pressures and tensions. The three key barriers and obstacles are: the need for secrecy; the need for speed; and the changing requirements of the intelligence community. In the day-to-day experience of impactful research these tensions locate themselves around the relative inflexibility of academics, who have university enforced timetables, an imperative to draw in research grant money and a lack of travel funding. There is a fundamental tension between information security, national security, and the imperative to publish and disseminate that is a hallmark of academia. It also does not necessarily follow that intelligence studies or security research can be applied directly to the business of the intelligence community.

The published outputs of academics are not generally written in a way that assists or supports decision making in government. Indeed, much of the mainstream international relations literature currently seems written to deliberately exclude the idea that it might be of use to officials: interestingly, the challenges to world views or pictures of reason have emanated from International Relations. Consequently, there has been a low-level and rumbling debate around whether academic research needs to be translated before it can be used by officials, or whether it should be written in such a way that the utility of it is drawn more clearly for a generalist or practitioner–expert audience. For academics, there are very clear career advantages to writing in a way that appeals to highly ranked peer-reviewed journals but which—consequently—excludes nearly all non-academic readers. As I know myself, there are few career advantages in being proficient at practitioner engagement, and it fits into the category of things I do because I enjoy and value it rather than because it is generating an instrumental end or career goal. There are, therefore, serious problems around the incentives for academics to engage with practitioners—and engagements, where they happen, are likely to require sensitive negotiations.

The simplest, and arguably most effective, forms of engagement are those involving in-house talks, lectures and discussions either held at a location in the academic community or within the national security estate. These events may be of varying size, depending on the complexity of the topic, the range of subject matter experts available, and the level of interest. It is reasonable to assume that specifically tailored and structured in-house events could offer high-level cost effectiveness in terms of the time available to government analysts. In this way, engagement between the two communities takes the form of a flexible liaison resource with the ability to gain high impact tailored to specific targeting. Such an approach also allows for flexibility around the level of sensitivity of a talk. On the national security estate, it is possible to host both unclassified and confidential (including classified) conversations. The limits of this are always clearly marked and communicated to participants. Academics are fond of the sanctity of a Chatham House Rule event (even if most of them still insist the one rule is plural) but very few have been formally security vetted (i.e. having been put through a vetting process by UK Security and Vetting, which is an office of the Foreign, Commonwealth & Development Office) and allocated a form of clearance, meaning the sort of information that it has been assessed they can be trusted to view. So, a passed Security Check (SC) would allow an academic to view materials up to SECRET, whereas

Developed Vetting (DV) allows material up to TOP SECRET. There are extended versions of the Developed Vetting, but that would be beyond the need of nearly all academics in all disciplines—bar some forms of sensitive engineering and those writing official histories.

The hosted workshop or equivalent keeps the security onus on the government department and its officials to ensure that official secrets are protected. This onus means that government departments are often unwilling to arrange events that make it clear what questions they are interested in. As an entirely fictitious example, an interest in hosting experts to discuss Chinese development or exploitation of 5G infrastructure would clearly hint at a preoccupation around future network security, although this would have been a more interesting and relevant topic five years ago, perhaps. The acknowledgement of a gap in knowledge is as relevant to understanding the state of the security community as it is to reading the knowledge they have.

Greater levels of embedded engagement—such as the Special Officer programme, or working in some form for an agency—are a good opportunity for the agency to exploit academic knowledge and gain targeted insights on classified materials, and they are a good opportunity for the academic to experience practitioner life on the inside, rather than a curated or carefully guarded snapshot of that life provided by workshops or interviews and the like. But embedded relationships require an agency to sponsor the academic's security clearances (which has a financial cost and a cost to officer time), it requires them to manage the academic, to provide them with physical passes, internal electronic passes and, if they are to gain access to the intranet, or equivalent, a laptop and telephone, as appropriate. Such a level of expenditure would require the agency to put forward what they describe as a business case to justify the cost against the anticipated gain. For the academic, they have to be intellectually and politically sold on the idea that this wish to assist the government's security effort—and that is by no means guaranteed across academia—they have to be willing to put themselves forward for the level of personal intrusion that a security clearance process entails, they have to manage the expectations of their university employer and gain consent for time away from the office, they have to be willing to accept the obligation that official secrecy and the surrounding processes entail, and they have to accept a partial curtailment of their normal freedoms to publish.

An academic—within the bounds of libel law, incitement, official secrecy and the needs of their employer—is free to publish what they can, where they can. A security-cleared academic has to be more careful not to publish anything that they have learned in the course of being attached to the intelligence community, and may even have to get their outputs approved for publication, which can be time consuming and awkward for the academic, who is expected to produce an agreed number of publications within an agreed amount of time (MacDonald, 2017). It is not entirely certain that these obligations on a cleared academic end when they are no longer engaging with their sponsor agency, which makes this a commitment that amounts to a paradigm shift. Sponsoring agencies will take a view on whether the academic can declare their engagement publicly, to their employer or in publications. Awkwardly, the agency's view might change during the course of the engagement depending upon the prevailing security situation and the situation at the academic's university, which—when a large amount of material is published online in some form—is hard to unknow once it has been released.

I spent the years of the Lessons Learned project, and several publications that followed it, advancing the argument that greater levels of cooperation between academics and the security community in the form of revolving doors and being embedded in the agencies would drive better outcomes for both communities. As time has gone on, I am now in the unhappy position of partially arguing against myself. I am no longer convinced that the benefits to both communities outweigh the financial and other costs of clearing and embedding academics. I think there is also merit to the intellectual argument that some form of air gap between the two communities allows academics to critique the work of the intelligence community without being compromised by embedded relationships, and allows the intelligence community to work on how to structure its engagements with academics to make the most of the intellectual capital available. Both sides should accept greater levels of risk to have more courageous intellectual encounters with each other to advance our collective knowledge. Better still, there would be a far greater emphasis on open source intelligence, which would diversify the pool of researchers and intellectual contributions available to officials, helping to widen their horizons beyond the very narrow confines of their existing world view.

A renewed effort to work on appropriate ways to systematically engage with research materials, and then to engage in open source deeper dives with researchers, is a more appropriate balance than currently exists. With the current incentive structures, and with cultures within the relevant academic disciplines being relatively hostile towards these kinds of embedded engagement, there is less instrumental gain for academics than if they were to attend an open source workshop. If my assessment carries weight, it should be seen as both a shame and a missed opportunity, but too many of the actors involved need reform to make the prospect of that happening in a reasonable time frame likely. Similarly, the risks presented by social media and the way that stories or rumours can be quickly escalated, and damage can be inflicted upon professional reputations, means that academics increasingly have to be cautious about whom they engage with and how they manage their reputations. In the last ten years I have worked with academic colleagues from both sides of the divide of enthusiastically working with or being ethically opposed to engaging with government and who have had their professional reputations dented by adverse publicity generated by mainstream media outlets, compounded by social media commentary. I have spared citing these examples to avoid causing further misery to colleagues I like and respect.

Concluding Thoughts

Academics in the Euro–Atlantic area systematically engage with all manner of practitioners, be they in private industry, public bodies or third-sector organisations, and it is now considered to be a professional norm (Flinders, 2020; Vincent, 2015). There are good moral, intellectual and practical reasons to promote this type of engagement, in addition to the contractual compulsion in the UK that is created by the presence of the impact agenda in the government's periodic Research Excellence Framework exercises.

For intelligence studies academics there are discipline specific opportunities and constraints to that engagement, mostly around personal and information security. For many intelligence studies academics the organisations they are engaging with are also the ones they study: the agencies are the referent object and that throws up a potential conflict of interest between the agencies and the engaging academic. Such conflicts of interest are not unique but they always feel more serious in intelligence because of the gravity of the issues that agencies deal with on a day-to-day basis. It is also true that the penalties for the transgressing academic are likely to be more severe, in legal and career terms. The classic UK Civil Service term 'going native' applies to academics working closely with practitioners: after a relatively short period of time, embedded academics internalise the working cultures and normative commitments of their practitioners.

So, whilst there are many synergies and benefits for national security agencies and the academic communities that work on these subjects from closer engagement, the notion of embedding academics in a way that would be reminiscent of the American revolving-door arrangements is overshadowed by the legal, ethical and organisational challenges there are to this. The recommendations of the Blackett and Butler inquiries both concluded that there needs to be a systematic approach to academic engagement and they both placed a clear imperative on government to act. But, save for the seven-year set of projects that Mike Goodman and I ran, and piecemeal academic board projects that have been run in the Ministry of Defence and Foreign, Commonwealth & Development Office, this is yet to be achieved in any meaningful way in government.

The UK's National Crime Agency has tried to tackle the problem of engagement through their Special Officer programme (https://www.nationalcrimeagency.gov.uk/careers/how-to-join-the-nca/nca-specials), which recruits niche capabilities from outside of the agency. Whilst this is not directly aimed at academics, it is said to include a number of academics. The sheer cost of clearing external experts, line managing them and ensuring information security will be considerable. The mission of academics, in particular, is different to salaried intelligence officers, and it is difficult to reconcile these distinct missions.

Ultimately, however, the lack of an overarching or coherent structure for engaging outside experts creates transaction costs for officials. The absence of robust processes around engagement (how to approach, how to engage and how to manage) is just beginning to reach an acceptable level of maturity across government departments. The absence of centrally held knowledge about intellectual capital in the UK is another significant barrier, with the more usual mechanism for engagement being whom the official knows, whom they have heard of, or whether Chatham House or RUSI can offer one of their experts. In 2017 the Cabinet Office opened a portal where academics could lodge the details of their research expertise and their contact details but it was poorly advertised. The professional associations— the Political Studies Association and British International Studies Association—also advertise opportunities for engagement, including those in parliament. This fractured picture does have the unintended effect of making it only those who are really determined to engage making the effort.

To find and vet academics (even in the most perfunctory way) to engage with does place a large transaction cost on government departments. The need for security clearance—and note my recommendations about reforming the intelligence community in the open source intelligence chapter (Chapter 4)—has the effect of reducing diversity in the pool of experts called upon. For example, if I were given the choice of consulting a Russianist who regularly travelled to Russia, spoke Russian and could read original Russian sources without translation, or a desk expert who never travelled to Russia and who relied upon Google Translate to read original sources, I would always choose the former. The latter is more likely to be capable of passing a security clearance process, which is why our notion of expertise and the way expertise is engaged should change.

Challenges similarly exist for the individual academic or expert, too. They are highly likely to be personally, intellectually and/or contractually keen to engage with government, but they will have the perennial problem of managing their host institution and potentially their departmental managers also. Managing teaching schedules, travel costs and the opportunity cost of reducing the amount of time that can be spent on high-yielding research income—which has become the goal of most research-intensive academics since the turn of the century—is difficult. Convincing managers that this is an activity that is adding value to the university is similarly tricky; also tricky is the potential to be misunderstood or mislabelled as a government official pretending to be an academic, rather than an academic seeking out knowledge exchange opportunities.

In terms of an ideal-type of relationship between academics and practitioners, I think a model that is premised upon iterative and ongoing support will be more effective than one that is premised on the production of open source context pieces or discreet essays. The ongoing engagement model is challenged by the requirement for security vetting, ongoing security concerns, dual line management, managing university leaders and the fact that currently there are no meaningful career incentive structures in place within academia to promote this kind of knowledge exchange, despite the rhetoric used in the field. Given that this kind of knowledge exchange has been a strong feature of academic life for at least fifteen years, that is somewhat disappointing. Engineering departments and the defence industries have created a system of 'sandboxing' academic interactions: that is, forming a contract with a cleared senior academic who manages a group of uncleared junior academics' completely clearly defined tasks that mean these junior colleagues are not burdened with the knowledge of the overarching project. Thus, the uncleared academics only pose the most minimal security risk to the overarching project.

A defence industries model of engagement is only really possible because of the generous amounts of money that are available to defence manufacturers and, by extension, engineering departments. The model is sound on its own terms, however, whilst not getting away from the inherent problems of serving to reinforce the existing logics that underpin government intelligence and its competitive mission in the domestic and international realm. If the pool of external experts is conditioned by who can be vetted, or who comes from the 'right kind' of institution or organisation, then it will remain narrow and unrepresentative. We hear a lot in popular discourse about the creation of online echo chambers, and how damaging these have been to our democracy and our societies (Auxier & Vitak,

2019; Zycher, 2018;). What I have described in this chapter about how external experts interact with intelligence officers is a discreet form of echo chamber: officials want to be challenged but only by so much, and root-and-branch changes to business are considered the stuff of heresy.

In research terms, the benefits of collaboration between the security community and academia we can see are mostly instrumental in nature: improved information resources, methods and validation techniques for both communities. Some of the benefits can be located in professional enrichment—from working with skilled professionals from outside a respective community bubble, and in improving professional techniques—but mostly should be located in the immersion in different types of professional culture. But counter to my earlier publications on this issue, it is now my assessment that the barriers and challenges to the relationships between academics and practitioners outweigh the possible benefits, certainly to the engaging academic. Managing two sets of entirely autonomous and de-linked line management, the necessity for vetting and ongoing security measures, the impact these relationships have on an academic reputation, and so on, mean that there is far greater utility—sadly— in remaining outside any formalised relationships with practitioners and instead providing workshop context, or discreet one-off pieces of work. That is a dismal conclusion when the potential gains for both communities are large and have the potential to alter the course of research undertaken by the fields of intelligence studies, defence studies and international relations, increasing and enriching the pool of knowledge available to inform national security decision-making. But after fifteen years, the structures are still nowhere near being in place to support such endeavours, however great the need.

The homogenising effect of the relationship between outside expertise and intelligence is wider than the research piece. Profitable opportunities have been found in education and training within the UK's university system to members of the intelligence, security, and law enforcement community (Goodman & Omand, 2008). The engagements enjoyed, for example, by King's College London with the Ministry of Defence at the UK Defence Academy and the Royal College of Defence Studies, by Brunel University with the

UK Ministry of Defence, and the University of Leicester with the NATO Defence College, have produced very strong research and professional exchange (built upon a long history of interaction with academia) and are replicable within the national security community, even if only in a virtual form due to the financial resources required in such initiatives. I describe this as a homogenising effect, because these programmes are all designed to produce better officers within the structures that already exist, to bring in international partners into these homogenised views, rather than to question the effectiveness of this operating model, to teach deep understandings of the competitors and adversaries and to challenge in an uncomfortable way: all things that I think are necessary to improve the way we do intelligence.

References

Aldrich, R. (2010) *GCHQ*. London: Harper Collins.

Auxier, B. and Vitak, J. (2019) 'Factors motivating customization and echo chamber creation within digital news environments'. *Social Media + Society* 5 (2), 1–13.

Bandola-Gill, J., Flinders, M. and Anderson, A. (2021) 'Co-option, control and criticality: The politics of relevance regimes for the future of political science'. *European Political Science* 20 (1), 218–236.

Bean, H., de Werd, P. and Ivan, C. (2021) 'Critical intelligence studies: Introduction to the special issue'. *Intelligence and National Security* 36 (4), 467–475.

Baron Butler of Brockwell, FERB (2004) 'Review of Intelligence on Weapons of Mass Destruction'. United Kingdom: Stationery Office.

The Cabinet Office (no date) https://www.gov.uk/government/groups/joint-intelligence-organisation#:~:text=Professional%20Head%20of%20Intelligence%20Assessment%20(PHIA)&text=The%20post%20and%20associated%20team,1%2C700%20intelligence%20analysts%20across%20government

Davies, P. (2012) *Intelligence and Government in Britain and the United States: A Comparative Perspective*. Westport, CT: ABC-Clio/Praeger.

Der Derian, J. (1993) 'Anti-diplomacy, intelligence theory and surveillance practice'. *Intelligence and National Security* 8 (3), 29–51.

Devanny, J., Dover, R., Goodman, M. S. and Omand, D. (2018) 'Why the British Government must invest in the next generation of intelligence analysts'. *The RUSI Journal* 163 (6), 78–89.

Dexter, H., Phythian, M. and Strachan-Morris, D. (2017) 'The what, why, who, and how of teaching intelligence: The Leicester approach'. *Intelligence and National Security* 32 (7), 920–934.

Dover, R. and Goodman, M. (2011) *Learning from the Secret Past: Cases in British Intelligence History.* Washington, DC: Georgetown University Press.

———— (2019) 'Between Lucky Jim and George Smiley: The public policy role of intelligence scholars'. In L. M. Gearon (ed.) *The Routledge International Handbook of Universities, Security and Intelligence Studies* (pp. 343–351). London: Routledge.

Dover, R., Goodman, M. S., & White, M. (2017). 'Two Worlds, One Common Pursuit: Why Greater Engagement with the Academic Community Could Benefit the UK's National Security'. In *The Palgrave Handbook of Security, Risk and Intelligence* (pp. 461-477). Palgrave Macmillan, London.

Flinders, M. (2020) 'The relevance of political science and the public responsibility of political scientists'. LSE Impact of Social Sciences [Blog].

Goodman, M. and Omand, D. (2008) 'What analysts need to understand: The Kings Intelligence Studies Programme'. *Studies in Intelligence* 52 (4), 57–65.

International Institute for Strategic Studies. (2008) *The Military Balance.* London: IISS.

ISA Intelligence Studies Section. (2020) 'ISA Intelligence Studies Section'. 4 March. Retrieved from International Studies Association: https://www.isanet.org/ISA/Sections/ISS

Kent, Sherman. (1949) *Strategic Intelligence for American World Policy.* New York, NY: Princeton University Press.

MacDonald, R. (2017) '"Impact", research and slaying Zombies: The pressures and possibilities of the REF'. *International Journal of Sociology and Social Policy* 37 (11–12), 696–710.

Mundheim, R. (1980) 'Conflict of interest and the former government employee: Rethinking the revolving door'. *Creighton Law Review* 14 (3), 707–721.

National Union of Students. (2021) 'National Union of Students'. 4 March. Retrieved from National Union of Student: Connect: https://www.nusconnect.org.uk/campaigns/preventing-prevent-we-are-students-not-suspects, accessed 3 January 2022.

Phythian, M. (2018) 'Profiles in intelligence: An interview with Professor Richard J. Aldrich'. *Intelligence and National Security* 33 (7), 939–953.

Rathmell, A. (2002) 'Towards Postmodern Intelligence'. *Intelligence and National Security* 17 (3), 87–104.

UK Civil Service (2016) 'Civil Service—Intelligence Analysis Profession'. 7 November. Retrieved from Civil Service Vocations: www.gov. uk/government/organisations/civil-service-intelligence-analysis-profession/about, accessed 3 January 2022.

UK Government (2015) 'What Works network membership requirements'. https://www.gov.uk/government/publications/what-works-network-membership-requirements

Vincent, A. (2015) 'The ideological context of impact'. *Political Studies Review* 13 (4), 474–484.

Zycher, B. (2018) *The Climate Empire Strikes Out: The Perils of Policy Analysis in an Echo Chamber*. Washington, DC: American Enterprise Institute.

4

OPEN SOURCE INTELLIGENCE AND
THE DIGITAL AGE[1]

What You Need to Know...

*Open source intelligence (OSINT) is decision support that is
generated from publicly available information for intelligence
purposes. It comprises no less than 80% of the information collected
by intelligence agencies (and it may be up to 95%), but the majority
of it remains unaccessible because much of the raw open source
information (OSIF) remains in our minds and is not collectable
using technical intelligence. That which is collected (e.g. social
media posts) is mostly warehoused and unassessed. Where OSINT
is used by intelligence agencies, it augments covertly acquired
information as part of an 'all source' mix, but is not currently
utilised as a foundation for the more effective collection of covert
sources. The current structure and purpose of government intelligence
agencies does not lend itself to utilising OSINT effectively: they are
funded and configured to focus on covert intelligence. Similarly, the
main consumers of intelligence—the Core Executive, defence and
security realms—do not see intelligence as decision support but as a
privileged form of news gathering. Refinements to the requirements,
collection management, processing and analysis, and the use of
modern presentational techniques, would help to resolve some of
this under-use or misuse. The purpose of intelligence is to provide*

support to the decision-making process at every level of government across all functional areas (e.g. public health, trade, immigration) not just military and security concerns. The existential threats that society faces are not from interstate violence, nor from terrorism: according to the United Nations they are from poverty, infectious diseases and climate change, as well as from transnational crime. These are threats that can be more effectively illuminated using OSINT sources and techniques and, moreover, provide a better value for money proposition than the current machinery of intelligence.

***

Open source intelligence (OSINT) is a form of intelligence collection management that involves finding, selecting, and acquiring information from publicly available sources and analyzing it to produce actionable intelligence. In the intelligence community (IC), the term "open" refers to overt, publicly available sources (as opposed to covert or classified sources); it is not necessarily related to open source software or public intelligence.

(Moitra et al., 2019)

***

There is a seduction to seeking out difficult-to-reach, covertly acquired intelligence. Similar seductions lay in creating expensive global networks to disrupt and help facilitate regime changes, to engage in extrajudicial assassinations from drone platforms, or to prosecute systemic patterns of rendition and torture. The human condition tends towards knowing secrets or information that others do not know and towards acting with impunity when no limits are placed on human action. There is a running joke within Whitehall that to get a Minister's attention you need to present them with documents marked Top Secret. As with all clichés and jokes, there is bound to be an element of truth nested within this absurd premise. The paradox of open source intelligence is that it does not meet the criteria of being covert enough to be attractive to the prurient, whilst also being the mainstay of most governmental intelligence activity. Often overlooked is the political, cultural and economic value of OSINT, which can be used to educate parliament, allies and adversaries, the media, and one's own public, without fear of disclosing a secret.

As with other catch-all terms in the intelligence lexicon, open source intelligence is now attached to a whole host of activities, up to and including—in the UK context—the covert use of public data in support of covert human intelligence source (CHIS) operations (National Police Chiefs Council, 2015). Prior to the internet age, open source intelligence had been associated with institutions like BBC Monitoring which monitored (and still monitors) radio and television broadcasts around the world, whilst the Federal Research Division in the US is an open source analysis bureau that uses the US Library of Congress. During the Cold War, the East German Stasi (The Ministry for State Security) had a unit dedicated to reading open access materials from the West, as a recognition of the understanding this might provide them about their adversaries.

The idea that there is more to be done with open source intelligence is not new. In America, the 1996 Aspin–Brown Commission recommended that there should be a greater use of openly available sources, whilst in the UK the 2004 Butler Report (which followed the invasion of Iraq) and the 2011 Blackett Review (which examined how the government responded to high impact risks) both recommended that greater use be made of the intellectual capital that is openly available (Government Office for Science, 2011; Johnson, 1995; Privy Council, 2004). Following these recommendations there have been movements within the transatlantic intelligence community to incorporate open source intelligence in their assessments but only within their existing frameworks and the recommendation implied by the 9/11 Commission (which explicitly recommended an Open Source Agency for the USA) of there being a need to share, not just a need to know, has made slow progress against the cultural norms of the community.

The notion of better utilisation of open sources has tended to find niche support but there are some signs of it gaining wider traction, and in 2016 the CIA renamed its Open Source unit the Open Source Enterprise. There are debates in OSINT literature around whether open source intelligence is intelligence at all, and nearly all conclude that it is (Hulnick, 2010; Steele, 2007). However, accepting that it is, they query whether accessing information behind paywall databases would count as being an open source (Schaurer & Störger, 2010). It is, after all, not truly open. But the public availability of the resource (regardless of payment) has meant that the consensus is that these sorts of behind-a-paywall resources do count as open source information. The widening of this definition brings into the open source mix all manner of business due-diligence databases, academic journals, trade press outlets amongst the many sources of alternative information. Similarly, there are debates around whether using alias accounts or impersonations to access materials is really open source intelligence or whether the use of covert techniques places this sort of activity under covert action (Wells & Gibson, 2017). Official guidance in the UK places covert interventions, impersonations and so on at the higher end of an ascending scale of OSINT operations: Overt OSINT Investigation or Research, Core OSINT Investigation or Research, Covert and Advanced OSINT Investigation or Research, Covert Internet and Networks Investigations (including impersonation, hacking) and Undercover Online or Covert Internet Investigations (Home Office, 2014).

Governments that are competitors or adversaries of the Euro–Atlantic area have also used a spectrum of open source intelligence techniques. The Chinese, Iranian, North Korean and Russian governments have been particularly active, and non-state actors and activists have fulsomely engaged, too (Zegart & Morell, 2019). The development of open source techniques in law enforcement intelligence is better developed than in national security intelligence (even with the founding of the American Director of National Intelligence's Open Source Center in 2005, now Open Source Enterprise) because of the requirements of validation in open court settings and the utility it has provided to law enforcers in triangulating evidence and bringing prosecutions. There have been strong advances in the tools available to all investigators and a greater use of private software solutions in government investigations, such as the use of Dataminr, which is used extensively in providing real-time information to crisis responders (Dataminr, 2020).

The utility of bulk collection, albeit not open source collection, was highlighted in February 2020 when a report by *The Washington*

Post revealed that the CIA had bought a Swiss company called Crypto AG during the Cold War, which supplied encryption machines to governments around the world, and which had placed backdoors that allowed American officers to intercept the diplomatic communications of those nations. The unparalleled insight it had provided into the inner communications of governments world wide led it to be described as 'the intelligence coup of the century' (Miller, 2020). This echoed the story, in 1988, by British investigative reporter Duncan Campbell, about the National Security Agency's bulk collection programme (Campbell, 1988). Twelve years on, the Campbell story was confirmed and extended by the European Parliament's investigation into ECHELON, which demonstrated the extent to which bulk collection can transform the intelligence picture.

The intelligence collection that Campbell and the European Parliament were focused on was not open source intelligence, but it provided a tantalising glimpse of where the NSA and GCHQ would then go when the internet became more widely used by the public. British and American agencies further increased their investment and emphasis on communications intelligence during this period as developments in the underpinning technology meant it was relatively easy to do, and it similarly had the advantage of catching targets off-guard, thinking they were having private discussions when—in fact—they were communicating in plain sight of the NSA and GCHQ.

The easy charms of bulk collection intelligence were further evidenced by the Snowden revelations, where the level of NSA intrusion into private communications and internet traffic was (as described in Chapter 8) beyond that imagined even by filmmakers. By contrast, open source intelligence, which is intelligence collected from publicly available sources, is commonly and erroneously thought of as something that citizens can do, and as something that will always remain in the unclassified realm: this is only partly true. In terms of conducting open source investigations, there are ways for private citizens to do their own thing. The online open source organisation Bellingcat has produced its own open source intelligence toolkit that it has made available as a Google Docs resource, and it is perfectly possible to utilise their techniques and the repositories they suggest to participate.

Open source intelligence bureaus have rapidly gained credibility, and a large number of online opponents and detractors have attempted to undermine their activities and reputation by lazily describing them as undisclosed government intelligence assets, even when there is yet to be any evidence of this. These bureaux have been cited frequently in international events, where governments have been perceived to be flat-out lying, or obscuring their role in events: the downing of MH370, the Skripal poisoning, the Iranian downing of an airliner in 2020, and evidence of war crimes in the 2022 Ukraine conflict are all examples of this (Bellingcat, 2022; Sheppard, 2018). The vulnerability in this crowdsourcing of intelligence was laid bare in February 2020 when the TerraServer open source satellite imagery service, beloved of human rights activists, journalists and investigators, suddenly disappeared, leaving only expensive or gated services remaining (Gordon, 2020).

The facets that make open source intelligence classified are the originating requirements (what is the question being answered), what sources are being examined (which would provide insights into the questions), the analysis done to those sources, and the end product. It is the intelligence cycle wrapped around the information, rather than the sources drawn in on their own, that create the classification. Edward Snowden's insights around the NSA and GCHQ's capability to intercept nearly all internet traffic suggested a far larger role for open source information (as well as covertly gathered communications intelligence) in the intelligence mix than had been previously assumed. The furore around Huawei's suggested role in the core infrastructure of the 5G networks of the Five Eye nations can be attributed to the extent to which these developed intelligence partners understand the vulnerability and exploitability of these core networks. Miller's story about the CIA buying Crypto AG in the Cold War and therefore having access to privileged communications around the world rather suggests that the US intelligence community—in particular—is aware of the benefits that might be delivered to the Chinese government of such an arrangement: something that Huawei itself was very quick to point out in February 2020 (Huawei, 2020). The UK's position of allowing Huawei to contribute to the peripheral network—and it seems unlikely that in 5G there are such things as core and peripheral networks—is down to the political desire to hedge defying the US, who are implacably opposed, and offending China, with whom good future trade arrangements will be key post-Brexit (Reuters, 2020). Regardless of 5G networks, the 'all source mix' that scholars and analysts describe is now far more heavily weighted in favour of open, rather than closed sources. It was often cited as being 70%–30% in favour of open sources, whilst post-Snowden we could safely revise this figure upwards and towards 95%. Whilst the shift in this balance is relatively uncontested, scholars still maintain that human intelligence is an under-resourced and under-served aspect of intelligence activity, often providing shortcuts to critical information around the intentions of adversaries that cannot easily be gleaned from electronic interception.

In the field of open source intelligence, the rapid development of networked technologies and societal interconnectivity since 2000 has led to a somewhat paradoxical entrenchment of intelligence as a government-led practice. It is paradoxical because of the weight of data being produced, stored and analysed by private corporations, something we could frame around a question of whether Google (via search, email and cloud servers), Facebook (via social networking, profiling and web analysis) or Amazon (via cloud servers) are better placed to conduct large data-set analysis than the intelligence agencies, if tasked appropriately. It is possible to conceive of a parallel intelligence machinery utilising the storage and processing capabilities nested within these three multinational companies to generate an intelligence capability to rival those of governments. The former Director of GCHQ in the UK—Sir David Omand—told the Cheltenham Literary Festival in October 2019:

> the internet companies know more about me, you, everyone in the hall than any intelligence agency ever could or should know about us… The Cambridge Analytica scandal, the way in which our personal data which is freely given in return for having an internet free at the point of use so we can do our searches and

so on … that information is monetised, it is sold [to political campaigns]. This is truly dangerous. I think it's a major threat to democracy and it's uncontrollable… There is nobody in GCHQ monitoring the British population. You need to get access to bulk data, a big haystack, in order to find particular things … patterns or IP addresses of terrorists or whatever it might be. But please preserve us from a situation in which we are under surveillance. Surveillance is persistent observation of the population, or a big chunk of the population. Thankfully that doesn't happen here. (Brown, 2019)

And whilst Sir David is correct that particular sorts of collection require warrants, it has been said that the agencies are able to self-certify some warrants, in some circumstances, and that the technical capacity to conduct surveillance, as he defines it, certainly does exist. There might also be a case for the provision of verified or validated public service information, as part of the intelligence services decision support function, given the revelations around the major internet content and social connectivity services—Amazon, Facebook, Google, MeetUp, Twitter, and YouTube—being found to manipulate (or personalise, to use their lingua franca) information, changing the search results based on payments, or politically sifting results and effectively deplatforming those with unpalatable views (Rogers, 2020). The cultural dissonance between the UK and US over this pattern of activities is observable, where an absolutist freedom of speech only resonates in the US, whereas the UK is more accepting of controls on these freedoms.

We might also question whether the entrenchment into secret government intelligence is as paradoxical in the context of the fundamental shift in social and economic relations that the internet has produced (creating transnational interest groups, and communities of the willing, whilst reducing reliance upon government services and information), and because of the development of 'always-on' networked communications and tracking: my smartphone knows every message I send and receive, it also knows where I go and the networks know who I was near at the time.

Whilst Facebook and Google talk of liberating the individual to connect more widely, to have access to more information and to be able to leverage their connections, the relationship between governments and the citizenry on both sides of the Atlantic has moved in precisely the opposite direction. There has been a marked reduction in the emphasis on the rights of the individual in favour of the interests of the state, certainly since the attacks on New York in 2001 and on London in 2005. So closely entwined are the British and American intelligence agencies in terms of open source intelligence and bulk collection in terms of strategic disposition, technology, methods and assessment, that they can be reasonably spoken of in the same context (Scott, 2012). So, the public's understanding—on both sides of the Atlantic—that they have privacy rights, and that there are limits to what can be done with their data for national security reasons, now has very little relationship with what the agencies consider to be proportionate use and lawful purpose. A good and contemporary example of this comes in the form of the mismatched expectations around the news that the UK's Metropolitan Police Service is to start using facial recognition technology across London, despite the field trials demonstrating serious flaws with the technological underpinnings, despite concerns that the use of this technology might be shown to be unlawful, and despite the similarly strongly expressed concerns about the ethical efficacy of this decision (Dodd, 2020; Fussey & Murray, 2019). For intelligence services, the individual is supplicant to the needs of the whole. For citizens, a confused intellectual pathology rules: the individual is king, unless state power is focused on 'them' 'over there', in which case the absence of empathy means that the individual cannot imagine themselves as being part of 'them', even though they might reasonably be so under a system of near dragnet surveillance.

In theory, for governments the central purpose of intelligence is in the value it can add in terms of decision support. In fact, governments on both sides of the Atlantic appear to have gone down the rabbit hole of favouring covert intelligence gathering operations, and the use of secrecy to hide indiscretions from their own legislatures, rather than to protect sources and methods (Blakeley & Raphael, 2020). The erroneous spread into wider functions and roles, including into proxy policy roles and external disruption roles, has taken the agencies away from their original purpose, and now affects the way that the public, intelligence officers and public policy officials think about the business of intelligence. Data warehousing is not an intelligence function, but it is in this current era. Diplomacy is not an intelligence function, but intelligence officers regularly perform quasi-diplomatic functions. The CIA and MI6 have found themselves accused of quasi-military activities against third countries, including inappropriate treatment of foreign nationals (Einolf, 2022).

The extension of intelligence activities beyond decision support—which has occurred during the lifetime of these agencies—has had a negative impact on their public standing, as greater understanding of their involvement in issues like Iraq, the mistreatment of detainees, and of accusations of involvement in partisan political matters, most notably in the US, has been widely discussed in public forums. As noted in Chapter 1 on disruption, government intelligence has been subject to a form of politicisation where it is expected to be able to be utilised by governing parties on issues broadly of use to them, whilst simultaneously being the object of scorn. This has brought intelligence services closer to the widespread public discontent with politicians, political parties and public officials and—therefore—the growing gap between governments and the citizenry (Adams, Green & Milazzo, 2011).

All too often the activities of governments are described in terms of them being a hindrance or intrusion into everyday life as opposed to being facilitative, enabling or supportive. In part, this is due to the success of neoliberal thinkers in the 1980s creating a dominant narrative around the private sector equating to efficiency, vibrancy and innovation and the public sector equating to inefficiency, reactionary mindsets and gilded lives for public sector workers (Jutel, 2019). These clichés have stuck despite the endless evidence that the UK's corporate culture (amongst multinational enterprises) is every bit as monolithic as the pen portrait of the public sector suggests. The dislocation of the public from politicians has some of its antecedents in the satire movement of the 1960s, in the move to politics dominated by television (where the human frailties of politicians became more obvious), the 'sleaze' of the 1990s around extra-marital affairs and financial corruption (Whiteley *et al.*, 2013), the perceived misuse of intelligence in building the case for war against Iraq in 2003 (which had the impact of hindering the public case for David Cameron's government to attack Syria in 2013, and ultimately prevented them from doing so), the MPs expenses scandal in 2009 (Pattie & Johnston, 2012), and—somewhat ironically—the Liberal Democrats decision to support the Conservative Party in a coalition government and thus go against their own tuition fees pledge (Dommett, 2013). Whilst it is difficult to attribute causation here, this overall dislocation has strong correlation. In this chapter, there is—therefore—a watermark that ties political legitimacy to the ability of intelligence agencies to perform the role of decision support, and to maintain the social contract around the use of open source data for intelligence purposes: a reworking of the notion of policing with consent. This argument can be advanced further to suggest that the adventurous and expansive roles that British and American intelligence agencies played in Iraq and in the war on terror and its associated activities have served to the reduce the legitimacy of the governments they serve, which in turn has undermined the effectiveness of intelligence for both governments and citizens alike.

For services so deeply entwined with the state that Peter Hennessy once described them as the hidden wiring of the state, the agencies have been strongly impacted by the attempts to control public spending on both sides of the Atlantic following the financial crisis of 2008 onwards (Hennessy, 1996). The historically high deficits and corresponding measures to control these deficits have generated considerable commentary as to where the burdens should fall to reduce the level of indebtedness: Should governments seek to generate additional taxation revenues, or should they seek to cut spending (which proportionately impact on the lower socio-economic groupings). Mixed in with this have been a wider public understanding about various governments' use of intelligence to support trade and business activity (Dover, 2007), the use of intelligence to identify, contain and roll back political dissent (Lubbers, 2012), and the over-reaching of those agencies into the private space to do so, something that has become starker with electronic and communications intelligence and the recent developments regarding facial recognition techniques (Hill, 2020). The Snowden revelations and the subsequent commentary and fallout, and the reporting of Kashmir Hill in *The New York Times*, have provided us with insights into the systems of surveillance that are fundamentally misaligned with the public's understanding of open and closed source intelligence activities. These developments have run ahead of where legislators thought they had legislated up to and which they thought they were overseeing through the various scrutiny committees. When the Snowden leaks dropped, President Obama initiated a review of intelligence practices, whilst his successor pursued a bifurcated line on the work of the intelligence services (The White House, 2014). Scholars have also used this moment to think further on what the limits of intelligence activity should be. Academics have been slightly more cautious than intelligence officials about what is proportionate and appropriate. Intelligence officers have been keen to continue to push what is reasonable, within the existing statutory and regulatory frameworks (Bellaby, 2014; Galliott & Reed, 2016; Phythian & Omand, 2018), whilst intelligence officers have been keen to continue to push what is reasonable. All these factors have coalesced to move the intelligence community from being part of 'us' and serving 'us' for an estimated $75bn in the US and £17bn in the UK, to occupying an outsider position as 'them'.

Intelligence as Decision Support: Not Only Secrets Are Intelligence

One of the most persistent features of the discourse around intelligence is that secrets equate to intelligence. Various intelligence grandees and intelligence studies scholars have suggested variations on this theme, be it that government information is intelligence (Kent, 1949), that privileged government information is intelligence (Dover, 2007), that secret government information is intelligence (Herman, 1996), that secret government information that leads to the tasking of a government asset is intelligence (Ferris, 2005) and that intelligence is an umbrella term for government activity in the secret space (Gill & Phythian, 2012). The latter of these is closest, I think, to encompassing what the business of intelligence is to traditional practitioners. The collection of information (be it covertly or via open source methods) is a technical exercise, using a wide array of techniques and technologies. The increasing dominance of warehoused data and large-*n* analytics, which occupies the majority of intelligence community time and attention, is not, therefore, intelligence per se. This poses a question about the role and purpose of intelligence agencies, when the predominant activity is one that often appears to be preparatory or peripheral.

When intelligence efforts are homed in upon the decision-support function, it creates an output that can be measured. The impact of an assessment upon on a decision can be measured for immediate impact and for its impact over time. For British and American intelligence communities everything that carries a classification (in terms of what information has been collected, how it was collected, and why it was collected) *is* intelligence. It might otherwise be described as merely classified information, rather than intelligence. The collection and warehousing of vast quantities of data, the majority—99% in the case of the National Security Agency—of which remains unanalysed, has been done because the technical facilities existed to collect and store it. These activities are not undertaken because they serve an immediate strategic or operational end-state: it is hoped that they will play an important role in future operations when the relevant technologies and techniques have matured.

Indeed, as one evaluates the totality of the technical underpinnings of modern intelligence, what one finds is a very great deal of money spent on technical collection and storage, and virtually nothing on human-to-human operations, on open source collection, on processing, or on sense-making tools for the individual analyst or analytic team.

As noted in the introductory remarks to this chapter, the majority of the information used by British and American intelligence agencies is open source in nature. It is difficult to evidence this point from intelligence repositories because they are closed and classified, but there have been multiple public utterances from Directors of Central Intelligence (DCI) and intelligence managers in the UK that reinforce this point (Gibson, 2004). President Truman's original vision for the CIA was that it should be a centralised aggregator of the intelligence collected from across the great breadth of the US intelligence system. Truman's belief in this form of institution came from his perceived need to make sense of assessments and recommendations that he viewed as often conflicting with each other, thus making his job as a decision-maker more complicated. He further concluded that these conflicting assessments more often than not looked like they were positioning for influence or resources (Truman, 1963).[2]

Intelligence bureaucracies have been no different from other parts of government in seeking to reaffirm their utility to decision makers and thus securing larger numbers of staff and larger shares of the government's financial resources as a consequence. The Cold War provided an ideal platform for both US and British intelligence to ask for more generous resourcing to meet the assessed threat presented by the Soviet Union. The end of the Cold War saw both communities suffer from the mooted peace dividend, only to recover their losses in recognition of the complex fight against global jihadism. Whilst there is no denying the reality of the threats presented by Soviet and jihadist aggression, the imperative to pull in further resource has conditioned much of the bureaucratic posturing of intelligence agencies. The existential quality of the Cold War and the Global War on Terror, and how easy it has been to focus upon these two broad threat matrices, distracted the intelligence community away from its responsibility to provide decision support to senior policy officials, to advise on how to adequately respond to the complexity that defines the international system, and to assess other contemporary and emergent threats (Fuller & Snyder, 2009). Instead, intelligence became synonymous with often violent disruption and dislocation, including in several cases regime changes across the globe. Activities that became seen by analysts and commentators as having been misguided or inappropriate precisely because of the lack of raw, and assessed, intelligence should have been core business for these agencies, and that would have assisted them in understanding and managing the complexity of international politics and conflict.

The idea that the international system is complex in a way that requires advanced 'systems' approaches to understanding it is an underdeveloped but important line of thought. Systems approaches have their antecedents in the highly individualised work of Buckminster Fuller and Mario Bunge who, from hard-science backgrounds, argued that only systems analysis could accurately provide details of emergent threats and patterns in the international system, which would highlight hitherto unrecognised competitive behaviours (Bunge, 1999; Fuller, 1979). They also noted that a systems approach demonstrated that the international system tends towards disequilibrium, rather than stability, which is a core element of policy planning and diplomatic practice. If we accept the premise that the international system might not be as we imagine it is, then we also have to accept that government policy might well be aimed at factors that are not intrinsically part of the analytical problem (Cairney, 2012). Adopting a systems approach might, incidentally, provide governments with reasons to warehouse the quantities of data they already do, and which are capable of providing more scientifically rigorous assessments of threat.

Following a line of thought spurred by systems analysis, which has been under-explored in the social scientific literature, provides the conclusion that the intelligence assessments produced at the moment are prompting governments to look in the wrong direction. Stephen Marrin describes this phenomenon as 'information push' (Marrin, 2009): namely, that the intelligence community—the producer of intelligence—has also tended towards setting the priorities for the customers of intelligence. The intelligence community is producing assessments for what it thinks the policy community should be interested in, or what it wants policy makers to be interested in. This takes intelligence agencies away from being agents of decision support and, instead, places them as collecting, analysing and disseminating products of their own choice, whilst being able to claim that this is serving the policy community and the interests of the electorate. This potential confusion in the intelligence community's core purpose has been long identified in the margins by producers as well as commentators. The careful 'delineation' of the intelligence producer from the policy-making process was seen as essential to avoid partiality or issue bias in the production of intelligence as long ago as 1976 (Forbush, Chase & Goldberg, 1976). Another way of looking at the failure of our established modern intelligence agencies is to consider the argument that they do not complete their assessments using holistic analytics (all threats, all policies, all timelines from historical to near and far futures). Contemporary agencies also confine themselves to a narrow reading and assessment of an issue, rather than branching out to consider the true-cost or through-life-cost analytics which would provide a different balance of assessment and risk. Downing Street's call—in December 2019—for super-forecasters to join their policy unit is emblematic of a shift in the right direction, even if it was a temporary move tied to Dominic Cummings' tenure and insights. These laudable efforts were marred by the immediate furore over the first of Downing Street's forecasting recruits being publicly associated with eugenics (Taylor, 2020). There were voices in government bureaucracies on both sides of the Atlantic in the 1990s and 2000s that were attempting to shift governmental thinking about emergent threats and the vulnerabilities that were present in public health, illegal immigration, and data integrity and cyber-security as the challenges of the future. These opportunities were missed by governments, who either marginalised these voices or closed the units they worked in.

In allowing intelligence agencies to change their structural role from decision support to information suppliers, governments have given far greater space for the agencies to take on their own (often disguised) political roles. The agencies have become semi-autonomous norm entrepreneurs, guided by multiple bureaucratic imperatives to seek the marginal outcomes that justify the budgetary, human and technical resources they demand. In this respect the agencies have adopted a form of Keynesian investment to maintain the broad base of technological and analytical support industries that have located themselves around, and which feed off, the intelligence community. This is the intelligence equivalent of the military industrial complex phenomenon and adds to the friction and barriers in trying to reform the agencies or their roles.

Does the Collection of Secrets for the Core Executive Justify the Entire Activity?

One of the lines of resistance to serious reflection about what intelligence is for has been the notion of competitive advantage for states. One of Prime Minister's Blair's justifications for war with Iraq was that the government knew important and secret intelligence to which the public was not privy. The implication was that if only the public were able to view this information they, too, would see that war was justified (Pfiffner & Phythian, 2008). The position of collecting and providing secret and competitive materials for the executive has been used by senior intelligence figures and—in the UK—by intelligence customers as being sufficient justification for their budgets (Lowenthal, 2012). However, the claim that all intelligence activity is justified because of the information supplied to the executive, be it the president in the US or the prime minister, National Security Committee and individual ministers in the UK, is partly undermined by the growing list of incidences where the product delivered was later shown to be critically inaccurate or underdeveloped, where agencies were the witting or unwitting ciphers for foreign influence, or where the agencies' expansion into policy areas was shown to be counterproductive—be it in terms of the quality of product that could be achieved from this perspective or the political fallout from the presence of the intelligence community working on those issues.

Focusing upon the intelligence spending of the US and UK, the US spends roughly $210 million per day and the UK spends £70 million a day on a straight-line equation. If we exclude some capital spending costs on building new infrastructure or acquiring new IT systems, to take two examples, the typical consulting rate for Ivy League, or in the UK Russell Group, professorial faculty is circa $2,000/£1,500 per day, which in turn equates to 102,500 professorial consultancy days in the US and 34,200 consultancy days in the UK. The quantity of what we might reasonably assume is world-class open source information that is vested in that equivalent consultancy spend is impressive in absolute and relative terms. What added value might we find in the intelligence agencies, over and above open source equivalents? And, more particularly, what added value might we find when mapped across the critical functions of decision support, providing competitive advantage in the international system, horizon scanning for international challenges and threats, responding to aggression from adversaries (which is another form of decision support) and understanding competing cultures? The relationship between this primary reservoir of open source intelligence and the agencies has been underdeveloped and is often fitful for reasons of culture, control and purpose. But what can be concluded is that whilst the information revolution has provided us with unparalleled access to knowledge drawn from across the globe, this has yet to be appropriately harnessed by the government level intelligence community, which has remained wedded to its existing methods and organisational architectures.

The move into alternative roles and away from the classic decision-support roles, which are well suited to open source intelligence, has seen a chronic under-investment in the analytical communities in the US and UK, hovering at an estimated 10%. Given the importance of analysis and assessment work to intelligence and decision support, this is a terribly small percentage. There has also been a limited discussion within think tanks and research institutes around the quality of the analytical pool: the average age of analysts has reduced markedly since 2000, often leaving newly graduated officers in positions of considerable influence, whilst experienced officers have either faced redundancy (certainly in the case of Sovietologists, which now would seem a grave error given the activism of the Russian state and the paucity of analytical expertise on Russia) or have sought careers on better terms outside government circles. In the case of cyber security experts, this has led to their being able to command more than double their public salaries on day one of their move into the private sector. The private security marketplace is now busy with former intelligence officers and analysts seeking to apply and sell their methods into new challenges.

As noted in Chapter 3, intelligence communities have been resistant to the notion that they can deal openly with outsiders, and so the relationship between the two sides has been ad hoc and often fitful. The rationale for this is based around a risk aversion to possible leakages, or vulnerabilities in getting openly close to unvetted sources of knowledge and expertise. Several websites have sprung up to reveal the links between academics and the intelligence community, which will not smooth the path to cooperation. Having reviewed my own entry on one of these websites, it was inaccurate and drew some rather lurid inferences from evidence I gave in 2012 to a Parliamentary Select Committee, which was entirely capable of being balanced by using evidence I provided to the Defence Select Committee in 2018 and 2019.

A classic intelligence view of outsider sources is to have them within an informant frame of reference: to think of the provider of information as doing so against the wishes of the target (so being a traitor), as a source being listened to or surveilled (a target), or as an external contractor or reservist (hired help). This focus on an essentially exploitative and exclusionary taxonomy of external actors means that the intelligence community is largely ineffective in its quest to harvest knowledge from external nodes of information in the open source space, including from academics, civil society actors, business people (and especially those running small and medium-sized enterprises), local government officers, legacy and new media figures, defence workers, and from those in third-sector industries. But, as the UK Arts and Humanities Research Council grant I held with Michael Goodman at King's College London demonstrated, with the appropriate controls academic experts can provide open source insights and challenge to a government community. The problems—even of commissioning scholars who would not pass clearance for government employment—are not insurmountable, nor are they particularly burdensome.

One of the key outputs of the British and American intelligence agencies are the daily briefing notes, and updates on intelligence actions that have taken place. The symbolism of the morning briefing as the blue riband activity of intelligence agencies is unlikely to lose its cachet despite President Trump's reluctance to read even the shortest briefing notes, preferring—instead—to consume his news from the television (Wolff, 2019). It has been noted on both sides of the Atlantic that the role of the intelligence analyst has been reduced from providing analysis to focusing on providing a rolling log of events or news. This function does not provide decision support to senior leaders, at the same time as there is no other capability mandated to achieve the desired end of timely, relevant, reliable decision support.

The opportunity that is currently being missed is the chance to access a measured and integrated set of methodologies to identify useful questions and then—as a consequence—to shape valuable answers to those questions. Answering questions in the moment—questions the Executive knows they need an answer to—is far removed from the current practice of 'We will tell you what we think you need to know.' Jan Herring, the first National Intelligence Officer for Science & Technology in the USA, distinguished—in what is known as the 'Herring Triangle'—among four levels of intelligence investment: recurring monitoring of all topics big and small (40% need, 10% cost); shared help desk providing tailored answers in the moment (30% need, 20% cost); primary research and experts on demand (20% need, 30% cost); and strategic forecasting, in breadth and depth, across all relevant languages (10% need, 40% cost). None of the intelligence agencies across the Atlantic area currently does this, and yet the Herring Triangle remains a sound articulation of intelligence priorities.

If we were to evaluate our intelligence machinery in the context of decision support, we would look to see to what extent the state uses its intelligence agencies to garner various kinds of advantage and forewarning in the international system. Such a review would look to focus on the timeliness, precision, effect and through-life cost of intelligence. It might also look to do so from the perspective of the target, the perspective of the recipient, and from the perspective of how the utility of the activity can be maximised for the public and the practitioner. The sheer quantity of open source information available across languages, borders and time—be it from scraped sources or via external experts—is such that it would be possible to evaluate the current knowledge produced by the agencies from an all-source mix. For example, the Chinese government employs a unit to scour academic journals and published conference papers to gather up and assess what can be used from these sources that is not already part of government knowledge.

As many commentators have noted, a key flaw in our intelligence systems is the dislocation created by the form of American business-school managerialism of meeting key performance indicators, including the financial metrics laid out annually, versus the servant-of-the-state obligations that are around advancing the cause of the nation and ensuring it is better prepared to deal with the complexities in the international and domestic systems. So, it is not just the core executive who require decision-support, it is Cabinet Secretaries (US), Junior Ministers (UK) and further down to bureau and branch chiefs and their individual country or topic desk officers; and the need to address the lack of open source support was a high-level recommendation of the 9/11 Commission's Report in 2004 (National Commission On Terrorist Attacks Upon The United States). Neither the US Congress nor the Houses of Parliament in the UK receives intelligence support across their public policy functions. Consequently their ability to effectively oversee and check the government, or to consider whether government spending is appropriate, is fundamentally compromised. Both the US Congress and the UK Parliament are heavily dependent upon the diligent work of the Congressional Research Service (CRS) in the US and the parliamentary researchers in the UK. Both organisations do a highly credible job in the context of their resourcing and remit— but neither produces 'decision-support'. Legislators also make use of external experts providing testimony in investigative committees, but this can be subject to the known reliability of the expert and whether they are known to parliamentary staff. In the UK, oral evidence is often triggered by the submission of formal, written evidence, something that forms a permanent record in the legislative bodies' archives. Legislators, often assisted by the gatekeeping role of their advisors or aides, are subjected to a large number of external contacts from lobbyists and interest groups. So large is the number that is often difficult for legislators to discriminate between information that is delivered to them with integrity and that which is delivered to meet the needs of a narrow sectoral interest. There has been consistent commentary about the poor level of debate and scrutiny in the US and UK legislatures, and yet the structural reasons for this remain unaddressed, falling back upon the hidden wisdom of the democratic mandate.

Whilst governments talk of evidence-based policy making, the reality has been that evidence forms only a small part of the overall mix (Cairney, 2016; Sanderson, 2002). Whilst there is an industrial effort in government bureaucracies to solve public policy problems as they occur, to scan horizons for the future problems and, in the case of intelligence agencies, to scan for future threats, these are done within tightly constrained institutional and cultural framings. Knowledge is produced for particular organisations with particular structural obligations. Without reorientating intelligence activity more towards a decision support function, then, our intelligence agencies will remain in the business of generating secrets, only some of which will contribute to decisions that legislators and the core executive make and to the national interest.

It may be that in the long run the greatest value of OSINT will be to mobilise public opinion to the point that political decisions will need to be upon verifiable evidence, rather than what we seem to have today, where 'pay to play' lobbying yields a disproportionate impact upon the policy process. The attitude articulated so well by Henry Kissinger, that 'Intelligence is not all that important in the exercise of power, and is often, in post of fact, useless', feels like a sentiment that belongs to the politicians of our times. Realistically, intelligence is not making a difference at the strategic, operational, tactical or technical (acquisition) levels, outside militarised conceptions of security activity. But we must be forced to conclude that, without novel forms of oversight and a public demand for evidence-based decision-making, the business of government intelligence will remain a spending programme that seeks to secure its budget and perform against targets set in the militarised security realm.

Nearly all intelligence agencies contain an open source unit. These tend to be staffed by a relatively modest number of staff, and conversations with them tend to centre around the latest software solution that their senior officers have been sold, which has given rise to greater expectations. Whilst it would disrupt the intelligence architecture, there is a case to be made for a dedicated Open Source Agency, which would have the intelligence community and legislators as its customers. Such an agency would provide politicians and their security officials with something that Berkowitz and Goodman describe as a platform of 'best truths' (Berkowitz & Goodman, 2002). And there are (now ageing) indications that a better connection to open source intelligence would reframe the view of governments on both sides of the Atlantic regarding risk and threat in the international system. The 2004 United Nations High-Level Panel on Threats, Challenges, and Change listed poverty as its top global threat, followed by infectious diseases and environmental degradation, which gives the impression of this panel being way ahead of its time in terms of the threats it identified and their continuing relevance to today, where the list would not be radically different (United Nations, 2004). The threat presented by the economic dislocation between those who produce and consume and those who own has become wider rather than narrower since 2004. The threat presented by the Ebola and COVID-19 viruses, as well as the climate crisis that has belatedly come to dominate headlines and public discourse, all point to the stability of the UN's initial assessment. Interstate violence, terrorism and organised crime, which are the mainstays of intelligence agency activities, fell outside the top four hierarchically listed threats. Whilst there has been an increase in terrorist activities since 2004, and the Russian invasion of Ukraine refocuses our attention eastwards, the magnitude of threat (globally) is not sufficient to radically rewrite the 2004 assessment. A greater focus on open source intelligence may well equip our governments to address more effectively those issues that are objectively more threatening to us over the long term.

Concluding Thoughts: The Public Craft of Intelligence

Public commentary around intelligence operations and the business of intelligence generally has been a large part of how UK and US government activity has been discussed since the 1980s. The public's perception of intelligence has had very little to do with the ways in which core intelligence products can support decision making in government. The public has been fed a diet of adventurous overseas operations, treachery and stories of how technologies are infringing our privacy and civil liberties. There is a reinforcing cycle of certainty between the ways that successive administrations and their agencies have cast their role, and essentially their primacy over all intelligence activities, and the way that media outlets, academics and popular cultural sources have reinforced these positions. These (false) certainties have been allowed to grow, even in a time when computing power, data warehousing and the ability of non-state actors to *do* assessments and analysis clearly rivals that of government agencies. These are certainties that have been advanced and doubled-down at a time when the current zeitgeist is to question (and reject) established forms of authority, and to distrust the judgment of those in authority.

Richard Aldrich and Chris Moran talk of the irrelevance of secrecy in the modern era, of a movement towards 'delayed disclosure'. This ties into the historical development of open source intelligence and the rearguard actions of government agencies to maintain a dominance in the intelligence world. Intelligence as a form of diplomacy is just diplomacy. Intelligence as special operations and disruption is just a form of special operations. The business of intelligence should be around providing warning notice and advantage in decision making to the core executive and to legislators.

The current configuration of intelligence agencies and their roles is premised upon providing secrets to the executive. And the agencies satisfy this requirement, whist not challenging the core assumptions or disrupting the projection of 'our' values. As with its armed forces, the US intelligence community has managed to create a parallel form of military–industrial complex (MIC) where the technological needs of the sector are driven—in part—by the requirements of technology vendors and the wider community of developers and sub-contractors involved in the MIC (Giroux, 2007; Lemieux, 2018; National Commission for the Review of the Research and Development Programs of the United States Intelligence Community, 2013). Whilst a smaller market, the UK has—as with most things in politics, economics and culture—followed the US lead, and the increased demand for technological solutions in intelligence has, in turn, created a vibrant market and support structure that includes a large number of small and medium-sized companies and the universities (GCHQ, 2018). The absence of effective lines of accountability and oversight on both sides of the Atlantic exacerbates the tendency towards technology and operational types that are done because they *can* be done, rather than because it serves a useful national security purpose for them to be done. The absence of adequate independent political oversight (although it is not clear that political oversight even in an intrusive form is particularly useful, as we can see from the amount of time the Prime Minister's Office spent blocking the Intelligence and Security Committee's report on Russian interference in 2019) and transparent audit processes has contributed to the current perception of the intelligence services having 'gone rogue' in one form or another (Intelligence and Security Committee of Parliament, 2020).

An intelligence community aimed at providing decision-support—throughout the various tiers of government activity, from the strategic all the way down to the technical level—should seek to:

(1) Develop requirements and manage their all-source collection and production consonant with a complex analytic model that integrates the broadest understanding of threats across core government policy areas. The shift here is away from narrow security threats to areas that are more representative of threats to the nation, but which also require intelligence input into the policy responses.

(2) Systematically utilise open source resources such as trade publications, the academic literature and private sector expertise to produce intellectually deep and broad intelligence essential to defining national security strategy, which then informs military and security planning processes. This has been particularly timely given the publication in 2021 of the UK's *Integrated Security, Defence and Foreign Policy Review*, which had been flagged as a root-and-branch look at the way the UK conceives and configures its response to security challenges (Howe, 2020).

(3) Produce timely and diverse intelligence-led decision support to condition the acquisition of security assets, be they military assets, security assets, law enforcement capabilities and associated areas. This should be done more widely than considering kinetic threats (military or terrorist actions), but in terms of information and influence operations and in responding to the hyper-competitive threat across industrial areas such engineering and trade in terms of designs, materials, industry partners, and supply chain vulnerability. This activity should

also include an element of counterintelligence capability against those who seek to diminish these capabilities domestically.

(4) Produce timely, culturally sensitive and accurate intelligence to support complex operations.

Many in the intelligence community might feel that they already do this. And some might. But this is not the stable practice within the community. Nor is it new to express these concerns or critiques. The critiques of the intelligence cycle, institutional silos and stovepipes in national intelligence communities and the production of synthetic or low-value intelligence product—that is almost immediately archived—are well drawn. These critiques have not resulted in significant reforms within the intelligence community nor in the role that intelligence plays in government decision making. Thus, reforms have not occurred to make intelligence work as it should, but more to reform intelligence activities as they already are. A move towards further capitalising on open source strands would improve the technical quality of the intelligence product and also improve the value for money equation that is often at the forefront of policy makers' minds. As noted in Chapter 2, the current intelligence staffing model, which is understandably preoccupied with secrecy, does not lend itself to bringing in external expertise, and so a change to this model and an emphasis on counterintelligence and connectivity would be a useful innovation inside a new Open Source Agency or, less ambitiously, within the existing open source functions of the agencies.

So, intelligence (as it exists within and outside government) continues to evolve as a craft. The availability of sources of information from which intelligence assessments can be made continues to grow. And this liberalisation of information sources and toolboxes of open source techniques, like those of Bellingcat and the Pathfinder programme run by Arno Reuser, has allowed for more citizen participants in high-end open source intelligence. There is, of course, a great deal of unhelpful noise created by the 'sense and feel' of armchair commentators, as we are discovering in the analysis of the Russian invasion of Ukraine. The ubiquity of the internet and of the means by which to distribute assessments will have the effect of removing the state's monopoly over intelligence. A public craft of intelligence is as relevant to my decision making, as an individual, as it to a government's. The impact of the growing range of intelligence activities, from covert collection, back-channel diplomacy, to covert and sometimes violent disruption, to warehousing personal data that is never analysed, has provided the rationale for intelligence as an exclusively government activity. A change of emphasis in the role of intelligence agencies would open up this space to wider societal challenges, and to stronger uses of the vast pool of open sources that can be used as a platform for evidence-based decision making. It might also provide a more internationalised and holistic view of social and political relations.

References

Adams, J., Green, J. and Milazzo, C. (2011) 'Has the British public depolarized along with political elites? An American perspective on British public opinion'. *Comparative Political Studies* 45 (4), 507–530.

Bellaby, Ross (2014) *The Ethics of Intelligence: A New Framework*. Abingdon: Routledge.

Bellingcat (2022) 'Hospitals bombed and apartments destroyed: Mapping incidents of civilian harm in Ukraine'. *Bellingcat*. 17 March. https://www.bellingcat.com/news/2022/03/17/hospitals-bombed-and-apartments-destroyed-mapping-incidents-of-civilian-harm-in-ukraine/

Berkowitz, Bruce and Goodman, Allan (2002) *Best Truths: Intelligence in an Information Age*. New Haven, CT: Yale University Press.

Blakeley, R. and Raphael, S. (2020) 'Accountability, denial and the future-proofing of British torture'. *International Affairs* 96 (3), 691–709.

Brown, Mark (2019) 'Tech firms know more about us than any spy agency—ex-GCHQ chief'. *The Guardian*, 8 October.

Bunge, Mario (1999) *Social Science under Debate: A Philosophical Perspective*. Toronto: University of Toronto Press.

Cairney, Paul (2012) 'Complexity theory in political science and public policy'. *Political Studies Review* 10 (3), 346–358.

———. (2016) *The Politics of Evidence-based Policymaking*. London: Springer.

Campbell, Duncan (1988) 'Somebody's listening'. *New Statesman*, 12 August, 10–12.

Dataminr (2020) Dataminr homepage. 13 February. Accessed 13 February 2020. https://www.dataminr.com/

Dodd, Vikram (2020) 'Met police to begin using live facial recognition cameras in London'. *The Guardian*, 24 January.

Dommett, Katharine (2013) 'A miserable little compromise? Exploring Liberal Democrat fortunes in the UK coalition'. *The Political Quarterly* 84 (2), 218–227.

Dover, Robert (2007) 'For Queen and company: The role of Intelligence in the UK's arms trade'. *Political Studies* 55 (4), 638–708.

Einolf, C. J. (2022) 'How torture fails: Evidence of misinformation from torture-induced confessions in Iraq'. *Journal of Global Security Studies* 1–19.

Ferris, John (2005) *Intelligence and Strategy: Selected Essays.* Abingdon: Routledge.

Forbush, R., Chase, G. and Goldberg, R. (1976) 'CIA intelligence support for foreign and national security policy making'. *Studies in Intelligence* Volume 20.

Fuller, Buckminster (1979) *Synergetics: Explorations in the Geometry of Thinking.* London: Macmillan.

Fuller, R. and Snyder, J. (2009) *Ideas and Integrities: A Spontaneous Autobiographical Disclosure.* New York, NY: Lars Muller Publishers.

Fussey, Pete and Murray, Daragh (2019) *Independent Report on the London Metropolitan Police Service's Trial of Live Facial Recognition Technology.* Colchester: Human Rights Centre, University of Essex.

Galliott, Jai and Reed, Warren (2016) *Ethics and the Future of Spying: Technology, National Security and Intelligence Collection.* Abingdon: Routledge.

GCHQ (2018) 'GCHQ director speaks at the launch of the National Cyber Security Centre's second annual review'. GCHQ. 16 October. Accessed 13 February 2020. https://www.gchq.gov.uk/news/gchq-director-speaks-launch-national-cyber-security-centres-second-annual-review

Gibson, Stevyn (2004) 'Open source intelligence'. *The RUSI Journal* 149 (1), 16–22.

Gill, Peter and Phythian, Mark (2012) *Intelligence in an Insecure World. 2nd edition.* London: Polity Press.

Giroux, Henry (2007) *University in Chains: Confronting the Military–Industrial–Academic Complex.* London: Routledge.

Gordon, Aaron (2020) 'Satellite imagery service used by human rights investigators abruptly shuts down'. *Vice.* 4 February. Accessed 6 February 2020. https://www.vice.com/en_us/article/xgqggw/satellite-imagery-service-used-by-human-rights-investigators-abruptly-shuts-down

Government Office for Science (2011) *Blackett Review of High Impact, Low Probability Events.* London: HMSO.

Hennessy, Peter (1996) *The Hidden Wiring: Unearthing the British Constitution.* London: Phoenix.

Herman, Michael (1996) *Intelligence Power in Peace and War.* Cambridge: Cambridge University Press.

Hill, Kashmir (2020) 'The secretive company that might end privacy as we know it'. *The New York Times*, 18 January.

Home Office (2014) *Covert Human Intelligence Sources. Codes of Practice. Pursuant to Section 71 of the Regulation of Investigatory Powers Act 2000.* London: The Stationary Office. Accessed 13 February 2020. https:// www.legislation.gov.uk/ukdsi/2014/9780111118580

Howe, Earl (2020) *Integrated Security, Defence and Foreign Policy Review.* 8 January. Accessed 13 February 2020. https://hansard.parliament. uk/Lords/2020-01-08/debates/FD784319-97FA-4222-A44C-B205972F8949/IntegratedSecurityDefenceAndForeignPolicyReview

Huawei (2020) Tweet concerning the CIA and Crypto AG. 12 February.

Hulnick, Arthur (2010) 'The dilemma of open sources intelligence: Is OSINT really intelligence?' In Loch K. Johnson (ed.) *The Oxford Handbook of National Security Intelligence* (pp. 229–241). Oxford: Oxford University Press.

Intelligence and Security Committee of Parliament (2020) *Russia.* Parliamentary Inquiry. London: HMSO.

Johnson, Loch K. (1995) 'The Aspin–Brown intelligence inquiry: Behind the closed doors of a blue ribbon commission'. *Studies in Intelligence* 48 (3), 1–20.

Jutel, Olivier (2019) 'Civility, subversion and technocratic class consciousness: Reconstituting truth in the journalistic field'. In Rosemary Overell and Brett Nicholls (eds) *Post-Truth and the Mediation of Reality: New Conjectures* (pp. 177–202). Zurich: Springer.

Kent, Sherman (1949) *Strategic Intelligence for American World Policy.* New York, NY: Princeton University Press.

Lemieux, Frederic (2018) *Intelligence and State Surveillance in Modern Societies: An International Perspective.* Bingley: Emerald.

Lowenthal, Mark (2012) *Intelligence: From Secrets to Policy. 5th edition.* New York, NY: Sage.

Lubbers, Eveline (2012) *Secret Manoeuvres in the Dark: Corporate and Police Spying on Activists.* London: Pluto Press.

Marrin, Steve (2009) 'Intelligence analysis and decision making'. In Peter Gill, Steve Marrin and Mark Phythian (eds) *Intelligence Theory: Key Questions and Debates* (pp. 131–150). Abingdon: Routledge.

Miller, Greg (2020) 'The intelligence coup of the century'. *The Washington Post*, 12 February.

Moitra, Abha, Bracewell, David, Gustafson, Steven, Baylor, Michael and Chau, Tina (2019) 'Systems and methods for facilitating the gathering of open source intelligence'. United States of America Patent US10235421B2. 19 March.

National Commission for the Review of the Research and Development Programs of the United States Intelligence Community (2013) *Special Topic White Paper: The IC's Role within US Cyber R&D*. Special Report. Washington, DC: NCRRDP.

National Commission on Terrorist Attacks Upon The United States (2004) *The 9/11 Commission Report: Final Report of the National Commission on Terrorist Attacks upon the United States*. Washington, DC: National Commission on Terrorist Attacks upon the United States. https://lccn. loc.gov/2004356401

National Police Chiefs Council (2015) 'NPCC guidance on Open source investigation/research'. Kent and Essex Police. *Suffolk Police*. Accessed 13 February 2020. https://www.suffolk.police.uk/sites/suffolk/files/003525-16_npcc_guidance_redacted.pdf

Pattie, Charles and Johnston, Ron (2012) 'The electoral impact of the UK 2009 MPs' expenses scandal'. *Political Studies* 60 (4), 730–750.

Pfiffner, James P. and Phythian, Mark (eds) (2008) *Intelligence and National Security Policymaking on Iraq: British and American Perspectives*. Manchester: Manchester University Press.

Phythian, Mark and Omand, David (2018) *Principled Spying: The Ethics of Secret Intelligence*. Washington, DC: Georgetown University Press.

Privy Council (2004) *Review of Intelligence on Weapons of Mass Destruction*. London: HMSO.

Reuters (2020) 'Trump "apoplectic" with UK's Johnson over Huawei decision: FT'. *The New York Times*, 7 February. Accessed 7 February 2020. https://www.nytimes.com/reuters/2020/02/06/technology/06reuters-britain-usa-huawei-trump.html

Rogers, R. (2020) 'Deplatforming: Following extreme internet celebrities to Telegram and alternative social media'. *European Journal of Communication* 35 (3), 213–229.

Sanderson, Ian (2002) 'Evaluation, policy learning and evidence-based policy making'. *Public Administration* 80 (1), 1–22.

Schaurer, Florian and Störger, Jan (2010) *The Evolution of Open Source Intelligence*. Zurich: ETH.

Scott, Len (2012) 'Reflections on the age of intelligence'. *Intelligence and National Security* 27 (5), 617–624.

Sheppard, Lindsey (2018) 'Organizational legitimacy and open source intelligence'. In Margaret Kosal (ed.) *Technology and the Intelligence Community* (pp.155–177). Zurich: Springer.

Steele, Robert (2007) 'Open source intelligence'. In Loch K. Johnson (ed.) *Hanbook of Intelligence Studies* (pp. 129–147). Abingdon: Routledge.

——— (2013) 'The evolving craft of intelligence'. In Robert Dover, Michael Goodman and Claudia Hillebrand (eds) *Routledge Companion to Intelligence Studies* (pp.71–84). Abingdon: Routledge.

Taylor, M. (2020) 'Build bridges to the future'. *RSA Journal* 22–27.

The White House (2014) 'Remarks by the President on Review of Signals Intelligence'. Office of the Press Secretary, 17 January. Accessed 6 November 2019. http://www.whitehouse.gov/the-press-office/2014/01/17/remarks- president-review-signals-intelligence

Truman, Harry S. (1963) 'Limit CIA role to intelligence'. *The Washington Post*, 22 December, p. A11.

United Nations (2004) *A More Secure World: Our Shared Responsibility.* New York, NY: United Nations.

Wells, Douglas and Gibson, Helen (2017) 'OSINT from a UK perspective: Considerations from the law enforcement and military domains'. In *Proceedings Estonian Academy of Security Sciences, 16: From Research to Security Union* (pp. 84–113). Tallin: Estonian Academy of Security Sciences.

Whiteley, P., Clarke, H. D., Sanders, D. and Stewart, M. (2013) 'Why do voters lose trust in governments? Public perceptions of government honesty and trustworthiness 1997–2013'. Paper presented at the conference on Citizens and Politics in Britain Today: Still a civic culture? London School of Economics, 26 September.

Wolff, Michael (2019) *Fire and Fury: Inside the Trump White House.* New York, NY: Abacus.

Zegart, Amy and Morell, Michael (2019) 'Spies, lies, and algorithms: Why US intelligence agencies must adapt or fail'. *Foreign Affairs* 98, 85–91.

5

INTELLIGENCE AGENCIES AND HYBRID WARS

What You Need to Know...

Intelligence agencies have found themselves at the interface between the opportunities afforded by greater access to information, and the hazards and vulnerabilities presented by hostile actors engaging in information conflict. There is an arms race underway between competitor states concerning who can gain a critical advantage in the information space, with 5G infrastructure and quantum computing promising the means by which to better understand an adversary and to break an adversary's cryptography, thus creating a critical advantage to those possessing such technology. Where there are opportunities in the information space, these have presented their own challenges: namely, the difficulty of making sense of vast collections of data, and the negative impact on the relationship between the agencies and the public. The public's trust in public authorities, in expert opinion, and in verifiable evidence has been rapidly eroded since 2003, leaving societal level vulnerabilities in the West. Intelligence officers are not immune to these trends and agencies have begun to take steps to insulate analytical processes from the impact of disinformation. Intelligence services find themselves unable to make compelling cases to the public to justify further intrusions into public privacy, without adequate support from politicians and in a context where technology companies have

141

been able to leap ahead of where regulation and oversight sits to do what intelligence officers are currently prevented from doing.

***

The modern political and security era exists in the 'internet age', 'the social media age', 'the big data age' and the era of populist politics. There is truth in and to all these labels, and to the notion that what impacts upon wider society must also impact upon intelligence officers, agencies and intelligence practice. Broadly, there are two connected phenomena at play: (1) the development and growth, in terms of usage and use cases, of electronic communication, storage and analytical technologies; and (2) the disruption to established political (and social and economic) cultures in the post-industrial world. These connected developments have—as this chapter expands upon—generated opportunities for intelligence agencies to increase the amount of data they are able to collect and analyse, to increase their capacity for situational awareness, and to conduct inquiries and investigations, even if some of the clearer advantages are to be found in investigations rather than in pre-emption.

For intelligence agencies and officers, the technological and political disruption has offered great advantages—in terms of collection, retention and analysis—but unwieldy challenges because of the difficulties in sifting, sorting and making sense of such vast information trails and in finding information that is important, as opposed to just more noise. The technological revolution has also posed challenges to essential elements of intelligence activity, such as human intelligence (who can go off grid now?) and the retention of secrets. But these developments have placed great challenges on counterintelligence defences (both of agencies and the infrastructure they are charged with protecting) and to running covert human intelligence operations, due to the norms of social media presence and activity, on counter-subversion in the manipulation of politics and of public narratives, and in developing technologies and techniques to collect and analyse useful information, rather than finding the enhanced quantities of collected information a positive hindrance. When it comes to recruitment, and in simple terms, an officer with no social media profiles is potentially as problematic as one with a hearty life on social media over many years. The notion that people who engage in all the opportunities that are there to be had on social media and internet dating sites have not engaged in activities that would present a vetting risk (be it through personal conduct or exploitable information) is difficult to square. Consequently, there is a balance to be struck between the need for potential officers to look 'real' enough in the digital world not to raise suspicions from our adversary's counterintelligence officers and not so open as to present an exploitable risk.

In the wider technology, innovation and business studies literature, and particularly in mainstream publications, there has been a largely uncritical belief that disruptive (non-security related) commercial technology has been and is a good thing, that 'connecting people' and providing 'smarter search' are unquestionable positives. Furthermore, there is a widely held belief that the disruptors who use technology to change society are at the cutting edge of modernisation, vanguard of a new industrial revolution. Some of this has been tempered by 'scandals' or 'revelations', like those which accompanied Edward Snowden, the insights into how Google collects and uses data, or the seemingly never-ending set of revelations around the Facebook platform, but whilst these revelations seem sufficient to prompt users to change behaviour, there has been very little in reported drop-off in uptake or in the use of these platforms, demonstrating the level of dependence that society has developed upon these companion technologies (and continues to have), by which we mean those technologies that reside in the pockets of consumers, or follow them through the day.

For those campaigners who complain about the extent of government intelligence surveillance and intrusion, if they are not also complaining about the level of intrusion into the privacy of individuals from the private sector, then they have missed the wider-ranging and troubling dimension of the picture. This is because the public sector does not have the range of powers and legal underpinnings to make the full use of the coercive end-use tools available to them, whilst some significant actors in the private sector have occupied unregulated spaces and latterly have been found to have gone beyond the confines of the weakly defined regulations that exist. And that is before we consider the impact that the ability to curate news and information to the public has on the public debate.

The public have acquiesced to the overwhelming private sector use of these technologies in a social contract that exchanges access to services for private data. They have not acquiesced to the state doing the same in exchange for enhanced security, be it short-term or longer-term. The widespread need for instant gratification has led the public to wilfully ignore the vulnerabilities created by the commercial exchange of data for service provision, whilst the longer-term security gain is viewed with far greater scepticism. This might be due to historical notions of the state as coercive or illiberal; or that, in contrast to the open-shirt wearing, young, middle-class beanbag-wielding folk of Silicon Valley, the state looks repressive, whilst tech entrepreneurs look fun or approachable.

So, whilst it is safe to leave the critiques of the business and finance implications of these technological and economic disruptions to another publication, my argument here is that in the political sphere this disruption has had a mostly negative set of perceived consequences, undermining truth and integrity and placing discourse, identity and security under tension. Of course, one could argue that this generation of political actors has neither more nor less integrity than previous generations, it merely has access to far more effective tools for behaving in an age-old way. For intelligence agencies, the consequences have been a faster moving and more technically difficult set of propositions to resolve. In terms of collection, many of the mitigations are technical and require research and development effort. In human intelligence collection, some of the mitigations require a reframing of practice. For some practitioners there is a line of thinking that HUMINT and SIGINT are now unified because of the all-pervading nature of our communication technologies, but this is a debate between traditional models of intelligence officer and those who create technologies for these agencies. For analysis, there are not only profound challenges to the speed of analytical practice, but also to the interpretation of raw intelligence which, in the increasingly digital age, is subject to systematic mis- and disinformation campaigns. And latterly, the use of intelligence in the policy realm is subject to prevailing political norms, oversight and regulatory lag, and thus the autocratic tendencies that have become mainstream are as much a challenge to intelligence agencies as the zeal of technology creators who have been more interested in the art of the possible than ethical appropriateness. These technologists have been operating with a development curve that is far in excess of where society and legislators' understanding has reached.

The Opportunities for Intelligence Agencies

The key opportunities to intelligence agencies and officers within this technological revolution have been in the amount and the depth of raw intelligence that can be collected, stored and computer analysed. This raw intelligence includes telephony records, electronic communication records, location data, social networking data, direct intercept of voice (be it on calls or VOIP or, in the case of PRISM, of rooms using telephone microphones (Lee, 2015)), transaction data, car and people movement data, CCTV data (Gates, 2011) and so on and so forth. The sheer weight of data that these 'always on' feeds generate has created entirely new analytical problems in terms of processing capacity, sense-making, and signalling false positives and negatives, but it has also spurred new technological insights into voice, gait and facial pattern matching, and of course the rapid sifting of very large-n datasets, and generating notions of 'normal', both in societal terms and for individuals—it is possible to assess when an individual is doing something differently, and therefore possibly acting suspiciously (Du & Maki, 2019). So, there are additional avenues into individual targets that were previously impossible (or more difficult), but there is also a range of tools, techniques and technologies that allow a meta-level analysis of data to provide some generalisable behavioural security rules to understand patterns of behaviour that give rise to concerns or which might trigger investigations and so on.[1] As was seen with an over-reliance on SIGINT and ELINT at the turn of the century, there is a danger of losing analogue intelligence techniques (e.g. intuition, forms of corroboration, etc.) to data-driven, and therefore computer-driven, solutions: a false assessment of the financial efficiency and accuracy of data-driven analysis.

Whilst the democratisation of travel and the liberalisation of migration (although now under threat and tension) have led to targets being able to move across the globe easily and cheaply, with some extra-judicial operations being able to be prosecuted without effective counterintelligence (Urban, 2018) or longer-term sleeper operations also being able to operate covertly for years (Lucas, 2012), the truth is that the movement of people and objects across the globe is recorded and can be monitored in a way that would have been unthinkable only twenty years ago. As a response to atrocities such as the Lockerbie aircraft bombing, and indeed the 9/11 attacks, the US Department of Homeland Security utilised their dominant market position to insist upon a data-sharing scheme across the transatlantic area called Passenger Name Record (PNR), for access to US airspace and airports (Argomaniz, 2009). This allows—at the point of booking—the US authorities, and whomever they share the intelligence with, to cross-reference travel plans with known terrorists or those who had come under suspicion in some way. The PNR is, however, a dragnet, catching all of us who travel, not just targeting on those who might fall under suspicion. The negotiations between the US and the EU were protracted and often ill-tempered. European legislators—for good historical and cultural reasons— were deeply uneasy about the data of their citizens being 'hoovered up' in this way, and were particularly exercised about the length of time that data would be retained and what guarantees would be in place to ensure that the data was not passed onto third countries (and therefore what those countries might do with it) (Di Matteo, 2017). PNR data is, however, not restricted to international air travel: it also applies to movements by train and by sea as well.

The PNR initiative was as much about doing something because the technical capability existed to collect, retain and analyse these data as it was about addressing a real security concern. The $n =$ of these data also allows for meta-level analysis to occur, to create an assessment of 'normal' behaviours and 'outlier' behaviours (at the individual and group level), which can then be flagged and responded to by domestic security agencies, creating any number of false positives. Equally, it has led to other types of traditional transaction becoming labelled as suspicious, such as paying for train tickets in cash rather than by credit or debit card, something that should not necessarily trigger an alert, given that it is a legal means of purchasing a train ticket. The act of using legal tender has been given a value loading because it is more difficult to track, and we can see in the field of general commerce that the use of physical cash is being subject to incentivisation (both positive and negative), with the encouragement for users to use traceable 'contactless' card payment systems (Jones, 2019). Use of these contactless non-cash methods has seen variable uptake across Europe, with very high levels of uptake in Sweden (Arvidsson, 2019) but correspondingly low levels of uptake in Germany (Korella & Li, 2018), with one of the non-technical reasons for this variation being the historic experience of German governments having too much insight into the personal life of individual citizens.

In a similar vein, the monitoring of monetary transfers, in part as a response to the terrorist threat, has offered a historically unprecedented set of insights into the transactions and conduct of individuals, within and across borders. There is, of course, a reasonable rationale for why international monetary transfers have increased in number in the last twenty years, as cheaper and freer movement of labour has allowed migrant workers to send remittances back to family members in countries of origin. But those involved in the operational and logistical lines of terrorist activities were adept at using international money transfer services to facilitate their activities. After 9/11 most NATO nations sought to enact laws that allowed them greater levels of lawful intrusion into banking activities. The 2010 SWIFT affair (De Goede, 2012; Suda, 2018) (which involved the US acquisition of EU citizen's financial data) demonstrated a level of intelligence capability that at once raises questions around why other sorts of financial malfeasance go undetected or undealt with, but also moved terrorist logistics lines away from international financial instruments and towards other types of financial transaction, be they via a Hawala system of moving money between intermediaries on promissory notes, or via assets in freeports, making surveillance and detection far more complicated for security agencies (Dover, 2016). The improvements to the technologies underpinning financial surveillance have resulted in far greater surveillance of and enforcement against the general citizenry. The UK HMRC's 'Connect' computer system is a good, contemporary example of how data analytics and 'big data' can be used to improve enforcement practice (Petit, 2018). Connect draws in feeds from the banking sector, financial services such as loans, and credit cards, and spreads into social media to make assessments of whether the declared income matches up to the spending patterns of the individual. Greater levels of international interconnection or information sharing in the tax space (which is threatened by Brexit) has also allowed the tax authorities to detect when individuals have offshore financial interests and to raise a question about whether undeclared earnings exist there for tax purposes (HMRC, 2019). The case for using these technologies is to improve the percentage collection rate of revenues, but we should observe that the UK government's 'Connect' system does a very similar job to private sector data aggregation and analysis services, such as Experian and Equifax in credit referencing, supermarket 'club-cards', and major insurance brokers, all of whom collect and analyse similar data as the HMRC but for different reasons, and without some of the political oversight of a government agency; and—as a whole—a track record of leaks and vulnerabilities that is unenviable (Bloomberg, 2019).

The other major line of benefits to intelligence agencies comes in communications technologies. The ability to intercept communications (be they telephony, instant messaging, emails, files), to intercept voice (via the reported mechanism of PRISM, or voice recognition CCTV), and to exploit vulnerabilities in the technologies of the 'internet of things' to track whereabouts, social networks and patterns of behaviour, is a significant improvement on the mostly analogue techniques of the Cold War. Where these electronic vulnerabilities can be exploited by domestic agencies, they can of course also be exploited by adversary and by friendly but competitor agencies, and so part of the underlying debate around the Snowden revelations, around previous debates over whether China and Russia are able to intercept undersea internet traffic in transit, and also around the somewhat loud and persistent debate about Huawei and their 5G networking infrastructure, is the sense that whilst 'friendly' agencies might be able to understand their publics in a far more detailed way, so might adversaries and competitors from less open nations, putting them at a clear strategic advantage, particularly in the event of future hostilities, particularly if one considers how little the allied nations will know about the publics of Russia, China and North Korea in response due to legislative and technical barriers to prevent information leakage. The extent of the knowledge (be it personalised or meta level) that is capable of being lawfully intercepted is large, but of a comparative (if not reduced) scale to that of the handset manufacturers, data carriers and app providers, as shown by the recent scandals that have enveloped Facebook, amongst others (Schneble, Elger & Shaw, 2018). So, there continue to be questions about what appropriate controls can be placed around the data generated by companion devices (smartphones and Internet of Things peripherals), and by applications whose business model seems premised upon the collection, aggregation and sale of data, rather than the service they are providing (Zhubov, 2019).

The final major class of opportunity for intelligence agencies is located in the management of public narrative and operational spaces. This is an opportunity that seems to have been significantly grasped by the Russian government in what has been variously described by observers and analysts as information war or hybrid conflict (Gioe, 2018; Seely, 2018). Where the Russian government and its energetic Western supporters are correct is in the observation that the NATO powers engage in a range of activities that are not entirely dissimilar to the Russian modus operandi. This is a clash between regimes who believe strongly in their version of the truth. Understanding these truths, and why actors believe in them and act in reliance of them, is key to challenging and countering them. In the UK, there is a military doctrinal underpinning for non-violent operations, which include the utilisation of media channels and psychological profiling, known as '77 Brigade' (UK Ministry of Defence, 2019b). The United States and Israel, amongst many nations, are also highly engaged in this area. In the winter of 2018 there was a hack and public dissemination (albeit via the unindexed web first) of internal documents of a British foreign and defence policy charity, the Institute for Statecraft, which had been partly funded by the UK Foreign, Commonwealth & Development Office to identify and counter Russian misinformation campaigns, but who were accused by the Russian state media and a large number of online commentators of carrying out precisely the sort of mis- and disinformation campaign that the Russian state had been accused of, most notably over the previous three years.[2] The particular project to highlight Russian disinformation was called 'the Integrity Initiative' and this phrase has become—on social media platforms—synonymous with 'deep state' activities, in part because of the presence in the core staff of people whom activists say have intelligence backgrounds, and because of the activities the initiative is said to have involved (Sputnik, 2018, 2019). The incident resulted in urgent questions and a debate in the House of Commons (Thornberry, 2018), principally to discover whether public money had been used to fund a charity in what was alleged to be hybrid warfare. Since November 2018 the phrase has been used to describe any perceived Western government media manipulation; on Twitter alone the hashtag was used more than 120 thousand times between 23 November 2018 and 28 February 2019, and was still being used at the submission date of this book.[3]

As with all elements of the contemporary information war, there are grains of truth buried somewhere in the conspiracy. The Foreign, Commonwealth & Development Office had funded an educational charity that researched into 'hybrid warfare' (a term that continues to be contested and which is perhaps premised upon a misunderstanding of the Gerasimov doctrine). It had focused upon Russian misinformation campaigns (and this was the stated purpose) and upon Chinese and North Korean activities (presumably for the normative reasons of the 'other' being bad whilst 'our' activities are value neutral, and equally for reasons of national allegiance). It had not examined—as far as I can tell—the counter-efforts of NATO members, nor has this been done outside the campaigner groups. So, we do not currently know whether—in cyberspace—the modus operandi of allied or adversary intelligence and security agencies (or their contractors) are similar, or whether there are national ways of war in this area. My educated suspicion is that there are common threads with national variations.

At the time of writing there does appear to be a single or prevailing modus operandi for adversary mis- and disinformation campaigns that sit within the broader umbrella of hybrid warfare. Previously it was thought that these information operations operated with combined human and 'bot' accounts to generate misinformation and a critical mass of messages to overwhelm or undermine the official narrative, something that would then be amplified by fellow travellers or by those inadvertently amplifying these messages, which in turn would be picked up by various parts of the legacy media (e.g. broadcast television and online and paper-based press outlets). The originating moment was seen, therefore, to emerge on regular social media platforms such as Twitter and Facebook (House of Commons: Digital, Culture, Media and Sport Committee, 2019), whilst the Institute for Strategic Dialogue places those originating moments (albeit in the particular context of German elections) as coming from platforms such as 4Chan[4] and Reddit[5] (Institute for Strategic Dialogue, 2019). This fits within the conceptual framework of the 'hybrid media system' as framed by Andrew Chadwick (Chadwick, 2013). In terms of information warfare, the hybrid media system and earlier researchers have missed that these campaigns actually begin in forums on the unindexed part of the world wide web, otherwise known as 'the dark web' (Dover, 2020). These forums share leads, rumours, documents, and so on. The challenge for those seeking to counter these attacks is to accurately assess whether they are viewing government-sponsored coordination, sophisticated non-government coordination (and the Venn diagram between those two groups might be interestingly close), amateur attempts, or—intriguingly— denial and deception strategies. Far from there being an organic or organically viral quality to the early moments of social media coordination, messages and strategies are developed in unindexed forums and are then brought to the public and indexed level (be it via social media, private messaging, dissemination to journalists).

If we extend the 'viral' metaphor slightly, we can find utility in finding and identifying 'patient zero' in a messaging campaign, as this provides more information about the motivations and origins of the campaign, its aims and likely trajectory. But just as in epidemiology, finding this 'patient zero' is technically difficult: when I tried to find patient zero in the messaging around four terrorism incidents, I had confidence that I had managed it once, and my confidence subsided in that instance as well. Working under an understanding of information campaigns that begin in the indexed web, these efforts were also pointless. By the time these campaigns have found their way to the indexed web, they have been rinsed of much of the data that would make the patient zero analysis interesting. The use of the term 'rinsing' is to deliberately evoke the term from the practice of money laundering, where money is seen to become progressively 'cleaner' when it is moved through a variety of accounts or a variety of asset classes before it emerges at the end as 'clean money'. This is similar to the way that disinformation campaigns treat the journey of information, and the two disciplines could learn from each other.

So, my reconceptualisation of this modus operandi is that for regime or state-based information campaigns, the originating sources (who push out to non-state-based accelerators) are capable of being found in the unindexed web, mostly in forums. These accelerators then bring these messages to the indexed web, and social media, and push these messages out using a combination of familiar channels (accounts) and often new 'bot' accounts to provide the messaging with trending heft. Legacy media which is aligned through ideology or ownership will then pick up these trends and further rinse and legitimise them by reporting on them, in skeleton format to begin with and then via invited academic and think-tank research experts in interview and talk-show formats, which then spurs further online commentary and may eventually break these messages out into unaligned legacy media outlets, by which time the message can be considered to be virtually mainstreamed. In parallel, during these campaigns, a significant and active quotient of individuals will be engaged in open source intelligence investigations or activism journalism, to do what they market as digging further into a story. They do this using a range of internet tools and, freedom of information requests and so on that has been labelled as 'lawfare' by some, and the 'instrumentalisation of the law for strategic ends' by others (Dover, 2019; Sari, 2019). What these accounts (be they individuals or 'bots') are often doing is picking up fragments of information and narrating around them. By the time these fragments and this narration has entered its third reformulation it is has reached beyond the point where it is logically connected to the original fragment of information. As an analytical technique it is perilously close to the logic of conspiracy theories, and indeed the logic of populist politics, where there will always be a tiny kernel of evidence that sparks the narrative but the narrative's end point will be significantly removed from where the evidence sits. Having scraped a considerable quantity of social media data[6] it is clear to me that once a disinformation theme takes hold on the large social media channels it is then also used to re-position other narratives that the collective behind the theme find awkward. So, narratives around individuals are re-shaped to produce favourable or unfavourable re-casting, the narratives around particular episodes are re-historicised in the light of the new, and largely unrelated data to provide 'new insights' as the activists see it. But the extent of the re-shaping endeavour, and the standardised way it is produced from a shard of tangential evidence, suggests to me that it is a mistake (per Brandolini) to focus on the micro-movements in the narrative, but one should home in on the far broader questions of 'What are these campaigns trying to achieve?' and 'What are these campaigns trying to distract us from?' In the case of Russia, both these questions are pertinent, whilst with China and North Korea it is the former question that might be more productive.

The opportunity and challenge to intelligence agencies from this form of information campaigning sits in the ability to shape the operational environment at one end, and being unable to wrestle back control of the narrative, at the other. There has been a strong and understandable argument within the literature that, by paying these former campaigns credence, they are given greater influence: the impact of the UK television channel 'RT' (formerly called Russia Today) with its very small viewing figures is undoubtedly overdrawn, but we have seen the impact of disinformation upon election and referendum campaigns both in the UK and wider world (Yablokov, 2015). The impact of narratives around immigration (in the case of Brexit and elections in Germany, Sweden, Denmark, France and the United States), in the 2018 case of the Salisbury chemical poisonings and, more recently, around the COVID-19 pandemic, has been to undermine certainty in both authority and 'facts' in the minds of the public. In undermining these certainties the ground is then fertile for adversary countries to build upon these schisms to further undermine our national resilience and our ability to respond collectively (UK Ministry of Defence, 2019a). There is currently inadequate understanding of the mechanisms of influence (of 'what works'), and indeed how these campaigns are being prosecuted. This research gap fits between information and computer sciences, political communication, strategic studies, psychology (personal and social), sociology and the practitioner field of counterintelligence and psychological operations and it can only be satisfactorily addressed in collaborative forms by these fields.

The Challenges to Intelligence

The main challenge to intelligence activity in this modern era comes from the underpinning and ongoing disruptions to technology, finance and society. The Snowden revelations demonstrated how technological possibility, coupled with a lack of ethical and legal oversight and control, can lead to curiosity or possibility-led collection of intelligence that is disproportionate to the threat it presents and itself can form a threat to social relationships. Snowden demonstrated—in the main—a pattern of collection for collection's sake. The impact of this—as it rippled out into common understanding—was to undermine the sophisticated tools for situations when they are used for entirely appropriate and proportionate targeting (Walsh & Miller, 2016). Overall, however, the interconnectedness of everyday life across the globe, not just in the post-industrial Global North, has provided an unprecedented opportunity for intelligence agencies—particularly those engaged in signals and electronic intelligence—to gain access to the inner lives of their own citizens and those of other nations. With this opportunity has come the challenge of making sense of hitherto unimaginably large datasets, and those who are engaged in subversive activities have constantly iterated their technology and techniques, creating a form of arms race akin to that which was seen during periods of the twentieth century in conventional and then nuclear technology. This analogy holds true for non-state-based actors, who have prosecuted Vietnam-style 'wars of the flea', finding increasingly ingenious ways to gain advantage over state-based intelligence actors. In communication terms, we see relevant evidence in the use of darknet forums in the early part of this century, the utilisation of video-game communication platforms as a means of passing targeting data to each other as a means by which to avoid detection, without having to go 'toe to toe' with state-based agencies in developing high-end technology (Podhradsky, D'Ovidio & Casey, 2012).

Part of the success of these groups has been in their use of the high-end technology developed by neoliberal economies against their countries. In finance terms, the use of international wire transfers was quickly replaced after 9/11 and by improvements to financial tracking by the US and British authorities by a combination of analogue—and ancient—money transfer practices, complemented by moves into cryptocurrency, which require considerable processing power to de-anonymise. Asymmetric actors have also been at the forefront—and preceding some of the behaviours of populists—of developing effective communication doctrine, in one guise utilising hacking and dark-web propagation as a means to break stories into the social and legacy media of the indexed web and effectively crowd-sourcing social media attacks and mobs, whilst, in another guise, adopting high-end production values for propaganda videos, and being ahead of Western militaries in breaking stories quickly and thus asserting message control and timeliness: two core facets of effective public communication.

There is an important and ongoing corrective to what has become bracketed under the Snowden revelations, which is the growth of surveillance capitalism (Bellamy-Foster & McChesney, 2014; Zhubov, 2019). This form of capitalism is in many respects far more disruptive than anything that government agencies have hitherto attempted to do with electronic surveillance. Thus far, so officials claim, European and North American governments have been more preoccupied with attempting to disrupt and prosecute those involved in threats to people, property and national security and thus have not had the resource to engage in other types of oppressive activity. This claim might be viewed with some healthy scepticism following the Snowden revelations (Bellamy-Foster & McChesney, 2014; Dencik & Cable, 2017; Lyon, 2015), the ongoing UK inquiry, headed by Sir John Mitting, into enhanced surveillance into activist groups (the vast majority of which appear to have been law-abiding and peaceful) (Casciani, 2019; Schlembach, 2016; Undercover Policing Inquiry, 2018), and the British government's previous history in these activities, notably the Ministry of Defence's Information Research Department (1948–77), which operated to counter communist activism and propaganda (Wilford, 1998). It is a weak argument to suggest that 'yes, we have the capability, but we're just too busy to use it'. This is particularly the case in an era where authoritarian-inflected populists are coming to power across the globe, who are far less concerned about confining themselves to proportionate and reserved uses of intrusive capabilities. In the private sphere, however, there is enough evidence to suggest that this form of surveillance capitalism is having a profound impact upon our social relationships, on how youngsters and young adults are forming their core identity, on commerce and economic relations, and in terms of how well understood we are as citizens by data owners and data analysers, predominantly those in the advertising sphere, sufficient to cause forms of social disruption, and therefore presenting an attractive target for manipulation by adversaries.

A technology columnist, Kashmir Hill, carried out an interesting experiment to test whether it is possible to function in post-industrial society without drawing upon the services (or underpinning architectural services—e.g. data hubs, web-hosting) of Amazon, Apple, Facebook, Google and Microsoft (Hill, 2019). To do this she inserted code into her connected devices to block them communicating with services from any of those five companies, and to do so over a period of six weeks, although she only blocked all five together in the final week. What Hill discovered was that the vast majority of the services she used (essentially all of them), were dependent upon one of these big five companies. Even when she attempted to use workarounds, such as using the privacy search engine DuckDuckGo, she discovered that it was underpinned by Amazon's web servers and was thus unavailable to her. When Hill wanted to transfer a media file for work, she discovered that the workarounds of Mozilla[7] and even Onionshare[8] were premised upon Google and Amazon web services, thus excluding them as well. Consequently, Hill concluded that it is technically possible to avoid the big internet companies but the cost in time and expertise to do so is considerable and prohibitive (Hill, 2019).

From an intelligence and security perspective we should note the concentration of web services, and therefore data capture, for nearly every member of society with access to interconnected technology. The personalised delivery of information to users, based upon preferences, usage and interest, means that the news I read is likely to be very different from the news my students read, or that the non-academics I socialise with read (Bakshy, Messing & Adamic, 2015). So, one of the inherent powers of these big five internet companies is the ability to shape the political space via the algorithms they are utilising for search and the push for data.

The delivery of personalised news, and the absence of cross-cutting news (as per Bakshy, Messing & Adamic), may partly account for the starkly polarised news environment we are witnessing currently. There is also a popular misconception of these algorithms as being somehow value-neutral or 'objective' because they are utilised by computing technology. They have—of course—been programmed by humans and are therefore a scaled manifestation of the experiences, education, conscious and unconscious biases of the programmers who programmed them. The values of the programmer, and the way that information is distributed and delivered, are not only capable of delivering change to the political culture but also to the values and understandings of the citizenry and the law enforcement and security officials who are drawn from society. In a fascinating article, Landon-Murray and Anderson tie together the increasing prevalence of the internet as a source of information, intelligence and neuroscience to suggest that the internet is having a fundamental impact upon the ability of intelligence analysts to effectively sift, sort and understand evidence (Landon-Murray & Anderson, 2013). This argument can now be extended to suggest that actually the big five internet firms have the ability to partially shape intelligence officer's understanding of the world and of events, through the way they sift, sort and deliver information, through the absence of classified material or the need to reach policy makers in a way that aligns to their knowledge base. The types of surveillance society commonly associated with George Orwell's Big Brother dystopia (1949), or the fictionalised account of East Germany's Stasi in the film *The Lives of Others* (2006), look somewhat tame compared to the potential held within the main internet and technology companies.

The dominance of so few companies places them in a peculiarly strong position in regard to understanding all strata of society, down to the level of individual granularity. They are so strong in this regard, because it is this data and their understanding of it that they have successfully monetised (Skeggs & Yuill, 2016; Zajc, 2015)—and they have not been passive in this monetisation or in improvements to their respective offers to monetise it. There is evidence and commentary on the techniques deployed by some of these companies to ensure that users keep interacting with these services, including—for example—the deployment of techniques to manipulate dopamine responses in individual users (Błachnioa, Przepiorkaa & Pantic, 2016). These companies are also technically able to control the flow of information (Schelter & Kunegis, 2018), be it to governments or the public, something that could have a significant strategic impact or, less seriously, an ongoing impact upon politics or unfolding events. As noted previously, our understanding of how messages impact upon citizens is underdeveloped, and our understanding of how citizens would respond to being bombarded with critical messages, or a messaging vacuum, is similarly poorly understood. But the literature has now begun to reflect a discussion and growing concern about how internet companies are able to have an impact upon the political views and the voting actions of their users, both in terms of search and in terms of social media aggregation (Diakopoulos *et al.*, 2018; Robertson *et al.*, 2018; Rose, 2017).

State-based actors, on the other hand, have engaged in day-to-day cyber attacks on each other, which amounts to a low-intensity conflict, and constant subversion (Betz, 2017; Opara, Mahfouz & Holloway, 2017). And it is to subversion and destabilisation that these activities really owe their origins: the micro-impact, or the overt intended outcome, seems less important than to create an over-arching culture of subversion and destabilisation. So, whilst there has been considerable Chinese and North Korean activity in stealing intellectual property from Western nations, which has enhanced the manufacturing base of China in particular, the aim is far more meta than the theft of the particular IP (Beckett, 2017). Hacks and attacks against persons of interest (be they politicians, journalists, academics or even film industry workers—as per North Korea's hack and revelations against Sony Pictures in 2014) are again aimed at more general subversion and destabilisation (Inkster, 2015). In a similar vein, the active courting of Western politicians, journalists, academics and other influencers with money, travel and advantage has had the impact of creating a cadre of fellow travellers who serve to advance the interests of their patron, in a way that sometimes conflicts with the interests of their own nation (David-Fox, 2003; Gioe, 2018; Parton, 2019). So, we can observe an information and influence conflict that has become more structured, better organised and more richly financed than in previous eras.

There is evidence of an ongoing arms race in the heavy spending on paradigm shifting technology, such as quantum computing, which would render current cryptography entirely obsolete (Farouk *et al.*, 2018; Mosca, 2018). Breakthrough technologies such as fifth-generation networks (5G), which accelerate the utility and adoption of the 'internet of things' and with it 'smart home' and 'smart cities' initiatives (Li, Xu & Zhao, 2018), provide those engaged in intrusive surveillance with a hitherto unprecedented set of data points that help to construct profiles of individuals and wider societal groups. The potential of quantum computing to break standard cryptography could be highly disruptive because economic transactions, communications and sensitive and personally identifiable data have become so heavily premised upon them being encrypted.

The evolution of mobile phones into 'companion devices', those with which we are constantly interacting, has reduced our collective capacity to operate in traditional analogue ways or, indeed, just ways that do not involve some form of interaction with an electronic or communicating device. The notion of neuroplasticity in this field, of how the brains of individuals are being physically transformed by the collective inability to focus on longer-form research, to cope with silence, or boredom, is an emerging area of research that impacts upon our understanding of the citizenry and indeed of intelligence analysts (Dongwon, 2015; Montag & Diefenbach, 2018). Similarly, we expect intelligence analysts to be able to simultaneously provide well thought through and clear product, but also to be closely following technological developments, something that is undermined by the rate of technological–generational change in information technologies, in terms of hardware, techniques, tools, attack vectors and so on.

The Challenge of Finding Truths

Political disruption has been assisted by internet-enabled platforms (Gerbaudo, 2018; Krämer, 2017). This has commonly been felt to be in the way they facilitate the creation of shared identities, of 'community', the sharing of core or important information, the coordination of actions and events, and the reporting of actions against the shared identity. These highlighted mechanisms under-report the extent to which these dynamics are impacted by considerations of the hybrid media system (that is, the extent to which the legacy media and new media are related and are synergistic) and the extent to which there is influence or even control over narratives by classic or traditional interest groupings. Moreover, the extent to which messages impact upon citizens (and the mechanisms by which they do so) is an area of research that has yet to come to maturity, but I am actively working on it. In my view this will be an important component of the impact these disruptive platforms and politics have had on the security of the nation and the sanctity of our democracy. These dynamics are very similar to the dynamics observed earlier in this chapter around state-based information warfare campaigns and their utilisation of private sector communications platforms.

Modern-day populists have demonstrated a strong willingness to break rules. They have also showed a considerable disregard for the truth. They have a facility for the evocation of myth, and for very accurately tapping into the illiberal fears of the population (Groza & Groza, 2017; Kelsey, 2016). Some of this facility is not through political 'feel' or 'touch' but through the utilisation of data analytical techniques and large-*n* datasets of personally identifiable data, i.e. a reapplication of marketing techniques into the political communications sphere (Ruppert, Isin & Bigo, 2017; Ward, 2018).

Populism is also a response to an established political system that has run ahead—in terms of sentiment on some issues—of its population and these populist actors serve as a particularly stark form of market correction.

Expertise and Illiberalism

The rise of so-called populists across the globe has been typified by a strong disconnection from verifiable evidence—which is the stock-in-trade of intelligence agencies—whilst simultaneously impugning those who make evidence-based claims and refutations of populist claims with evidence. As the computer programmer Alberto Brandolini somewhat caustically—but accurately—claimed: 'The amount of energy necessary to refute bullshit is an order of magnitude bigger than it is to produce it.' (Brandolini, 2013). Brandolini's law, as it is now known, is highly applicable to populist politics and to modern political discourse. The amount of effort required to correct important errors of fact or detail would result in a loss of momentum and impetus on the part of those having to correct them. The hybrid media system—which is the reinforcing system of social and legacy media outlets—provides key advantages to populists who are less careful with the accuracy of their messaging. Furthermore, a recent study of how stories proliferate online (Vosoughi, Roy & Aral, 2018) provided evidence for the old truism that lies spread more quickly than truths. Some influential contemporary politicians have gone out of their way to compound these effects through discrediting those who have dedicated their professional lives to understand whatever subject it is under discussion. So, for example, the current UK Environment Secretary Michael Gove claimed in the 'Brexit' referendum campaign that 'the people have had enough of experts', which was a meme that took hold during the campaign, as a means to undermine the overwhelming majority of academic economists who assessed a negative impact to the British economy from Brexit (*Financial Times*, 2016). During and since the referendum result, every expert assessment—including those of the Bank of England and the UK's Treasury—has been dismissed by leave campaigners with a catch-all term of 'project fear' (Halligan & Lyons, 2017).

Similarly, there is a vast number of examples of where the settled assessment of the climate change discipline has been challenged, not with science but with variations of emotional response and revisionist history (Lewandowsky, Oberauer & Gignac, 2013; McCright & Dunlap, 2011; Oreskes, 2018). In the US presidential election (including in the primaries) there were accusations levelled at candidates around their probity, family histories and so on that had literally no basis in evidence at all (but which helped to inform narratives that voters seemed wedded to) and, indeed, the election has been haunted by the investigations into the alleged involvement of foreign powers seeking to interfere with the election process. But these trends are important to understanding the challenges that face security officials in this modern era. The trends are suggestive of the way that some elements of our political classes are able to systematically reject evidence and evidence-based assessments in favour of value-based positions. That this can happen is itself suggestive of a wider dysfunction in our political and security culture between evidence-based and value-based decision making. This reduces the effectiveness of intelligence agencies, but also reduces the attractiveness of careers and diminishes the calibre of applicants. The notion that intelligence occurs with the consent of the people will become strained if the cultural gap concerning the primacy of evidence is allowed to continue. Such a rejection of evidence-based assessment, not only by the policy sphere but by the public, undermines the work of intelligence agencies and the collective credibility they depend upon.

Value-based voting is not new (Barnea & Schwartz, 1998; Schwartz, Caprara & Vecchione, 2010). Part of the explanation for 'champagne socialists' and 'working-class Tories' can be found in value-based voting patterns, rather than those which premise rational maximisation of economic interests, for example. We can see the same pattern in why some consumers display brand loyalty when they believe the brand aligns to values they identify strongly with (Gyrd-Jones & Kornumb, 2013; Ross & Harradine, 2011). The populists who won the referendum campaign in 2016, and the US presidential race in the same year understand—far better than their competitors—not only the values of a critical base of support but also how to articulate messages to that base of support. And so there is an additional critical challenge to intelligence and security in this age of populism, which is that there is a significant gap between 'elite sentiment' and the sentiment of the ordinary citizen. We take for granted—in universities, as well as in policy-making circles—that the various equality agendas that have developed over the last century and a half, and which have been variously legislated during that time, are universalized norms, or on their way to being so. There is now quite good evidence to suggest that this is not the case, and it is 'populist' discourse that has understood this far more effectively than 'establishment' actors. We can select some emblematic examples from across the breadth of experience of 'ordinary' citizens to illustrate this point.

Immigration and the attendant freedom of movement (of labour, for lifestyle and for living) were assumed to be a significant positive of the European Union project. The ability to access by 2018 twenty-eight different economic markets, with relatively few restrictions, was unprecedented in modern history, and in 2018 20.4 million EU citizens were living in EU countries different from those they were born in (EUROSTAT, 2019). But whilst the political classes, and indeed those placed at the strategic end of business and commerce, viewed this as an unalloyed good, the public—particularly under conditions of financial restraint and austerity—did not (de Vreese & Boomgaarden, 2005; Gietel-Basten, 2016). Some of this negative view seems to have been informed by the perception of not sharing in the economic benefits of globalisation and, therefore, being on the outside of the globalisation of finance and commerce (Colantone & Stanig, 2018). And whilst it is not particularly easy or popular to say so, immigration was not an issue that was neatly aggregated in the minds of the electorate between EU immigration and non-EU immigration, which was and is governed by separate regimes. Indeed, the entanglement in the popular mindset between domestic radicalisation, 'foreign fighters', returning fighters and wider population displacement from the Middle Eastern warzones into Europe, was repeatedly cited during the referendum campaign—and since—as the most persuasive reason for casting a vote for leave, even though it had little to do with EU immigration policy (Goodwin &

Millazo, 2017; Veltri *et al.*, 2019). This was further, and deliberately, entangled by leave campaigners who cited—in poster adverts, and through directly targeted adverts on platforms such as Facebook— that remaining in the EU would open up the prospect of uncontrolled immigration from Turkey, playing on racial and religious sensitivities (Ker-Lindsay, 2018). The reality—as experienced through the ballot box—was that 'the establishment' was far more comfortable with immigration than the public, and the referendum represented an opportunity to express that dissatisfaction tangibly. In turn this has left the security establishment with a weight of public expectations to police the perceived security threat of non-EU nationals, as a mirror to the preferences of the public, even if the security establishment's risk assessments tell that the risks from these communities are no higher than those of established communities.

We can see similar disjuncture in the establishment and legislated view of protected identity characteristics and religiosity, in which the freedom to declare one's own (gender) identity, sexuality or to practise religion, with all the associated practices and symbology, runs contrary to the views of a sizeable cleavage of society. The legislated view is clear, but the popular acceptance of these differences from a constructed, perceived or held homogenous norm is not as clear, and forms part of the discourse of discontentment even amongst those who one might characterise themselves as belonging to 'middle England' and 'middle America' in all other ways. And this is important in several ways:

(1) the official and public understanding of what are and are not acceptable views (and by extension what are extreme views) are currently unaligned;

(2) such a mis-alignment serves to alienate those whose views are now unacceptable (but which had been normatively acceptable, and indeed been largely unchallenged, over the previous fifty years) and it also serves to alienate those protected from these views because it highlights difference and creates an impetus to seek redress. And it is this that has—in part—driven electoral backlash: the phenomena of 'We are not listened to by the Westminster bubble'; and

(3) there is a hitherto underexplored set of impacts around preferences and views of intelligence officers, in absolute terms and in relative terms when norms shift, and how these impact upon their performance.

Politicisation represents an important challenge to intelligence activity from populist politics. This challenge might include co-option of officers and agencies or—perhaps more strangely—in the case of the United States currently, alienation, and a wider undermining of the credibility of intelligence activity, the undermining of expertise and a creative tension or malleability of narratives.

The structural underpinnings of this populist age create a second line of challenge that is wider than the populists themselves: the international interconnectedness of transnational interest groups or networks, the sharing of techniques, expertise and resource across national boundaries, and the arms race in technologies and techniques that requires a great deal of resource and expertise to maintain pace with, constantly allow opportunities for competitor groups and states. This has now taken on the dynamics of a quasi-arms race, crystallised by the prospect of quantum computing and by the strong moves by the US, Australia and the UK against Huawei's 5G networking equipment (Zhang, 2018). Perhaps the greatest mistake made thus far by agencies, with a strong steer from the political elites, has been to avoid calling out the serious damage that populism and its structural underpinnings has done to the established systems of governance in the countries affected. The preference for the line that our democracies are not only intact but are robust and flourishing has allowed competitor nations and groupings greater latitude to continue inflicting harm upon our political systems and political culture.

Conclusion

For the first time in modern history there have been and still are leaders of post-industrial nations with whom it is challenging or hazardous to share intelligence (Balls, 2018; Schindler, 2017). Depending on future electoral fortunes, this might serve to undermine established international intelligence liaison, such as the Five Eyes group, or even the NATO alliance. Domestically, the unwillingness to share might hinder the investigation or curtailment of security threats. The story in February 2020—that was denied by both the Home Secretary and MI5—that the latter denied the former access to some intelligence is an early warning about the impact such distrust can have on intelligence security (Weatherby, 2020). Strained relations in this part of government might further impact upon the definition of subversion (and therefore what might qualify as activities requiring curtailment), might be subject to significant change, depending on the political beliefs of those in government. Again, we can call on the contemporary example of the protest group Extinction Rebellion being included in the radicalisation handbook for police officers in the UK as an example of where there is an expansion of the definition of subversion (Dodd & Grierson, 2020). The preference amongst populists for current and historical world leaders who are described as being 'strong' or 'autocratic', depending on your stance, raises the prospect of the advances in surveillance technologies and techniques being used in the internal capture of the apparatuses of state. So, whilst government intelligence activity has always necessarily been political—despite the widely held view and position that it is not—it may well play a far more significant political role in the medium to long term, in policing the boundaries and curtailing the excesses of populists, albeit still within a position of 'not being political'.

The increased politicisation of security and surveillance comes through in the advanced uses of data analytics, which may result in a widening of the scope of investigations but also in the constant prompting for investigation and prosecution of opponents that follows the modus operandi of information warfare described earlier in this chapter. Security is—therefore—not subject to logically consistent narratives. There is a constant set of constitutional questions around the positioning of intelligence and security actors guarding our democracies and our democratic institutions that are becoming more pressing: for activists this debate would centre on the appropriate role, scope and powers of intelligence agencies to interfere across analogue and digital channels. For those who do not see themselves as activists per se, the debate would focus on the ways in which foreign powers utilise open platforms, our institutions and domestic citizens to advance their strategic ends, and this has become more pressing in the light of populists being more willing to break norms and rules. The disruption of our politics is as much about the hidden wiring of the state (the security and intelligence services) as it about conspiracies around the activities of the 'deep state', which is a pejorative code for the same actors (O'Neil, 2017). Intelligence is political, but not party political. It is an open question as to whether society recognises the apolitical but political role of the intelligence agencies in trying to secure the continuation of our particular form of politics and constitutional settlement. We should also recognise that in discharging these responsibilities, the rapid development of transnational interconnected technologies, and the near parsimony of those technologies, is stretching traditional analogue, analytical and digital functions of intelligence, causing mistakes to be made and missteps to be taken. This is normal at any intersection between government agency and the public. The arrival of hybrid war—and that term is beginning to stretch so widely that it will rapidly lose currency—is a whole of government activity, really a whole of government plus a large number of actors and organisations activity. In that sense, we have all been co-opted into the projection of key values, norms and behaviours. We see—with how our agencies treat those who sit outside these norms or who advocate for radical change—how the state and these values have become a body politic: the immune system responds aggressively to those who seek to challenge it. The business of intelligence in the twenty-first century is, therefore, the management up and down of the many professional tribes that are engaged in these hybrid battles. We are all at war, now.

References

Argomaniz, J. (2009) 'When the EU is the "norm-taker": The Passenger Name Records Agreement and the EU's internalization of US border security norms'. *Journal of European Integration* 31 (1), 119–136.

Arvidsson, N. (2019) *Building a Cashless Society: The Swedish Route to the Future of Cash Payments.* Munich: Springer.

Bakshy, E., Messing, S. and Adamic, L. (2015) 'Exposure to ideologically diverse news and opinion on Facebook'. *Science* 348 (6239), 1130–1132.

Balls, K. (2018) 'Should the government share full intelligence with Corbyn?' *The Spectator*, 2 April.

Barnea, M. and Schwartz, S. (1998) 'Values and voting'. *Political Psychology* 19 (1), 17–40.

Beckett, P. (2017) 'Data and IP are the new nuclear: Facing up to state-sponsored threats'. *Network Security* 17–19.

Bellamy-Foster, J. and McChesney, R. (2014) 'Surveillance capitalism: Monopoly-finance capital, the military–industrial complex, and the digital age'. *Monthly Review:An Independent Socialist Magazine* 1 July, 1–6.

Betz, D. (2017) *Cyberspace and the State: Towards a Strategy for Cyber Power.* London: Routledge.

Błachnioa, A., Przepiorkaa, A. and Pantic, I. (2016) 'Association between Facebook addiction, self-esteem and life satisfaction: A cross-sectional study'. *Computers in Human Behavior* 55, 701–705.

Bloomberg (2019) 'The unfinished business of the Equifax hack'. *Bloomberg.* 29 January. Accessed 6 March 2019. https://www.bloomberg.com/opinion/articles/2019-01-29/equifax-hack-remains-unfinished-business

Brandolini, Alberto (2013) Twitter post. *Twitter.* 11 January.

Casciani, D. (2019) 'Secret document reveals police "blacklisting"'. *BBC News.* 6 March. Accessed 6 March 2019. https://www.bbc.co.uk/news/uk-47457330

Chadwick, A. (2013) *The Hybrid Media System: Politics and Power.* Oxford: Oxford University Press.

Colantone, I. and Stanig, P. (2018) 'Global competition and Brexit'. *American Political Science Review* 112 (2), 201–218.

David-Fox, M. (2003) 'The fellow travelers revisited: The "cultured West" through Soviet eyes'. *The Journal of Modern History* 75 (2), 300–335.

De Goede, M. (2012) 'The SWIFT affair and the global politics of European security'. *Journal of Common Market Studies* 50 (2), 214–230.

de Vreese, C. and Boomgaarden. H. (2005) 'Projecting EU referendums: Fear of immigration and support for European integration'. *European Union Politics* 56 (1), 9–82.

Dencik, L. and Cable, J. (2017) 'The advent of surveillance realism: Public opinion and activist responses to the Snowden leaks'. *International Journal of Communication* 11, 763–781.

Di Matteo, F. (2017). 'The massive and indiscriminate collection of passengers' data: A congenital defect within the EU PNR Directive?' *Diritti umani e diritto internazionale* 213–236.

Diakopoulos, N., Trielli, D., Stark, J. and Mussenden, S. (2018) 'I vote for—How search informs our choice of candidate'. In M. Moore and D. Tambini (eds) *Digital Dominance: The Power of Google, Amazon, Facebook, and Apple* (p. 22). New York, NY: Oxford University Press.

Dodd, Vikram and Grierson, Jamie (2020) 'Terrorism police list Extinction Rebellion as extremist ideology'. *The Guardian*, 10 January.

Dongwon, C. (2015) 'Physical activity level, sleep quality, attention control and self-regulated learning along to smartphone addiction among college students'. *Journal of the Korea Academia-Industrial Cooperation Society* 16 (1) 429–437.

Dover, R. (2016) Fixing financial plumbing: Tax, leaks and base erosion and profit shifting in Europe. *The International Spectator* 51(4), 40–50.

——— (2019) 'UK response to hybrid threats'. *UK Defence Select Committee*. 8 January. Accessed 1 March 2019. http://data.parliament.uk/writtenevidence/committeeevidence.svc/evidencedocument/defence-committee/uk-response-to-hybrid-threats/written/94257.pdf

——— (2020) 'SOCMINT: A shifting balance of opportunity'. *Intelligence and National Security* 35 (2), 216–232.

Du, L. and Maki, A. (2019) 'These cameras can spot shoplifters even before they steal'. Bloomberg. March 4. Accessed 7 March 2019. https://www.bloomberg.com/news/articles/2019-03-04/the-ai-cameras-that-can-spot-shoplifters-even-before-they-steal

EUROSTAT (2019) 'Migration and migrant population statistics'. 1 January. Accessed 5 March 2019. https://ec.europa.eu/eurostat/statistics-explained/index.php?title=Migration_and_migrant_population_statistics#Migration_flows:_2_million_non-EU_immigrants

Farouk, A., Tarawneh, O., Elhoseny, M., Batle, J., Naseri, Mosayeb, Hassanien, Aboul E. and Abedl-Aty, M. (2018) 'Quantum computing and cryptography: An overview'. In A. Hassanien, M. Elhoseny and J. Kacprzyk (eds) *Quantum Computing: An Environment for Intelligent Large Scale Real Application* (pp. 63–100). Munich: Springer.

Financial Times (2016) 'Britain has had enough of experts, says Gove'. *Financial Times*, 4 June.

Gates, K. (2011) *Our Biometric Future: Facial Recognition Technology and the Culture of Surveillance*. New York, NY: New York University Press.

Gerbaudo, P. (2018) 'From cyber-autonomism to cyber-populism: An ideological analysis of the evolution of digital activism'. *tripleC* 15 (2), 1–13.

Gietel-Basten, S. (2016) 'Why Brexit? The toxic mix of immigration and austerity'. *Population and Development Review* 42 (4), 673–680.

Gioe, D. (2018) 'Cyber operations and useful fools: The approach of Russian hybrid intelligence'. *Intelligence and National Security* 33 (7), 954–973.

Goodwin, M. and Millazo, C. (2017) 'Taking back control? Investigating the role of immigration in the 2016 vote for Brexit'. *British Journal of Politics and International Relations* 19 (3), 450–464.

Groza, T. and Groza, E. (2017) 'Populism: A factory of myths'. *Journal for the Study of Religions and Ideologies* 16 (48), 147–152.

Gyrd-Jones, R. and Kornumb, N. (2013) 'Managing the co-created brand: Value and cultural complementarity in online and offline multi-stakeholder ecosystems'. *Journal of Business Research* 66 (9), 1484–1493.

Halligan, Liam and Lyons, Gerald (2017) *Clean Brexit: Why Leaving the EU Still Makes Sense—Building a post-Brexit Economy for All.* London: Biteback.

Hill, Kashmir (2019) 'I cut the "Big Five" tech giants from my life. It was hell'. 7 February. Accessed 15 February 2019. https://gizmodo.com/i-cut-the-big-five-tech-giants-from-my-life-it-was-hel-1831304194

HMRC (2019) *Make a Disclosure using the Worldwide Disclosure Facility.* 8 February. Accessed 1 March 2019. https://www.gov.uk/guidance/worldwide-disclosure-facility-make-a-disclosure

House of Commons: Digital, Culture, Media and Sport Committee (2019) *Disinformation and 'Fake News': Final Report.* Parliamentary Inquiry, London: HMSO.

Inkster, N. (2015) 'Cyber attacks in La-La Land'. *Survival* 57 (1), 105–116.

Institute for Strategic Dialogue (2019) *The Battle for Bavaria: Online Information Campaigns in the 2018 Bavarian State Election.* London: Institute for Strategic Dialogue.

Jones, R. (2019) 'UK cash system "on the verge of collapse", report finds'. *The Guardian*, 6 March.

Kelsey, D. (2016) 'Hero mythology and right-wing populism'. *Journalism Studies* 17 (8), 971–988.

Ker-Lindsay, J. (2018) 'Turkey's EU accession as a factor in the 2016 Brexit referendum'. *Turkish Studies* 19 (1), 1–22.

Korella, J. and Li, W. (2018) 'Retail payment behaviour and the adoption of innovative payments: A comparative study in China and Germany'. *Journal of Payments Strategy & Systems* 12 (3), 245–265.

Krämer, B. (2017) 'Populist online practices: The function of the Internet in right-wing populism'. *Information, Communication & Society* 20 (9), 1293–1309.

Landon-Murray, M. and Anderson, I. (2013) 'Thinking in 140 characters: The internet, neuroplasticity, and intelligence analysis'. *Journal of Strategic Security* 6 (3), 73–82.

Lee, N. (2015) 'The afterlife of total information awareness and Edward Snowden's NSA leaks'. In N. Lee, *Counterterrorism and Cybersecurity* (pp. 151–182). Munich: Springer.

Lewandowsky, S., Oberauer, K. and Gignac, G. (2013) 'NASA faked the moon landing—therefore, (climate) science is a hoax: An anatomy of the motivated rejection of science'. *Psychological Science* 24 (5), 622–633.

Li, S., Xu, L. and Zhao, S. (2018) '5G internet of things: A survey'. *Journal of Industrial Information Integration* 10, 1–9.

Lucas, Edward (2012) *Deception: The Untold Story of East-West Espionage Today.* New York, NY: Bloomsbury.

Lyon, D. (2015) 'The Snowden stakes: Challenges for understanding surveillance today'. *Surveillance and Society* 13 (2), 139–152.

McCright, A. and Dunlap, R. (2011) 'Cool dudes: The denial of climate change among conservative white males in the United States'. *Global Environmental Change* 21 (4), 1163–1172.

Montag, C. and Diefenbach, S. (2018) 'Towards Homo Digitalis: Important research issues for psychology and the neurosciences at the dawn of the Internet of Things and the digital society'. *Sustainability* 10, 415–436.

Mosca, M. (2018) 'Cybersecurity in an era with quantum computers: Will we be ready?' *IEEE Security and Privacy* 16 (5), 38–41.

O'Neil, P. (2017) 'The deep state: An emerging concept in comparative politics'. *SSRN.* 20 November. Accessed 1 March 2019. https://ssrn.com/abstract=2313375

Opara, E. U., Mahfouz, A. Y. and Holloway, R. R. (2017) 'Network platforms, advanced persistence threat—The changing patterns of cyber-attacks'. *Journal of Forensic and Crime Investigation* 1 (1), 104–114.

Oreskes, N. (2018) 'The scientific consensus on climate change: How do we know we're not wrong?' In A. Winsberg and E. Lloyd (eds) *Climate Modelling* (pp. 31–64). New York, NY: Palgrave Macmillan.

Parton, C. (2019) *UK–China Relations: Where to Draw the Line between Influence and Interference?* Occasional Paper, London: RUSI.

Petit, N. (2018) 'Artificial intelligence and automated law enforcement: A review paper'. *SSRN* 1–12. https://ssrn.com/abstract=3145133

Podhradsky, A., D'Ovidio, R. and Casey, C. (2012) 'The Xbox 360 and steganography: How criminals and terrorists could be "going dark"'. In *Annual ADFSL Conference on Digital Forensics, Security and Law* (pp. 33–54). Richmond: ADFSL.

Robertson, R., Jiang, S., Joseph, K., Friedland, L., Lazer, D. and Wilson, C. (2018) 'Auditing partisan audience bias within Google Search'. *Proceedings of the ACM Human–Computer Interaction* 2 (CSCW), Article 148, 1–22.

Rose, Jonathan (2017) 'Brexit, Trump, and post-truth politics'. *Public Integrity* 19 (6), 555–558.

Ross, J. and Harradine, R. (2011) 'Fashion value brands: The relationship between identity and image'. *Journal of Fashion Marketing and Management: An International Journal* 15 (3), 306–325.

Ruppert, E., Isin, E. and Bigo, D. (2017) 'Data politics'. *Big Data and Society* 4 (2), 1–7.

Sari, A. (2019) 'Hybrid warfare: The legal challenges'. *UK Defence Select Committee.* 23 January. Accessed 5 March 2019. http://data.parliament. uk/writtenevidence/committeeevidence.svc/evidencedocument/ defence-committee/uk-response-to-hybrid-threats/written/95802. html

Schelter, S. and Kunegis, J. (2018) 'On the ubiquity of web tracking: Insights from a billion-page web crawl'. *Journal of Web Science* 4, 53–66.

Schindler, J. R. (2017) 'The spy revolt against Trump begins'. *Observer.* 12 February. Accessed 1 March 2019. https://observer.com/2017/02/ donald-trump-administration-mike-flynn-russian-embassy/

Schlembach, Raphael (2016) 'The Pitchford inquiry into undercover policing: Some lessons from the preliminary hearings'. *Papers from the British Criminology Conference* (pp. 57–73). London: British Society of Criminology.

Schneble, C., Elger, B. and Shaw, D. (2018) 'The Cambridge Analytica affair and internet-mediated research'. *EMBO Reports.* EMBO Rep. 19 (8), e46579. doi: 10.15252/embr.201846579

Schwartz, S., Caprara, G. V. and Vecchione, M. (2010) 'Basic personal values, core political values, and voting: A longitudinal analysis'. *Political Psychology* 31 (3), 421–452.

Seely, B. (2018) *A Definition of Contemporary Russian Conflict: How Does the Kremlin Wage War?* London: Henry Jackson Society.

Skeggs, B. and Yuill, S. (2016) 'Capital experimentation with person/a formation: How Facebook's monetization refigures the relationship between property, personhood and protest'. *Information, Communication and Society* 19 (3), 380–396.

Sputnik (2018) *Anonymous Exposes UK Hybrid Warfare.* 12 1. Accessed 7 March 2019. https://sputniknews.com/trend/anonymous_integrity_ initiative_2018/

——— (2019) 'Anonymous publishes new docs on Integrity Initiative's Institute for Statecraft'. *Sputnik.* 25 January. Accessed 7 March

2019. https://sputniknews.com/europe/201901251071818668-anonymous-integrity-initiative-statecraft/

Suda, Y. (2018) *The Politics of Data Transfer*. New York, NY: Routledge.

Thornberry, E. (2018) 'Institute for Statecraft: Integrity Initiative'. *Hansard*. 12 December. Accessed 7 March 2019. https://hansard.parliament.uk/commons/2018-12-12/debates/298F9A3C-307A-40ED-9CB1-3B2A98F14165/InstituteForStatecraftIntegrityInitiative

UK Ministry of Defence (2019a) 'UK response to hybrid threats'. UK Select Committee on Defence. 28 January. Accessed 5 March 2019. http://data.parliament.uk/writtenevidence/committeeevidence.svc/evidencedocument/defence-committee/uk-response-to-hybrid-threats/written/95802.html

———— (2019b) '77 Brigade: Influence and outreach'. 5 March. Accessed April 2021. https://www.army.mod.uk/who-we-are/formations-divisions-brigades/force-troops-command/77-brigade/

Undercover Policing Inquiry (2018) *UK Undercover Policing Inquiry*. 10 October. Accessed 15 February 2019. https://www.ucpi.org.uk/

Urban, Mark (2018) *The Skripal Files*. London: MacMillan.

Veltri, G., Redd, R., Mannarini, T. and Salvatore, S. (2019) 'The identity of Brexit: A cultural psychology analysis'. *Journal of Community and Applied Social Psychology* 29 (1), 18–31.

Vosoughi, S., Roy, D. and Aral, S. (2018) 'The spread of true and false news online'. *Science* 359 (6380), 1146–1151.

Walsh, P. and Miller, S. (2016) 'Rethinking "Five Eyes" security intelligence collection policies and practice post Snowden'. *Intelligence and National Security* 31 (3), 345–368.

Ward, K. (2018) 'Social networks, the 2016 US presidential election, and Kantian ethics: Applying the categorical imperative to Cambridge Analytica's behavioral microtargeting'. *Journal of Media Ethics* 33 (3), 133–148.

Weatherby, Bronwen (2020) 'Priti Patel 'absolutely livid' about claims MI5 doesn't trust her'. *The Evening Standard*, February 24.

Wilford, Hugh (1998) 'The Information Research Department: Britain's secret Cold War weapon revealed'. *Review of International Studies* 24 (3), 353–369.

Yablokov, I. (2015) 'Conspiracy theories as a Russian public diplomacy tool: The case of Russia Today (RT)'. *Politics* 35 (3–4), 301–315.

Zajc, M. (2015) 'The social media dispositive and monetization of user-generated content'. *The Information Society: An International Journal* 31 (1), 61–67.

Zhang, D. (2018) 'U.S. push on Huawei ripples through markets'. *The Washington Post*, 23 November.

Zhubov, S. (2019) *The Age of Surveillance Capitalism: The Fight for a Human Future at the New Frontier of Power.* London: Profile Books.

PART TWO

THE PUBLIC CONSUMPTION
OF INTELLIGENCE

6

THE EVOLVING RELATIONSHIP BETWEEN INTELLIGENCE AND THE MEDIA

What You Need to Know...

The relationship between intelligence agencies and the legacy media has been both symbiotic and subject to enduring tensions, in part due to the amount of shared practice, ethos and techniques between the two industries. The generation of stories or narratives around threats and challenges has traditionally been used to bolster the hegemony of the Five Eyes and NATO-aligned nations, both in terms of their actual security position and the world view they represent and protect. The emergence and disruption caused by internet platforms and the new media have merely served to exacerbate these pre-existing symbioses and tensions: intelligence agencies still try to positively shape the information environment and guard against the release of information that endangers national security interests and intelligence assets. The speed and traction of internet posting have provided the backdrop to a new era of information warfare, one in which Western governments have been overmatched by Chinese, Iranian, jihadist, North Korean and Russian adversaries. The media also forms an important part of the informal oversight of intelligence agencies and government intelligence activity. The effectiveness of this oversight has been hampered by the transformation in the business models of media companies, which has seen a broad divestment away from traditional investigative journalism. It has also been impacted by governments' use of surveillance and interception to disrupt investigations and the prosecution of journalists and their sources. Revelations have tended to come in large set-piece splashes with coordinated multi-jurisdictional releases to mitigate government action, but which have been criticised for not sufficiently mitigating the harm to government intelligence activity.

***

It is of the essence of a Secret Service that it must be secret, and if you once begin disclosure it is perfectly obvious to me as to honourable members opposite that there is no longer any Secret Service and you must do without it.

Chamberlain, 1924

***

Purpose of the Relationship

The relationship between intelligence and the media has—since the Second World War—been remarkably close. Indeed, Mike Goodman and I described intelligence officers and journalists as blood brothers, whilst David Leigh provided an excellent overview of the challenges of dealing with intelligence officers as a journalist (Dover & Goodman, 2009; Leigh, 2019, pp. 85–98). This runs contrary to the misperception that intelligence agencies are wedded to living away from the public gaze: a good number of intelligence officers are empowered to speak with media sources, albeit within controlled boundaries and with the need to debrief these contacts. This reflects the reality that shaping the operational environment is a key element of intelligence tradecraft and this has necessarily involved intelligence officers maintaining useful relationships with media outlets and specific journalists.

For intelligence agencies to maintain their budgets, and therefore their staffing and equipment levels, they also need to shape the public's understanding of the threats we face and what will be needed to counter these threats. This assessment is fed by the contemporary history of the 1990s, where a post-Cold War dividend saw large cuts to budgets and human resource across intelligence and security communities in the North Atlantic area (Leigh & Wegge, 2018, pp. 7–24). Maintaining the awareness of threat requires—in part—a productive and systematic relationship with media outlets, academics, cultural industries and other forms of civil society in addition to the government. Journalism (along with other businesses) was a useful cover trade for spies seeking to create operational legends during the Cold War: the infamous double agent Kim Philby was, for example, a journalist. The proximity of the two trades is not just philosophical but also has some practical benefits on occasion.

One of the best articulations of the closeness and yet tension in the relationship between intelligence and media organisations was made by CIA Director William Casey in 1986 when—in a briefing to the editors of America's largest newspapers—he noted the essential similarities in tradecraft between the communities. Casey also noted that both communities work to provide accurate information to help policy officials and the public make informed decisions and that the media also provides informal oversight. He also—importantly—noted what he described as a shared moral commitment of the communities to protect sources (Aldrich, 2009). But Casey had a warning for the media, which was later to echo the problems the intelligence community had with the Cablegate and Snowden affairs: investigative journalism had the potential to undermine high-value intelligence sources. Such revelations—Casey further argued—had given comfort to America's adversaries because they had undermined the valuable network of international liaison relationships between intelligence agencies and had similarly made some of the US's intelligence collection systems redundant (Aldrich, 2009). Tacitly, the advice was feel free to publish, but they should be aware of the damage done to the US interests at the same time.

The tension that Director Casey highlighted in his briefing goes to the heart of the relationship between media organisations and intelligence and security agencies. The media provides important mechanisms by which intelligence agencies can shape the operational environment, and by that I also mean shape the public's understanding of the challenge, or threat, of the legitimacy of an action or whatever it might be. This powerful collaborative moment between these two professional tribes—of collaboration between an intelligence organisation and a section of the media—helps to shape public understanding long into the future.

American intelligence agencies have enjoyed far closer relations with their press than MI5, MI6 and GCHQ have done in the UK. This is partly because the American Constitution affords journalists greater protections both to investigate and to print stories about the intelligence community, but it is also a reflection of the decisions made by US agencies to engage with the press, to shape issues but also to advance their own institutional advantages. As the Congressional Report—known as the 1976 Church Report—noted, the CIA had routinely run journalists and authors as agents, pushing information into the foreign media and even going to the lengths, via the UK's Information Research Department, of buying up favourable books and licensing their translation and publication in other jurisdictions (US Senate, 2020; Wilford, 1998). The public response to the Church Committee's report was hostile, and the activities were immediately reduced as a result, ending the paid relationships with journalists. The relative openness of the US system remained and this—in part—explains why more has been known and continues to be known about the American agencies over and above their British counterparts, where legal protections are less well defined, and where there is less budgetary advantage to be gained by initiating a public turf-war. In the UK, the agencies have relied upon their political leaders for support.

After the collapse of the Soviet Union in 1991, Western governments took the decision to extract what they saw as a peace dividend in reduced military costs. Throughout the 1990s, European governments—in particular—reduced their investment in military, security and intelligence forces. As events in Kosovo, Afghanistan, Iraq, Syria and now Ukraine show us, this dividend was entirely erroneous: the cost to our collective security vulnerability is far more costly than the savings made. These same governments also felt emboldened enough to cast a limited amount of light on their intelligence agencies, and thus open them up to more media scrutiny. Across the Western world this transparency manifested itself through the public acknowledgement of the work of agencies (avowal) and more public manifestations of statutory underpinning and regulation alongside developments in declassifying official archives, which included the operational history of agencies.

The terrorist attacks of 9/11 resulted in a large brake being put on official transparency, with Western governments seeking to re-grow their intelligence and security capabilities and to enact ever tighter rules around official secrecy. These expanded notions of state secrecy and intrusive surveillance have generated a greater demand for agencies to be held to account for their operations and the decisions they have taken in investigating particular communities, in placing surveillance on whole sections of society and engaging in violent coercion against suspects, when official forms of oversight and regulation failed to reveal, check or balance some of these assessed excesses.

Whilst freedom of information legislation in both the US (1966) and the UK (2000) has promised—and largely delivered—greater insights into the workings of governments, with the obvious caveat that intelligence agencies are protected under the legislation, these Acts have resulted in increased coverage and a societal expectation of openness, but little in the way of formal enhancements to oversight. New, digitally based media have offered, therefore, the prospect of a form of parallel or informal oversight over the intelligence services, where activists, citizen journalists and whistleblowers, protected by the judiciary, can come together to hold governments to account: something Richard Aldrich has described as 'regulation by revelation' (Aldrich, 2009). Internet-based platforms and communications have created what Andrew Chadwick has persuasively termed a hybrid media system allowing media and activist organisations to simultaneously release information about intelligence activities across international boundaries, without regulation (Chadwick, 2013). These have included the Cablegate leaks (2010—*El País*, *Der Spiegel*, *Le Monde*, *The Guardian*, *The New York Times*, WikiLeaks), the Snowden revelations (2013—*The Guardian*, *Der Spiegel*, *The Washington Post*, *The New York Times*, *O Globo*, *Le Monde*), and the Crypto AG story (2020—*The Washington Post*, Reuters and ZDF).

The presence of internationally coordinated media splashes can be cited as evidence that the electronically interconnected world will help hold governments to account, and thus produce better democratic outcomes. The positives of greater interconnection have been outweighed over the course of the last decade by the realisation—in part spurred by Snowden and commentaries like those of Shoshana Zuboff, who has focussed on the private sector pathologies of surveillance and control—that a pervasive form of semi-authoritarianism is sweeping the globe (Zuboff, 2019). On the one hand, governments and aligned actors are utilising electronic platforms and freedom of information pathways to overwhelm the public and the media with uninteresting but voluminous data, making one of the key challenges of being a citizen the problem of how to decipher what is important. On the other hand, governments increasingly try to throttle off the quantity of sensitive data available to the public, and to restrict the capacity of citizens to protest about issues such as change without being labelled as extremists (Grierson, 2020). Delineating the impact of these changing patterns of government information on the citizenry is exceptionally complicated. The extent to which the electorate is able to make sense of the myriad of data points and information feeds to identify issue salience and place an appropriate vote has always been something that academics think they can discern, but ultimately it rests upon which way their vote was cast in the previous election and a 'feel' or 'sense' of the candidates (Dennison, 2019). In an era where the extent of the data available to citizens is so large (and from a wide array of credible and unreliable sources), political salience has bifurcated into a small number of touchstone issues that become disproportionately persuasive during a campaign, and in fitness to govern. The same type of phenomenon has faced the intelligence agencies as well. Their capacity to intercept communications data, to store and to machine analyse it has increased exponentially, but the challenge of sifting the data for something useful remains very large and the technological arms race between those seeking to protect their privacy and those looking to lawfully interrupt it remains fierce. In other words, it is not clear that the surveillance capacity of state intelligence agencies is yet giving them a significant advantage, even if the potential is there for precisely that.

For investigative journalists (of which there are vanishingly few compared to the 1970s and 1980s), for academics and for activists the development of freedom of information legislation, coupled with the audit potential of electronically created and stored documents, promised greater insights into the inner workings of government. The 2003 Hutton Inquiry in the UK—covering the circumstances around the death of the defence scientist David Kelly—revealed, for the first time, that the electronic communications of civil servants were now fully disclosable to these sorts of inquiries (Hutton, 2004). Clamours for an investigation into the government's handling of the Covid pandemic focused on how recoverable messages were from private encrypted services (Hall, 2022). The Hutton Inquiry shed light on some communications that were never intended for public consumption and were exceptionally awkward for those sending and receiving them. But an inquiry is a special and well-resourced occasion, and for journalists, academics, interested citizens and the official archivists they often deal with, there is a great deal of presumed knowledge of government processes and systems required to make effective use of freedom of information legislation, accepting that it does not apply directly to the intelligence community. So, the promise of the liberalisation of official information has not been realised in practice, and the ability to monitor and counter those investigating government activities has increased. This has led to the paradoxical expansion of the security state, freed from effective oversight.

Within the official archives that journalists, activists, academics and research students operate, the digitisation of papers has made it technically simpler to piece together unofficial histories, where the archive exists, and to do so via electronic searches and digital documents rather than by manual trawls through the holdings. The majority of materials about intelligence and security is subject to security classification (from OFFICIAL to TOP SECRET, and variants above) and is then subject to the slow process of declassification, usually over prescribed periods of time. Over the course of the last forty years the US has oscillated between greater openness and greater secrecy, turn by turn. An Executive Order from President Clinton in 1995 allowed for all documents more than twenty-five years old to be declassified: something that was strongly opposed by the agencies and security conscious legislators (Department of Justice, 1995). Clinton's initiative created a massive backlog of files for which the responsible department or agency had requested a security exemption. The US Army applied for exemptions for 269 million pages of documents, whilst the CIA applied to have circa 150 million pages exempted. In the event, the agencies had to create their own security review clearing houses to help reduce the backlog and the end result was a large quantity of previously unseen material that helped roll back some of the mysteries of the agencies during the Cold War. In parallel to the declassification process, the development and popularisation of the internet helped to create informal alternative outlets for government documents that had often not made their way through formal declassification processes, such as John Young's Cryptome site (cryptome.org).

In 2000, the final full year of Clinton's administration, a swift reversal of the 1995 declassification policy occurred, which became known as reclassification. Whilst the reclassification under Clinton was quite modest, under his successor, George W. Bush, the reclassification process took on a similarly industrial scale as that of declassification only a few years earlier. In the space of three years the programme had looked at 43.4 million pages of documents held in the US National Archive, reclassifying previously open documents that many historians felt were neither sensitive nor particularly interesting. Declassification, and to a greater extent reclassification, are strong examples of the ways in which governments can shape the historic telling of particular episodes, but—more importantly— through that telling, shape the beliefs, values and behaviours of society by setting the contextual narrative.

Throughout the 2000s the reinstallation of tougher secrecy measures could also be seen in the evocation, on both sides of the Atlantic, of secrecy privilege in court cases where people were seeking redress for rendition and invasions of communications privacy, and in greater penalties and exemplification for those caught leaking government secrets. Examples of people who fell foul of these tighter restrictions included former MI6 officer Richard Tomlinson, who was subject to a European-wide manhunt for his unauthorised memoirs, which became freely available on the internet (Tomlinson, 2001). Similarly, 'the Tomlinson List', which does not seem to have had anything to do with Tomlinson, was published online, listing mostly retired and alleged MI6 officers, and which caused acute discomfort to those involved. This follows on from the problems MI5 had experienced in the 1990s with discontented ex-employees David Shayler and Annie Machon, who are still active in commenting on security issues online (Hollingsworth & Fielding, 1999; Machon, 2005).

Examples of the same phenomena in America include the extraordinary decision in 2008 to indict the Pulitzer Prize-winning reporter James Risen of *The New York Times*, who had revealed that the National Security Agency had failed to secure warrants for its interception of international communications that began or ended in the US, something required under federal law (Risen, 2016). Risen had further irritated and embarrassed the American security state through revealing the joint Israeli–American Operation Merlin, which aimed to disrupt Iranian nuclear proliferation but which had been uncovered by Iranian counterintelligence officers and had cost the lives of CIA agents in Iran. The context of the indictment was a souring of relations with Israel's Mossad, who were peaked about how leaky the US intelligence community had proven to be (Siskind, 2020). Somewhat ironically, given Risen's work on the NSA and wiretapping, arrests were affected on officers assumed to be his sources on the basis of phone record evidence. Jeffrey Sterling was later imprisoned for his role in the reporting and has recently written his account of the episode (Sterling, 2019). The overall impact of these crackdowns (and perhaps the intention, too) was to disincentivise investigative journalism and intelligence officers from maintaining contacts with journalists. The use of wiretap and communications intelligence also created a cottage industry in counterespionage and safe whistleblowing, including reversions to analogue forms of secret communications like secret ink, dead-letter drops and microdots.

The greatest international impact from a story came from Dana Priest's Pulitzer Prize-reporting in *The Washington Post* about the presence of secret CIA prisons across Europe (Mayer, 2008; Priest,

2005). Despite the acquiescence of European governments to these activities, and that they had used intelligence gathered in this way for their own security, the Council of Europe, the European Parliament and a clutch of member states held official and high-profile inquiries about the secret sites (Blakeley & Raphael, 2020; European Parliament, 2012; Marty, 2006). The American agencies felt aggrieved about the hypocrisy of the Europeans, whilst European agencies felt aggrieved about the leakiness of the US system. Neither seemed particularly vexed about the ethics of rendition and torture, and many legal cases persist as a result. The publicity also pressured European states to change their approach to the war on terror. Mary O. McCarthy, a CIA officer near to retirement, was dismissed for conducting undisclosed and unauthorised meetings with journalists but was not accused of being Dana Priest's key source. Some have seen McCarthy's dismissal as part of CIA Director Porter Goss's determination to end the wave of leaks, and as a signal to others that they might lose valuable retirement benefits if they are caught in authorised positions—again a chilling of the links between journalists and intelligence operatives (Johnstone & Shane, 2006). This might appear reasonable, but a general perception that these contacts are always inappropriate set the scene (some say) for the death of the British defence scientist David Kelly, who was allowed to be hounded for his contact with the journalist Andrew Gilligan, a contact whom—it turned out—was part and parcel of his day job (Baker, 2007; Hutton, 2004).

There are considerable benefits for both journalists and intelligence agencies from a close relationship between the two professions. Both fields are concerned with knowledge production, employ similar methodologies and are premised upon secret informants. Interestingly, both see themselves as losing out to the other in their often-tetchy relationship. Select journalists are able to write interesting stories, and intelligence officers have the opportunity to position issues and institutional interests as they wish. But the relationship is subject to cyclical trends and it has been conditioned by the prevailing political situation and the dominant events of the time. Investigative journalists have, turn by turn, been lauded for placing a check and balance on governmental over-reach, and harassed and occasionally prosecuted for breaches of secrecy laws during their investigative work, even when the court of public opinion has judged that the public interest is overwhelming. Good examples of these cases come from the examples noted above— James Risen and Dana Priest—but also from people like the British investigative journalist Duncan Campbell and the American author and former practitioner James Bamford, both of whom contributed to the public revelation of the ECHELON listening programme (Bamford, 2002; Campbell, 1988). Campbell was routinely arrested and harassed, with his home being searched numerous times to disrupt his investigations, whilst Bamford was periodically threatened with prosecution for his research (Dymydiuk, 2020).

The ubiquity of internet and social media platforms in everyday lives has disrupted the intelligence–media relationship. This relationship, which serves as a conduit for a dialogue to protect some particularly sensitive secrets whilst tacitly accepting that the media does play an oversight role, does not exist in the largely unregulated space of the indexed, and particularly the unindexed, internet. As noted earlier, media organisations have been careful to coordinate their large splashes across many jurisdictions, as a form of quasi-legal protection. They have worked with whistleblowers to carefully manage these exposés, to fulfil the whistleblower function without trying to fundamentally damage the reputation of the agencies. The internet has not heralded an end to official secrecy, even if Cablegate and Snowden seriously tested the ability of many governments (in coordination) to cope with the weight and number of revelations. Whilst the EU has sought to protect the position of the whistleblower in law, we know that the ability of a whistleblower to remain anonymous has been fundamentally undermined by advances in technology (European Parliament, 2019).

The notion that there are any secure means by which to transmit information from a whistleblower to the internet or to a trusted media source is a complete fallacy. The use of encrypted messaging services is undermined by the ability of agencies to intercept the inputs into a device being used for this purpose; layers of virtual-private-network (VPN) and TOR (The Onion Router) browser protection are also insufficient to protect the whistleblower and, in the wake of the 2020

Crypto AG revelations about tampering with cryptography machines during the Cold War, there was a slew of unverified assertions online that the US had developed TOR with backdoor weaknesses to do the same on this form of internet and had backdoors placed in computer equipment from the 1990s onwards to do the same. It is notable, however, that some whistleblower organisations conduct their business using 'burner phones' (unregistered single-use SIM cards), and dead-letter drops, in the style of Cold War dramas. The tension between secrecy and informal oversight looks set to continue, with the press playing the role of receiving leaks and converting them into journalism, but within the cyclical framework of legal and political bumps along the way.

The Management of the Relationship

As noted above, intelligence officers and journalists have more in common—whether they like it or not—than they have in opposition. In producing knowledge, to deadline, for distinct purposes via sources, be they informants, covert listening devices, honey-traps and so on, that they protect jealously they are, in many respects, two sides of the same coin. What is more, their professional interests overlap and so the relationship is often akin to competitive intelligence agencies engaged in 'spy games'. The stock-in trade of the media has been exposing treachery and intelligence failure. The revelations around the Cambridge Spy Ring damaged the UK's relationship with the US for well over a year, whilst the stories about the UK Minister for War, John Profumo, led to his exile from public life, the beginning of the end of Prime Minister MacMillan's government and the show-trial and suicide of Stephen Ward (Mangold, 2020). The failure to put the intelligence that was collected before 9/11 together created a thriving industry in reportage and commentary on intelligence failure, as did the similar assertions of failure prior to the Iraq War in 2003, the 2005 London bombings and subsequently the 2017 Manchester concert bombing and various smaller scale marauding attacks in Whitehall, near Parliament and on London Bridge and Borough Market. Far less prominence has been given to intelligence successes, which have largely gone unreported.

Intelligence agencies have sought to manage the challenges of the media's preference for reporting failures, reporting the odd and unresolved cases (such as that of the GCHQ officer Gareth Williams, who was found dead in a suitcase in 2010) and reporting on the more exciting aspects of intelligence tradecraft, by cultivating privileged relationships with trusted journalists to manage the delivery of more acceptable stories into the public arena. The management of trusted journalists was markedly different in the US in the Cold War up to 1976, where the Church Committee Report revealed that more than fifty journalists had been paid as agents, and were therefore working undercover. In the UK, the equivalent was the Foreign and Commonwealth Office's Information Research Department that sought to place stories across the world that were useful to particular operational or strategic ends. After the Church Committee, the practice of running journalists as agents requires Presidential approval, and during the more recent adventures in Iraq and Afghanistan the practice has all but stopped due to the unacceptable risk it was posing to regular journalists whose physical safety was routinely compromised by accusations of being run by intelligence agencies. The privileged relationships now are more informal and on the basis of trust, and where it is known that they will advance a public information service on an issue. The respective agencies' public information units are also far more visible in commenting on issues and 'getting ahead of the story' to shape the narrative, rather than being ambushed by the narratives of others. This has become particularly relevant in managing the rollercoaster of social media reportage and commentary. The assumed activities of the British Army's Brigade 77 information operations unit has been a popular jumping off point for online commentators seeking conspiracies about governmental control of internet information flows.

One of the other key elements of the relationship between the media and intelligence agencies is the ministerial interview: something the agencies have very little control over. Imagine the horror on the faces of senior intelligence officers in MI5 and counterterrorism policing watching a series of broadcast interviews where their new political boss continually refers to clamping down and attacking at source the scourge of counterterrorism, rather than terrorism, undermining a policy before its even been enacted, vividly brought to life by the online and viral video of the comedian Michael Spicer, acting up as the adviser in the next room (Spicer, 2020). The reliance on politicians and the set piece interview is an important element of the management of intelligence-media relations because it is a component of how the public make sense of intelligence activity, albeit refracted through their own experiences, education and biases. The necessity for secret operations, the derogations of privacy this often entails and whether the agencies are *winning* are important elements of the narrative formed and maintained in the media.

For the most part the agencies are passengers in the set piece political interview, at the mercy of the programme editors and how they have framed the underlying issue, what footage they have used and how they have recalled previous related successes or failures, and what talking-head expertise they have brought into provide the background, before being entirely reliant on the politician to competently put the case in the face of often aggressive and persistent questioning. A harried politician may fall back on the Blairite trope of 'if only you knew what I know', which is undoubtedly true, but which plays badly with the British public after the approach to the 2003 Iraq War and the so-called 'dodgy dossier' (McCormack, 2019). The public tend to think that politicians overstate the security threat, whilst activists continuously claim that all extensions to security law are a creeping development of an authoritarian state. The public facing role of the minister is to contribute in convincing the public that measures they are proposing will increase the sum total of security for the individual and at the community level, thus making the country a more attractive place to live in, do business with or invest in. Evoking superior knowledge through intelligence would play better if there were settled views—even in Parliament—about how our dominant security threats should be dealt with. That there is not makes it hazardous, if not understandable in the heat of an interview.

Consequently, the political interview is a game within a game, where the desired outcomes of the programme makers, the interviewer, the politician and the agency are all likely to be different, within degrees. There is also the potential trap of the inadvertent leak of intelligence information, because just as institutions like BBC Monitoring monitor broadcasts in other countries, competitors do the same to us. An example of this comes from the Crypto AG story that broke in February 2020 was the revelation that President Reagan had twice inadvertently compromised Operation Rubicon by revealing enough detail in interviews to alert, in one instance, the Argentinian government to the fact that their encrypted communications were being monitored (Miller, 2020). In more routine intelligence matters, such inadvertent leaks might undermine an operation, threaten the safety of officers or prejudice court proceedings: all undesirable outcomes.

From Analogue to Digital Eras

The move from the analogue era of newspapers and linear broadcasts, to the era of the internet, social media and streaming services (be they user generated platforms like YouTube and TikTok, or commercial streaming services like Netflix) has placed additional challenges on the intelligence community. The idiosyncratic and borderless communities that discuss national security and intelligence online, on Twitter, through Facebook or LinkedIn groups, all the way down to the darknet forums, allow the public to converse with active and retired officials, private intelligence workers, and keen amateurs. Closed groups have the potential to see sensitive material passed around, either deliberately or in someone seeking to correct a misunderstanding. Either way, they represent a vast expansion of the security officer's field of vision, providing additional horizons of concern and worry. Active officers on both sides of the Atlantic are restricted as to what social media services they can use, and they have to declare the social media they are active on for counterintelligence purposes. Those sites which receive leaks or opensource informing have only their consciences and legal liability through which to exercise some form of judgement over what and what not to publish. Those who are not deeply expert in security affairs will—in reality—have no accurate point of reference by which to gauge what is prohibitively sensitive, placing themselves and state assets in potential harm's way.

The second key dimension to the development of the digital media environment has been the ideological or information war component (Barber, 1995). Al-Qaeda were fond of noting that more than half of the battle in which they were engaged was a battle for the media, to help them capture the hearts and minds of Muslims that their war was morally justifiable and necessary. As a globally connected insurgent force, this was the creation of their framing logics, of their picture of reason confronting the accepted norms of Western society. This quasi-military doctrine was ahead of the doctrine of militarily superior Western armed forces who have more recently accepted that they are engaged in information conflicts (UK Ministry of Defence, 2021). The increasing sophistication of jihadist information operations placed a huge stress on relatively slow moving and reactive government public relations units, and similarly placed a strong tension on media outlets who became the battlefield in the information war, torn between sensationalist copy and not wishing to damage the government's efforts (Taylor, 2010).

The set of beheadings carried out by the British national Mohammed Emwazi, known in the media as Jihadi John, in 2014 and 2015, were filmed using high quality cameras and were electronically distributed (James, 2016; Verlaik, 2016). The strong production values allowed Western media outlets to faithfully reproduce these images on their front pages and on the television. The effect of this reproduction was to assist the polarisation of parts of British society, between those inspired by these images—even when they were framed as abhorrent—and those who were sickened by them and sought government action as a result of them (Friis, 2015). This most unpleasant of tactics seemed effective in illuminating the political, moral and ethical chasm between the broadly secular North Atlantic and those claiming religious justifications for their violence, which became intimately tied with beheadings, a historical anachronism (Koch, 2018). For media managers, the decision to print and broadcast or not to print and broadcast seemed doomed to moral traps on all sides.

The British media tends towards publication as a reflex and so the Jihadi John images were seen, and the impact was felt across society in the ways described. The reproduction of these images spurred a further debate about whether it is more appropriate to censor or ban publication of such images, and indeed to suck the oxygen out of terrorist attacks by consciously downplaying the events when they occur. In practice this would involve not speculating on casualties, the motives of the attackers, and by not describing them as terrorists, not using their names in reports, nor reporting on manifestos they may have left. This form of response was seen in the reporting of the far-right terror attack in New Zealand in March 2019 by Brendan Tarrant, where the attacker's name continues not to be broadcast, nor spoken of by the government and his manifesto has equally not been widely analysed nor reported (Bromell & Shanks, 2021). This is starkly different to previous attacks in the Western world, including those of Anders Breivik, whose name, courtroom antics and manifesto are widely circulated and known. Breivik was given the opportunity to create theatre—one of the core aims of terrorists—whilst Tarrant was not (Laugerud & Langballe, 2017).

For journalists covering national security issues, they have always faced considerable challenges. As just noted, the media have been accused of providing adversaries the oxygen of publicity. From faithfully reporting Russian disinformation to repeating the lines in Jihadist videos, journalists have opted to provide publics with a balanced view: the initial material and the counterpoint. And thus, it is difficult for them not to give these views oxygen when framed by journalistic impartiality, which itself is challenged by the fragmentation of the media and reversion to ideological positions. This is one of the underlying reasons behind journalists increasingly finding themselves the target of attacks, and why dangerous adversaries have moved towards filming and publishing their own footage. The media industry has taken centre stage in contemporary information warfare and between competing frames of logic.

The importance of the internet to our international adversaries is in the guidance it provides to those wishing to carry out attacks or subversive activities, and as a platform for raising and distributing funding (RUSI, 2017). These platforms have provided moral certainty to those considering participation, and whilst governments have struggled to engage in these activities without reputational loss, disrupting websites and webservers has provided temporary relief, albeit that the materials have been replicated on mirror sites almost immediately. Intelligence officers have vacillated between thinking it is more effective to leave sites where they are and monitor them and the traffic around them, or to disrupt them.

The Chinese, North Korean, Iranian and Russian governments have employed large groups of officers to engage in online debates, and to disrupt opponents, whilst Western governments have done something similar on a far smaller scale and with far less effect. The Russian unit is known by the unfortunate acronym IRA (Badawy *et al.*, 2019; Xia *et al.*, 2019) but is part of the military intelligence organisation the GRU. In Iran, these cyber operations are prosecuted the Islamic Revolutionary Guard Corps (IRGC), again a core part of the state's security apparatus. A similar picture can be observed in North Korea where the offensive cyber operations are conducted by Bureau 121, a part of the General Bureau of Reconnaissance, a wide-ranging intelligence and security organisation (Ji-Young, In & Gon, 2019). In contrast, 77 Brigade, the British Army unit dedicated to identifying, containing and prosecuting this activity is staffed by a relatively small number of reservists (Giegerich, 2016). In this area of information conflict, it is the emergent states who are currently fielding capabilities and strategic impacts that are proportionately larger than their physical military capabilities. They have also inflicted numerous embarrassing and awkward moments on those nations allied to the US. The British response—via 77 Brigade and GCHQ—has been relatively circumspect in contrast, but the newly published *Integrated Review of Security and Defence* makes it plain that the UK will be engaging in offensive cyber operations in the future and considers them to be an essential part of military activities in the future (UK Ministry of Defence, 2021). The partially successful subversion of the established information order is a reflection of how the playing field can be more ably levelled in the cyber realm, and that the dominance of the euroatlantic powers is not guaranteed.

The decision to disrupt or not disrupt, to push messages or not, have all had impacts upon the credibility of the agencies involved, something that is easily lost in an online environment, particularly when partial segments can be reproduced out of context and international audiences can all consume the same material. In managing crises, official communicators have often rested upon a primary need to provide validated information to maintain their credibility, but we found that this and a lack of coordination in which government agency was providing the authoritative voice provided a gap that competitors moved into, and it was these rival messages that had the longest term impact (Dover, Downey & Smith, 2019).

In the field of strategic intelligence and international relations, information war is also now a prominent feature and indeed could reasonably be deemed a sixth domain of war fighting (UK Joint Doctrine Centre, 2018). The UK's ongoing tensions with Russia have played out in various forms of information and misinformation campaigning via social media and legacy media platforms. The attempted assassination of former GRU Officer Sergei Skripal in Salisbury in March 2018 has been contested ever since, with even mainstream politicians casting some doubts on the veracity of the UK government's assertion that this can have only been a Russian state sponsored attempt on his life (Schofield, 2018). The longevity of the digital echoes of these stories is one of the strong features of this form of disinformation, with online activists, fellow-travellers or so-called 'useful idiots' linking all manner of stories to their narrative around the assassination attempt (Gioe, 2018). Similar levels of contestation around evidence and attribution have been found in the debates concerning chemical weapons and the Syrian civil war, something that has been starkly brought to life by a BBC radio-broadcast called *Mayday* in 2020, exploring the life and death of James LeMesurier and then returning for a one off special in April 2021 to explore the role of British academics in some of the information contest that continues to surround the so-called White Hats in Syria and the Syrian government's use of chemical weapons and torture in the civil war (BBC, 2021). This information contest is also discussed at greater length in the chapter on social media intelligence in this book.

The real challenge from the development of these digital domains has been the extent that the public have been swayed or convinced by digital disinformation, thus making their responses less predictable than before, and consequently generating a greater number of strategic shocks. And similarly, that the political elites have found processing the increased amounts of information now available to them highly problematic. In the US, President Trump was said not to favour the morning intelligence briefing, preferring the reporting on TV news (Wolfberg, 2017). The final Director of National Intelligence under President Trump, Richard Grenell, also stated that, with so much open source information available, he does not see much need for the intelligence community as a provider of information he thinks he can secure elsewhere at a lower cost (Editorial Board, 2020).[1] Similar developments have been suggested in the UK, where MI5 was forced to deny that they hold back intelligence from the Home Secretary, again suggesting that Priti Patel might be forced to seek her information elsewhere (Sparrow, 2020).

The impact of unverified information impacting upon strategic level decision-makers might be very pronounced, but very difficult to track. We know that year-on-year an increasingly large percentage of the population see the internet (and Facebook / Meta in particular) as their primary source of news information (Mosquera *et al.*, 2020). So, these government positions are a troubling echo of societal change. The barriers to entry to providing 'news' on the internet are low, and so the gatekeeping our adversaries—such as dissident groups and competitor states—faced from the legacy media no longer exist. Their platforms can also employ devices such as password protection as a means by which to suggest that the user is accessing verified information and protecting the community of users, and reinforcing a sense of the end-user receiving privileged information.

The Analogue and the Digital Eras Meet: The UK's D-Notice Committee

One feature of the relationship and dynamics between the British media and security community in security reporting is the most British invention, the D-Notice Committee, which is now more than 100 years old. The Committee has no legal nor constitutional weight, but there is evidence that it is treated by those who deal with it as if it did. Because it has no statutory basis, it is voluntary for both officials and media using it, and consequently its advice may formally be disregarded by both sides. Whilst the Committee's staff notionally reside in the Ministry of Defence, it is independent of all of its stakeholders and is staffed by one permanent Chair (a high-ranking and retired military officer) and has a membership of four additional officials and sixteen senior press and broadcasting representatives. Its advisory function augments rather than replaces official secrecy and aims to mitigate potential harm to the operations and officers engaged in security work. It is possible to argue that it also helps media outlets to avoid unpredictable and expensive litigation through a privileged avenue of consultation. In the last ten years we have seen that the alternative to court action in the UK is intelligence agency attention against journalists and media organisations. A notable example of this was the raid on *The Guardian's* offices connected with the Snowden revelations and the suggestion that they physically destroy their hard drives containing information from Snowden (Laughland, 2013).

The D-Notice system covers 'national security', but this is not adequately defined. Indeed, until the 1980s what the D-Notice Committee was and did was not well understood and only an official history by a former Chair Nick Wilkinson has helped to clarify its role (Wilkinson, 2009). The common misperception was that stories could be embargoed or blocked by a D-Notice, which reinforced a misperception that there was a secret, censoring committee underpinned by law (Sadler, 2018). In terms of defining national security, we might reasonably think of it covering issues around military, strategic and counterterrorism operations, for example. The Committee's core business are typified by its standing notices: Military Plans and Operations, Equipment (including nuclear weapons), Cryptology, Sensitive Sites, the intelligence community (made difficult by the growing trend of former insiders to publish autobiographies and 'inspired' novels) and Special Forces (again made difficult by a slew of popular autobiographical books). The very partial public understanding of the Committee and its remit makes its role look outsized: it also hints at the management of the respective professional tribes across the intelligence and media communities and with it a conditioning of important value-laden narratives.

According to the published accounts of its former Chairs, the D-Notice Committee also gets involved in other issues of national security, which emerge if the Chair is approached by a journalist or an official on a specific issue; but from the evidence provided by Wilkinson and Sadler this seems to have been interpreted by the Committee and its participants relatively loosely. The Committee has also served as a location to discuss what is and is not 'national security', thinking through harms to life and operations, as well how much of the information is already in the public domain. The question of whether information is already in the public domain has become more complicated with the advent of the internet and microblogging, which can see stories broken in real-time, across national boundaries. Legacy media outlets rightly see themselves as being placed at a far higher standard than new media outlets in this context (Starinsky, 2021).

In many respects the internet has merely speeded up something that was already observable. The development of communications delivered by railways, and by telegraph, then wires, and underwater cables saw the speed and range of communications increase and therefore a globalisation of information, including security information (Castells, 2010; Rosenberg, 2000). The timeframes are shorter, and consequently the day-in-day-out role of the Committee is more on mitigating the harm of elements of an emerging story than of preventing an entire story being published. This is very much an area that can be characterised as 'delayed disclosure', the Katharine Gun affair of the (partially inadvertent GCHQ whistleblower) was only fractionally delayed by the Committee who convinced the media not to publish details of the intelligence that had been leaked (Cram, 2009). The Gun affair became something of a cause celebre when the prosecution withdrew its case presumably to prevent further revelations in court and in 2019 Gun case was made into a very watchable film called *Official Secrets*.

The D-Notice Committee has played an important role as a forum in which senior officials and senior legacy media representatives can meet in person to discuss the difficult practical issues which security stories often present, and to overcome the cultural barriers that exist between them. Such a forum—however—provides grist to the mill of those who claim that mainstream narratives are reproduced and policed by these ostensibly separate branches working together.

On the government side, the tendency towards secrecy and non-disclosure obviously runs counter to the culture in the press which is for openness, transparency and public information (there are obviously other interpretations of press motivation, but this seems the most charitable). We might observe—however—that openness on issues that do not need to be secret allows the government more scope to define what issues really do need to remain secret. Limiting secrecy in this way helps to protect key national secrets. It also helps the work of the officials and the journalists within the D-Notice Committee, for example, to know what really should not be published and what can be shaped to be less harmful and so on.

The presence and activities of the D-Notice Committee does tell us something interesting about the development of the contemporary media and the challenges that have been thrown up by the internet age. The legacy media clearly still plays a significant role in shaping the national debate, be it directly with readers via their online readerships, or via politicians and the broadcast media responding to what they are saying. Their absolute role is—however—less than it was in the 1950s to 1990s, where they set the national debate. The legacy media might also—with justification—feel pinched that they are subject to D-Notice discussions when online outlets are not, and platforms like Cryptome, WikiLeaks, Bellingcat, and so on, are freer to publish than they are. These outlets miss out—if that is the correct term—on the privileged discussions between officials and journalists and must—therefore—be closer to everyday legal risks as a result.

The circulation of found-footage of particular first responders on social media from the 2017 bombing of the Ariana Grande concert sat in the unhappy place of being something that newspapers would think twice about publishing, but in the context of the Twitter-sphere it was shared freely. Analogously, there have been many incidents where well-known personalities have been said to have been protected by the UK courts, but that across the world in non-UK media outlets and social media these issues have been discussed very openly. The British citizen of the internet is a citizen of everywhere in such moments. These are the challenges of social media, but also of how to protect secrets. In the information contest between actors in the Global North and South (and inside these formations), some measure of control of information has historically been important. Consequently, these forms of state intervention do help to police the information sphere, and to condition and reproduce what the public (should) deem to be acceptable, and normal.

From WikiLeaks to Foreign Press Sources and Anything Goes

Publics on both sides of the Atlantic seem—on balance—to like (and value) a whistleblower. All the modern whistleblowers, or their facilitators, have been pilloried by their respective governments, but found favour in the court of public opinion. People like Edward Snowden can rightly say that they have set the tone for public discourse about privacy and the rights of governments to intercept internet and communications traffic, just as Chelsea Manning helped to augment a public debate about how the American military had prosecuted its campaign in Iraq. In terms of platforms, John Young's Cryptome seems to exercise quite close judgements about what and what not to post publicly, which is something that WikiLeaks also did in its earlier days, but its wholesale publication of Cablegate was met with some criticism that it had not given enough weight to the impact publication would have on the safety of individuals or for international relations (Reppy, 2014). The debate around whether Assange is a sympathetic character is irrelevant. Whether he is a journalist or not seems moot, but the quality of the treatment, or mistreatment, he is reportedly suffering at the time of writing augers badly for how governments are now viewing whistleblowing and revelations (Quinn, 2020). The treatment reported in *The Guardian* suggests there is something in the treatment of Assange that echoes that of detainees at Guantanamo Bay: that of conspicuous punishment and virtue signalling and containing colonial echoes.

The judgements about how much regulation there should be over the publication of material that can be deemed to be sensitive, is often calibrated in the context of how effectively a government or democracy is functioning. When a government seems to be operating with a degree of impunity, then the public seem to turn to the Courts and to the media, and now new media, for checks and balances.

When these sources are suppressed or side-stepped by government, then flash-point events tend to take on a size and momentum of their own, witness the start of the Arab Spring in Tunisia in 2011.

The changes in the way that even the legacy media operates, confronted by rolling news agenda, means that the production timetables have changed over the last thirty years and have dramatically sped up for all media outlets in the last ten years. For newspapers, their stories now appear online and therefore the articulation and design of a newspaper is one of the outputs of the journalism, not the output. For television and radio outlets, the need for content has pushed them towards talking head analysts and so-called 'hot takes'. Thus, the availability of talking head opinion and visual images, which has been assisted by the quality of portable recording equipment, has steered where media outlets have sought stories. The public's impression of intelligence and security operations, from journalists who have been embedded or have used footage from members of the public, is skewed towards the drama of the moment, rather than more sober forms of analysis. The ever closening proximity, in terms of production values and content, between popular culture and the news media on intelligence operations is also conditioning the public's response to these operations and of how they understand the world. In short, it reinforces the framing logics of the North Atlantic area.

The centrality of the media's role in shaping the public's view of intelligence has also come about because of the perceived failings in the official oversight mechanisms. These failings are—in part—a product of unreasonable expectations. The expectation that US intelligence oversight could stop the exceptional measures used in the war on terrorism, or effectively halt Russian electoral interference, or in the UK that foreign interference could be stopped by oversight mechanisms is unrealistic, but this appears to be the source of public discontent or apathy towards formal oversight mechanisms. In the gap left by formal oversight mechanisms have stepped journalists and activists, who see themselves as holding a torch up to the government's secret activities, but without a great deal of accountability for their evidence or the analysis that they bring to these investigations. Consequently, the media (be it legacy media or new media) have also deployed their own covert techniques, in using undercover journalists, stings, or agents to provide disclosures, but in doing so have damaged the relationships between the agencies and media organisations. The fact that this news environment exists and that media organisations have gone to extraordinary lengths to stand up investigative stories has left the intelligence community to work out how to operate as safely as possible within this context and has placed a greater emphasis on the agencies to provide more of their own media engagement, via press officers or their own social media accounts and webpages. In the US this has involved inviting journalists to secure sites to understand which elements of their stories are particularly sensitive and therefore should not be disclosed and how they can retain the exciting parts of their story without undermining national security interests. It is not clear if the UK intelligence community does the same, outside of the D-Notice Committee structure, but it is a sensible accommodation of the tensions between both communities.

As the internet and social media continue to be the places where the public gets its information about intelligence matters and operations, then they will continue to be a key battleground upon which the intelligence community fights to position the adversary and justify its actions. In having rigidly defined areas of transparency and secrecy it will be able to do this more effectively. The bold truth is—however—that the media and intelligence agencies working (deliberately or inadvertently) together produce a very strong narrative for the population to consume. Strong enough to create foundational stories and loyalties that persist for generations. The internet has already proved to be disruptive to this relationship, but it is a constantly evolving situation. It is the glorious paradox of intelligence in developed democracies that the dark corners of secrecy must exist in a society that prides itself on illumination and transparency.

References

Aldrich, R. (2009) 'Regulation by relevation?' In R. G. Dover, *Spinning Intelligence*. London: Hurst & Co.

Badawy, A., Addawood, A., Lerman, K. and Ferrara, E. (2019) 'Characterizing the 2016 Russian IRA influence campaign'. *Social Network Analysis and Mining* 9 (1), 1–11.

Baker, N. (2007) *The Strange Death of David Kelly.* London: Methuen.

Bamford, J. (2002) *Body of Secrets.* New York, NY: Doubleday.

Barber, B. (1995) *Jihad vs McWorld.* New York, NY: Times Books.

BBC (2021) *Intrigue.* 'Mayday: The evidence gatherers'. 6 April. Retrieved from BBC Sounds: https://www.bbc.co.uk/programmes/p08xh4ds, accessed 10 January 2022.

Blakeley, R. and Raphael, S. (2020) 'Accountability, denial and the future-proofing of British torture'. *International Affairs* 96 (3), 691–709.

Bromell, D. and Shanks, D. (2021) 'Censored! Developing a framework for making sound decisions fast'. *Policy Quarterly* 17 (1), 42–49.

Campbell, D. (1988) 'Somebody's listening....' *The New Statesman.* 12 August.

Castells, M. (2010) 'Globalisation, networking, urbanisation: Reflections on the spatial dynamics of the information age'. *Urban Studies* 47 (3), 2737–2745.

Chadwick, A. (2013) *Hybrid Media System: Power and Politics.* Oxford: Oxford University Press.

Chamberlain, A. (1924) Hansard CLXXIV. *Hansard*, 15 December, p. 674.

Cram, I. (2009) 'The disclosure of state secrets and dissent: Official Secrets, DA Notices and Freedom of Information'. In I. Cram, *Terror and the War on Dissent: Freedom of Expression in the Age of Al-Qaeda* (pp. 131–154). Berlin: Springer.

Dennison, J. (2019) 'A review of Public Issue Salience: Concepts, determinants and effects on voting'. *Political Studies Review* 17 (4), 436–446.

Department of Justice (1995) *Executive Order No. 12,95—Classified National Security Information.* 1 January. Retrieved from United States Department of Justice: https://www.justice.gov/oip/blog/foia-update-executive-order-12958-classified-national-security-information, accessed 3 January 2022.

Dover, R. and Goodman, M. (2009) 'Spooks and hacks: Blood brothers'. *British Journalism Review* 20 (4), 55–61.

Dover, R., Downey, J. and Smith, D. (2019) 'Communicating in a haze: The challenges of hybrid media and hybrid threats in crisis communication'. *Media, Communication and Cultural Studies Association* (p. 15). Stirling: Media, Communication and Cultural Studies Association.

Dymydiuk, J. (2020) 'Filling the information void: GCHQ, NSA and investigative journalism'. PhD thesis, Warwick University, Coventry.

Editorial Board (2020) 'Cripple the intelligence agencies? Not smart'. *The New York Times*, 21 February.

European Parliament (2012) *European Parliament resolution of 11 September 2012 on alleged transportation and illegal detention of prisoners in European countries by the CIA: follow-up of the European Parliament TDIP Committee report (2012/2033(INI))*. Brussels: European Parliament.

———— (2019) Directive (EU) 2019/1937 of the European Parliament and of the Council of 23 October 2019 on the protection of persons who report breaches of Union law. 26 November. Brussels: European Parliament.

Friis, S. (2015) '"Beyond anything we have ever seen": Beheading videos and the visibility of violence in the war against ISIS'. *International Affairs* 91 (4), 725–746.

Giegerich, B. (2016) 'Hybrid warfare and the changing character of conflict'. *Connections* 15 (2), 65–72.

Gioe, D. (2018) 'Cyber operations and useful fools: The approach of Russian hybrid intelligence'. *Intelligence and National Security* 33 (7), 954–973.

Grierson, J. (2020)' Extinction Rebellion guidance raises fresh concerns over Prevent'. *The Observer*, 12 January.

Hall, R. (2022) 'UK ministers accused of "government by WhatsApp" in court'. *The Guardian*, 23 March.

Hollingsworth, M. and Fielding, N. (1999) *Defending the Realm: MI5 and the Shayler Affair.* London: Andre Deutsch.

Hutton, Lord (2004) *Report of the Inquiry into the Circumstances Surrounding the Death of Dr David Kelly C.M.G.* London: The Stationery Office.

James, M. (2016) 'The colonial representation of Jihadi John: Matters of life and death in the "war on terror"'. *Soundings* 62, 138–149.

Ji-Young, K., In, L. and Gon, K. (2019) 'The all-purpose sword: North Korea's cyber operations and strategies'. In T. Minárik, S. Alatolu, S. Biondi, M. Signoretti, I. Tolga, and G. Visky (eds) *2019 11th International Conference on Cyber Conflict (CyCon)*(pp. 143–162). Tallin, Estonia: CCD COE Publications.

Johnstone, D. and Shane, S. (2006) 'CIA fires senior officer over leaks'. *The New York Times*, 22 April.

Koch, A. (2018) 'Jihadi beheading videos and their non-Jihadi echoes'. *Perspectives on Terrorism* 12 (3), 24–34.

Laugerud, S. and Langballe, Å. (2017) 'Turning the witness stand into a speaker's platform: Victim participation in the Norwegian legal system as exemplified by the trial against Anders Behring Breivik'. *Law & Society Review* 51 (2), 227–251.

Laughland, O. (2013) 'Smashing of *Guardian* hard drives over Snowden story "sinister", says Amnesty'. *The Guardian*, 21 August.

Leigh, D. (2019) *Investigative Journalism*. London: Palgrave MacMillan.

Leigh, I. and Wegge, N. (2018) *Intelligence Oversight in the Twenty-First Century: Accountability in a Changing World*. Abingdon: Routledge.

Machon, A. (2005) *Spies, Lies & Whistleblowers. MI5, MI6 and the Shayler Affair*. Lewes: The Book Guild Limited.

Mangold, T. (Director) (2020) *Keeler, Profumo, Ward and Me* [Motion picture].

Marty, D. (2006) *Alleged Secret Detentions and Unlawful Inter-state Transfers of Detainees Involving Council of Europe Member States*. Brussels: Council of Europe.

Mayer, J. (2008) *The Dark Side: The Inside Story of How the War on Terror Turned into a War on American Ideals*. New York, NY: Doubleday.

McConnell, M. (2007) *Remarks and Q&A by the Director of National Intelligence*. 13 November. Retrieved from Federation of American Scientists: https://fas.org/irp/dni/dni111307.pdf, accessed 28 December 2021.

McCormack, T. (2019) *Britain's War Powers: The Fall and Rise of Executive Authority*. London: Palgrave MacMillan.

Miller, G. (2020) 'The intelligence coup of the century'. *The Washington Post*, 11 February. Retrieved from *The Washington Post*. Accessed 28 December 2021.

Mosquera, R., Odunowo, M., McNamara, T., Guo, X. and Petrie, R. (2020) 'The economic effects of Facebook'. *Experimental Economics* 23 (2), 575–602.

Priest, D. (2005) 'CIA holds terror suspects in secret prisons'. *The Washington Post*, 2 November, p. 1.

Quinn, B. (2020) 'Julian Assange was "handcuffed 11 times and stripped naked"'. *The Guardian*, 26 February.

Reppy, J. (2014) 'WikiLeaks and state control of information in the cyber age'. In G. Giacomello (ed.) *Security in Cyberspace: Targeting Nations, Infrastructures, Individuals* (pp. 59–82). London: Bloomsbury.

Risen, J. (2016) *Pay Any Price: Greed, Power, and Endless War*. New York, NY: Houghton Mifflin.

Rosenberg, J. (2000) *The Follies of Globalisation Theory: Polemical Essays*. London: Verso.

RUSI (2017) *Social Media and Terrorist Finance: Vulnerabilities and Responses*. London: Royal United Services Institute.

Sadler, P. (2018) *National Security and the D-Notice System*. London: Routledge.

Schofield, K. (2018) 'Former shadow minister says Salisbury poisoning a "smokescreen" for government problems'. 5 April. Retrieved from Politics Home: https://www.politicshome.com/news/article/former-shadow-minister-says-salisbury-poisoning-a-smokescreen-for-government-problems, accessed 28 December 2021

Siskind, S. (2020) 'Israel and the Great Powers: The unsung Cold War role'. *Middle East Quarterly*, 27 (2), 1–7.

Sparrow, A. (2020) 'MI5 rejects claims that officials withhold intelligence from Priti Patel'. *The Observer*, 23 February.

Spicer, M. (2020) *The Man Next Door*. 4 February. Retrieved from Michael Spicer: https://youtu.be/xk4EMBXxG5A, accessed 14 February 2021.

Starinsky, S. (2021) 'From books to Facebook: How social media became the biggest publisher of our time'. *Publishing Research Quarterly* 37 (4), 657–670.

Sterling, J. (2019) *Unwanted Spy: The Persecution of an American Whistleblower*. New York, NY: PublicAffairs Press.

Taylor, P. (2010) 'Public diplomacy and the information war on terror'. In Inderjeet Parmar and Michael Cox (eds) *Soft Power and US Foreign Policy: Theoretical, Historical and Contemporary Perspectives* (pp. 152–164). Abingdon: Routledge

Tomlinson, R. (2001) *The Big Breach: From Top Secret to Maximum Security*. Paris: Cutting Edge Press.

UK Joint Doctrine Centre (2018) *JCN/18 Information Advantage*. London: Ministry of Defence.

UK Ministry of Defence (2021) *Global Britain in a Competitive Age: The Integrated Review of Security, Defence, Development and Foreign Policy*. London: HMSO.

US Senate (1976) Senate Select Committee to Study Governmental Operations with Respect to Intelligence Activities (The Church Committee): https://www.senate.gov/about/powers-procedures/investigations/church-committee.htm

US Senate (2020) *Intelligence Related Commissions*. 26 February. Retrieved from US Senate: https://www.intelligence.senate.gov/resources/intelligence-related-commissions, accessed 28 December 2021.

Verkaik, R. (2016) *Jihadi John: The Making of a Terrorist*. London: Simon & Schuster.

Wilford, H. (1998) 'The Information Research Department: Britain's secret Cold War weapon revealed'. *Review of International Studies* 24 (3), 353–369.

Wilkinson, N. (2009) *Secrecy and the Media: The Official History of the United Kingdom's D-Notice Committee*. London: Taylor & Francis.

Wolfberg, A. (2017) 'The president's daily brief: Managing the relationship between intelligence and the policymaker'. *Political Science Quarterly* 132 (2), 225–258.

Xia, Y., Lukito, J., Zhang, Y., Wells, C., Kim, S. J. and Tong, C. (2019) 'Disinformation, performed: Self-presentation of a Russian IRA account on Twitter'. *Information, Communication & Society* 22 (11), 1646–1664.

Zuboff, S. (2019) *The Age of Surveillance Capitalism.* London & New York: Profile Books.

7

SPYING ON SCREEN
REFLECTIONS FROM A HALL OF CIRCUS MIRRORS[1]

What You Need to Know...

Spies and espionage have been the backbone of a significant tranche of cinematic production and video games. These cultural artefacts have told us many things about the business of intelligence but, more particularly, have shone a light on how we feel about treachery, loyalty, our governments, gender politics, the 'other', and the glamour and seduction of the unknown. The chapter finds that very few cultural portrayals seek to portray intelligence authentically. Much of the cinematic output has focused on fanciful storylines, imperial grandeur, and one-dimensional accounts of conflict. The same has largely been true of video games loosely based around intelligence: they have followed the James Bond-esque tropes around special forces operations as intelligence. These interpretative snapshots of a reality compound and reinforce themselves over time and exposure, making it inconceivable to think of intelligence in other ways. The novel is one place where greater care has been taken by some writers to draw operational and psychological truths more authentically. There is much to learn about intelligence from these cultural artefacts: they are not instructional manuals but they do have an important contribution to make.

***

Intelligence agencies and intelligence officers are a product of the society they serve. Spy-drama, or intelligence, in popular cultural mediums are both a reflection of partial truths about tradecraft, part positioning of modern versions of morality plays, of good versus evil, or tragedy and of 'us' versus 'them', and part a reflection or contemplation upon contemporary fears and obsessions. In the first series of the American homeland-security drama *24*, the adversary hailed from the Balkans, a reflection of the US-led action against Serbia of the recent past. Post-9/11, subsequent series of *24* homed in on threats from Jihadists, including threats from foreign migrants, whilst the acclaimed eight-series *Homeland* (2011–20) evoked and echoed stories of a white jihadist threat, mixed in with Cold War counterintelligence tropes of double and triple agents. More recently, the highly cinematic production of John le Carré's *The Night Manager* (2016), mirrored societal concerns about the exploitation of globalised finance by rogue non-state actors, of gun running through Russia and the Balkans, and of our politics being rigged by internationally well connected people who live a life immeasurably remote to ordinary experience, whilst the British intelligence officers portrayed are equally down-to-earth and heroic. In October 2019, John le Carré published his novel *Agent Running in the Field*, a story of Brexit and tortured allegiances to Queen and country, and to Europe, but also evoking Cold War structures and alliances. Le Carré portrays a generational schism between an older generation steeped and blooded in the transatlantic alliance, and the younger rogue officer, Ed, who commits treason in line with his allegiance to a European ideal. Such narratives perfectly capture an element of the cultural conflict raging in the UK at the time of writing.

Because intelligence is a product of the society it serves, our current intelligence agencies are a mirror to our societal preferences and obsessions with tech-culture. As we consume more, in terms of physical devices and services that are paid for with cash or our data, we buy into the idea that this is making our lives more efficient, when in reality it is creating more knowledge about us and increasing the number of vulnerabilities we have to cyber-criminals, the cyber-units of adversary governments and—of course—our own authorities. Our consumerism—the desire to have the next piece of technology or innovation—is wrapped up in the economic system we all enjoy, which suggests that our happiness is dependent on things we are about to buy rather than the things we already have. This drives us towards ever more sophisticated and connected technologies but, as with the weight of literature about the Internet of Things, to technologies that are vulnerable to hacking and other types of intrusion. The public obsession with, and yet anxiety around, social media has provided government intelligence agencies with unparalleled insights into the public on a meta-level and into individuals on a micro-level, whilst failing to unseat the public's usage of these technologies. Similarly, whilst people outwardly suggest that they are uncomfortable with the level of intrusion possible into their lives, they do nothing to change their addiction to personal electronics. Those who deal with vulnerable whistleblowers suggest that the technical possibilities around intrusion mean that they tend to communicate with their leads via burner phones (one-use devices), and via old-school analogue means, typed communications and dead-letter drops. Persistent carping by Western politicians about the 'evils' of encryption (forgetting that there is no e-commerce or internet banking without it), or casting doubts on why anyone would want to use a virtual private network (to avoid being robbed whilst using the free WiFi in the coffee shop, perhaps) or a TOR browser, tie up closely with the consumerist culture to push for ever greater levels of openness and exploitability, things that are warmly welcomed by intelligence communities of all stripes and by private data brokerages and advertisers keen to sell more content.

This chapter and the following chapter, which focus on popular culture, make two key claims. The first is that the popular cultural depictions of intelligence provide a fragmentary and distorting view of the business of intelligence. It is a partial view of what intelligence agencies, officers and agent-assets are empowered to do, have the resource to do, and so on. It nearly always glamorises or valorises intelligence technologies and techniques, and imbues intelligence officers with unreasonable levels of energy and insight, and in the case of 24's Jack Bauer, a bladder that does not need relieving once over successive twenty-four hour periods. These fictionalised accounts give the public greater certainty that they understand intelligence work. My students have always been dismayed when I suggest that they watch the 2006 film *The Lives of Others* to get a better appreciation of the banality and tedium of certain types of intelligence work, and that the experience of preparing intelligence analysis might be closer to their experience of writing assignments—only more frequently and with a less obliging reader.

My second key argument is that popular culture also provides partial and fragmentary views of the issues, challenges and threats that intelligence agencies are charged with identifying, containing and rolling back. Fictionalised spy drama shapes audience responses to these threats—making it possible to lessen or amplify societal fears—a useful tool when looking to ease societal anxiety or, conversely, trying to create the conditions for collective action. This fragmentary view helps to create its own new realities on the ground: our enemies are not human, nor do they have human feelings or responses. To use the vernacular of the Second World War, they are framed as *Untermensch* (as sub-human), when we know from research carried out on war criminals that they are capable of normal human relationships and normal human responses. The gripping BBC podcast series *The Ratline* (2018) by Phillipe Sands, who investigated the story of the German SS officer Otto von Wächter to his demise just prior to a planned exfiltration to Argentina, provides an in-depth exposition of how those who facilitated some of the Nazi regime's worst excesses had relatable human frailties. Wächter's son is discussing his dad, a dad who performed normal dad-like tasks and with whom he had a good (in the context of the time) relationship. Similarly, those who have engaged in terrorist atrocities since 9/11 in Europe have often been described in the margins of the media afterwards, by those who knew them in their communities, as being pleasant but serious people. They have occasionally even been described as being fond of partying and so on. Reducing those we perceive as enemies or adversaries to single-dimensional characters (without seeking to excuse or mitigate their crimes) is to potentially miss the trigger points and motivations for the criminal acts, and the potential interception or de-escalation points. Games writers, cinema and TV screenwriters are operating within limited time parameters, and within established and formulaic commercial markets. There is very little appetite for sympathetic portrayals of terrorists or their logistics lines, or for positive portrayals of Russian intelligence, certainly outside academia anyway. But the route to prevention exists precisely in the human stories behind these characters.

To try and make sense of this area of intelligence life is worthy of a book-length treatment of its own. There are good books and PhD theses on these topics by accomplished scholars such as Jeremy Black, Toby Miller, Christopher Moran and the former practitioner turned writer Pierre Lethier. To keep this treatment manageable, I have divided the material on popular culture into two chapters (Chapters 7 and 8), both of which provide some lessons derived from popular culture's treatment of intelligence. This first chapter concerns spy fiction as a genre and its representation and impact on gender politics. The second of the two chapters examines what spy fiction tells us about our politics and values, and of the impact upon the business of intelligence, the so-called production, co-production and reproduction of knowledge.

The Making of a Genre

There is a spy-thriller popular culture genre that feeds through books, cinema, small-screen portrayals and video games. As with all genres, there are tropes and markers established over time that constitute the unofficial rules of the genre, and which are reworked, reinterpreted and sometimes parodied and mocked by subsequent films and the like. The extent to which the spy genre might be unique, because it combines storytelling with practitioner experience, can easily be overdrawn. Much of our cultural landscape is created by people who either have experience of the thing they are writing about or who have researched extensively into the subject. The spy genre is perceived to be different or unique in this regard because of the general aura of difference that intelligence engenders, partly because the subjects are either acutely dangerous or pertain to statecraft, and partly because official secrecy necessarily obscures our insights into the workings of the agencies and tradecraft. In other words, we think we gain insights into this secret world through the fictionalised depictions of it.

The traction of spy genres is, however, that the reality of the business of intelligence is all about the curation and manipulation of stories. It is collecting information to be able to tell a story to those who are able to respond to the reality it creates, and to deploy assets in response. Intelligence is about changing facts on the ground to create new stories. The strong connection between intelligence and the discovery and creation of narratives gives it its traction on the small and big screen, within radio plays and in books. These are time honoured tales of good versus evil, of individuals triumphing against the odds, of morality dramas and difficult choices.

In the cinema, the spy genre has been strongly informed by former intelligence officers telling fictionalised re-runs of their operational experiences, or dramatised versions of the experiences of those they managed or ran. Graham Greene (*The Confidential Agent* (1945) and *Our Man in Havana* (1959)) was an MI6 officer during the Second World War, and ran the double-cross agent Garbo, who was instrumental in the success of the D-Day Landings in 1944. Greene came close to being prosecuted for revealing tradecraft secrets in his literary work, and to some degree his books can be read as goading or sending-up the British intelligence machinery, which may well have contributed to the animosity felt towards him (Le Carré, 2017). Similarly, Lord Clanmorris (John Bingham) wrote police and spy thrillers whilst actively working as an MI5 counterintelligence and political subversion officer, and is said to have encouraged the young David Cornwell (John le Carré) in his early writing endeavours. Le Carré, himself, was both an MI5 and MI6 officer during his active service, which ran from the mid-1950s to 1964. He has noted that the inspiration for his best known and revered fictional creation—George Smiley—was in part inspired by working with John Bingham, and so the particularly cerebral game-playing that Smiley liked to engage in has its origins in lived professional experience. Frederick Forsyth (whose novels include *The Day of the Jackal* (1971), *The Odessa File* (1972), and *The Dogs of War* (1974), amongst others) has said publicly that he did unpaid work for MI6 between 1967 and 1987, whilst the former Director General of MI5 (1992–1996) Stella Rimington has written almost a dozen novels, including *At Risk* (2004), *Secret Asset* (2006), *Illegal*

Action (2007), and *Dead Line* (2008). In a public disagreement in 2019 between the former head of MI6, Sir Richard Dearlove, and John le Carré, the former claimed the latter has besmirched the good name of MI6 through negative portrayals of intelligence officers and MI6 throughout the Cold War. In the wide-ranging and well-constructed rebuttal, Le Carré testily noted the production and approval of flawed intelligence leading to the Iraq War under Dearlove, which he argued was far more damaging than any fictionalised account (Diver, T., 2019). Le Carré added further injury when he noted that the new terms and conditions of employment in MI6 now mean that any modern era officers lose all of their income from publishing back to MI6. In removing much of the incentive to put pen to paper, the British intelligence community has potentially deprived the spy-thriller genre of future entertaining and informed contributions, something that former high-ranking intelligence officers, like the former Director General Stella Rimington, have profited from.

In terms of spy cinema, one of the founding fathers of the genre was the legendary cinematographer Alfred Hitchcock, who dedicated roughly a third of his output (14 out of 53 films) to spy drama (Lethier, 2009). Hitchcock was a pioneer of many techniques that we now take for granted in cinema, and this was also the case in spy cinema, where he was similarly ahead of his time in working with former intelligence officers[2] to weave suspense, betrayal, puzzles and a well-developed mistrust of authority, into his offerings. Hitchcock has the less desirable honour of having also pioneered that most reliable of spy tropes: women being desirable and often willing participants in what might loosely be described as romantic liaisons (Allen, 2003). He also created the CIA film sub-genre, a set of films that has become emblematic of, and synonymous with, the public's identification of spy films since the 1960s, and which are drawn forward into the Jason Bourne franchise, for example, and are also focused heavily upon the increasing complexities of the Cold War, much as modern outputs have been concerned with the complexities of jihadist terrorism and Great Power politics.

In Hitchcock's *Torn Curtain* (1966)—which is a torturous watch—the film tells the fictional but resonant account of the theft of secret research into anti-ballistic missiles from a group of patriotic,

Soviet East German atomic scientists (Dynia, 1976; Kapsis, 1988). This story echoes the concerns at the time about anti-ballistic missile technology and also that the Soviet intelligence machine was highly capable, serving to heighten public fear. It is not clear what assistance or advice Hitchcock received from official circles but it is suggested by some that he was well connected with American intelligence and it would be reasonable to suppose that some of the narrative had a level of informed knowledge to it (Lethier, 2009). By 1969 Hitchcock had returned to depicting a vision of the Cold War with the film *Topaz*, an undramatic retelling of the Cuban Missile Crisis, covering the justified concerns about how close the US and USSR had got to sparking an all-out exchange of nuclear weapons (Corliss, 1970; Walker, 2004). *Topaz* acted as salve to the widespread sense of public relief in America and Europe that the immediate threat of nuclear war had been averted and was a cultural signal that the general threat from the Cold War was also reducing. The film plays into government agendas to show the Soviets as continuing to present a menace, and shows the benefits of the North Atlantic Alliance to our safety—the heroic lead in *Topaz* is a French intelligence officer. It presents the Cold War as NATO protagonists would want it presented.

The classic, Western telling of the Cuban Missile Crisis—both in popular culture and in academic accounts, barring those of scholars like Mark Laffey and Jutta Weldes—is that the sober and careful positioning by the US averted the conflict (Laffey & Weldes, 2008). This standard account is repeated in the 2000 release of *Thirteen Days*, which is viewed from the perspective of Kennedy's war cabinet. *Topaz*, *Thirteen Days* (directed by Roger Donaldson) and the 1974 docudrama *The Missiles of October* (directed by Anthony Page) offer a genre reinforcing comfort for American and European audiences that the US underwrites our collective security, doing so with superior technology (in this case imagery intelligence, which—in the story—may have been assisted by Russian double agents) and skill (through assessments staff, which actually was not the case in the Cuban crisis), and this is something that resonates in the majority of Western spy films. But these accounts miss, as Robert McNamara in Errol Morris' film *The Fog of War* (2003) demonstrates really strongly (as have decolonisation scholars), that history should account for the role of the Cuban government, and also for the highly developed role of the Soviets, highlighting the provocation of the US positioning a nuclear arsenal in Turkey, whilst also amplifying, in McNamara's case, the extent that de-escalation was down to several moments of good fortune and 'lucking out', rather than to skill. Pierre Lethier, perhaps utilising his former experiences as a French intelligence officer (Lethier, 2001), also noted in his PhD thesis on spy cinema that there was a considerable role for French intelligence in the crisis, both in support of and against the interests of the US, that has been missed almost entirely by the established histories (Lethier, 2010).

In stark contrast to *Topaz* and *Thirteen Days*, Stanley Kubrick's seminal film, *Dr Strangelove* (1964), satirised Cold War nuclear logics, sending up the notion of mutually assured destruction and highlighting the frailties of recognisable characters in the US defence system (Case, 2014; Krämer, 2017). *Dr Strangelove* has become more relevant in the last five years, as it inadvertently highlights the dominance of human decision making in any nuclear standoff at a time when electronic decision making (via machine learning systems) is being considered across a suite of public policy issues (Johnson, 2020).

The early construction of the essential components in the spy film genre, of the interweaving of fragmentary but recognisable or discoverable truths with fiction and high drama, coupled with the superiority of Western politics and culture, has been a mainstay of spy fiction since the era of Hitchcock. These devices are a key part of the spy genre's enduring traction with paying audiences, and they can be traced through the spy films that have been released up to the current day, with very few exceptions, which may partly explain the enduring public myths around intelligence.

Holding Out for a Hero? Gender and the Cultural Depiction of Intelligence

In the television adaptation (2018) of the John le Carré's novel *The Little Drummer Girl*, the actor Florence Pugh plays the idealistic Charlie, a jobbing amateur actor who gets caught up in the international network of left-wing activism and campaigning

Palestinian groups, or Palestinian terrorists, depending on your preferences (Silver, 1987). Charlie is courted and seduced by the dashing and emotionally unavailable Israeli intelligence officer Becker, played by occasional model and actor Alexander Skarsgård. Whilst Charlie is led by emotion, and a hint of rashness, she is given reserves of resilience, much as Le Carré's character Pru—the wife of the lead character Nat—is in the 2019 novel *Agent Running in the Field*. But whilst Charlie's smoking, for example, is contextualised by anxiety or fret, Becker's occurs as an aide to concentration. Becker is clearly emotionally involved and attached to Pugh's Charlie, but he is given the martial characteristics of discipline and focus, and he keeps his emotional palate obscured, whereas Charlie is seen as sexually available, malleable (she is sent in as a covert human source with and against the terrorists), whilst showing several flashes of steel—when undercover with the terrorist group, and at the paramilitary training camp in a story that is told in a non-linear, mosaic fashion (Martin, 2019). Le Carré has said that for the idealism and the emotional charge, he gained inspiration from the personality of his younger sister, but it is not reported whether she was flattered or dismayed by this characterisation (Le Carré, 2017).

Le Carré carried this characterisation into his final book, whilst he was alive, *Agent Running in the Field* with the character Florence. She is fiercely bright, unrefined (despite her schooling), rash, and yet shows moments of clarity and steel, particularly in understanding— in an unspoken way—how to play along with Nat's exfiltration plans. Coming off the back of the filming of *The Little Drummer Girl*, where Le Carré was effusive about the skills of his lead actor Florence Pugh, it is not unreasonable to think that the physical description and name of his fictional Florence was consciously or unconsciously inspired by the actor of the same name. In *24* (2001–10), the key female backroom character of Chloe O'Brien is emblematic of another spy fiction archetype: that is, a notionally asexual or dowdy but dedicated officer who is married to the office and their job. In the case of O'Brien we are led to assume that she has strong autistic personality traits—her response to killing an attacker in self-defence is to note her own lack of emotional engagement and her desire to 'process it later'. In the Melissa McCarthy film-parody *Spy*

(2015), she similarly plays a bookish and nerdy character, who falls into operational art almost by mistake, and for whom a key route to comedy is word-play, self-deprecation and slapstick. McCarthy's character is conspicuously married to the office but has a far keener sense of her own sexuality and a desire to escape. In the long-running American series *Homeland* (2011–20) the female lead, Carrie, played by Claire Danes, is given the rare opportunity for top billing, but can be seen to have been 'played' by the double agent Brody. Even within contemporary settings women—even when strong—are still vulnerable to established tropes: something that seeks to constrain the possibilities for young women growing up in Western societies.

The elephant in the room of any critique of gender and the cinema are Ian Fleming's *James Bond* novels and films, where female characters are almost exclusively there for the sexual gratification they can provide, including the office-based Moneypenny, who is both wedded to the office but overtly sexual: Bond's safe option at home (Vermaak & Le Clue, 2020). The exception to this, with perhaps the most notional of nods to the path-breaking MI5 Directors General, Stella Rimington and Eliza Manningham-Buller, is Judi Dench's 'M', who plays a professional mother figure to Bond, chastising but ultimately proud and protective. Thus it is, across nearly all spy genre, that the female characters conform to certain scripted and perhaps preordained types and tropes, depending on their age and positioning. This is disappointing but it helps to provide the essential framing of society that the operation of intelligence serves to reproduce.

It is perhaps simplistic to point to male characters falling into the same quasi-militaristic 'hero' category; instead it is possible to divide our male leads into several distinctive profiles: (1) the cerebral George Smiley; (2) the special operations executive, James Bond; and (3) the 'Nat'—a troubled soul, with keen interpersonal skills. The George Smiley character is bright enough to be at the top of any academic tree, and is particularly good at the sort of espionage and counterespionage games that characterise Cold War spy genres (Bradbury, 1990). Le Carré's George Smiley is the best example of this type of character, and he has clear resonances with real-life directors general of intelligence agencies, such as Allen Dulles of the CIA. Others have sought to emulate the Smiley figure, placing flawed omnipotence at the centre of the action: the characters of Johnny Worricker from *Page Eight* (2011) and Harry Pearce (MI5) and Oliver Mace (MI6) from the television series *Spooks* are particularly good examples of this.

The James Bond, special operations executive characters are the most populous of this genre, because they so clearly lend themselves to the sort of action sequences that attract large box office takings in the cinema. There is, as I remarked back in 2009, a compelling critique that neither Bond, nor his successors, are really intelligence officers at all (Dover, 2009). The Special Operations Executive (SOE) was, after all, a form of stay-behind army, or covert operation, rather than a producer of intelligence per se. Despite this historical anomaly and mischaracterisation, the viewing public certainly think of these characters as intelligence officers. Early spy cinema (pre-1980), which—as noted above—was dominated by the work of auteurs such as Alfred Hitchcock, assisted by his intelligence veteran screenwriters, crafted charming heroic characters who had the individualism we would later come to recognise in the Bond films and their successors. These classic characters also enjoyed a similar fractured relationship with their agencies, who strongly resisted their individualism. The characters of James Bond, Jason Bourne (of the *Bourne* film trilogy), Ethan Hunt from the six *Mission Impossible* films, as well as the parody figures of Dwayne 'The Rock' Johnson's character Robbie Wheirdicht in *Central Intelligence* (2016), Rowan Atkinson's *Johnny English* (2003, 2011 and 2018), and the two French *OSS 117* films (2006, 2009), all portray socially eloquent, individualistic, or even loner spies, fully versed in special operations skills, and able to overcome impressive (or entirely unrealistic) odds to prevail against their various enemies, including their home agencies. Such characters and stories overlap with aspects of military fiction writing and cinematic genre, but have their own niche in the spy thriller genre.

James Bond's Picture of Unreason

In the Second World War Winston Churchill famously said he wanted to set continental Europe alight with the SOE, a series of stay-behind armies and force multipliers (i.e. those who help train locals to carry out similar operations) to provide robust resistance to occupying Nazi armies and also to distract and degrade morale (Foot, 2011). The SOE was given free rein to conduct guerrilla operations, assassinations, and to arm and assist resistance movements as they saw fit. It was the perfect breeding ground for a different kind of intelligence-led special forces, a kind of asymmetric and nimble fighting force that we can see echoes of in our terrorist opponents today.

A notable exponent of this individualised licence to create havoc in Europe was an educated and charming character called Patrick Leigh Fermor, who quickly became a scourge of the German Wehrmacht on the island of Crete (Beevor, 2011; Davis, 2015). His initial 18-month tour of the island was in disguise as a local shepherd, and he famously trained and led a local team to kidnap the Werhmacht's island commander, General Kreipe (Fermor, 2014). For this operation Fermor earned a Distinguished Service Order medal, and the kidnapping became the basis for the Dirk Bogarde film, *Ill Met by Moonlight* (1957). Classically educated, polite and well dressed (in civilian guise), Leigh Fermor could have been, and indeed might have been, the template upon which the generic James Bond was modelled. As a fluent Greek speaker, he helped to organise the Cretan resistance in 1943–4, and when I travelled to Crete in 2006 there were still villagers in Anogia who spoke luridly about Fermor and their mixed feelings towards the British as a consequence of the kidnapping of Kreipe and the reprisals that followed. The consequences of Allied high adventures are rarely considered within popular cultural depictions, and find a niche place within the academic literature as well. The value-neutrality of our actions is a strong aspect of the media and popular cultural depictions of intelligence and security. Keeping the public at arm's length from the dirty business of fighting is, however, a pursuit with a long history.

The qualities that Fermor and the other members of the SOE showed during the Second World War were taken forward in two ways into the Cold War. The practical consequence was the so-called Gladio stay-behind armies, carefully revealed by the Swiss scholar Daniele Ganser; the cultural consequence was the amped-up portrayal of special operations spies, first in novel form and then in cinematic form with Ian Fleming's James Bond; and the characterisations were also a product of Fleming's experience in naval intelligence (Ganser, 2005). Until very recently it was thought that Fleming had a somewhat marginal career as a naval desk officer, but new archive research suggests that he was somewhat more important to the Allied war effort than he had been given credit for (McCrisken & Moran, 2018). The titular Bond character and some of the generic forms of exploit, that are repeated throughout the cinema series, are likely to have been informed by episodes that occurred and could be fictionalised throughout the SOE's Second World War experience.

The irony is, of course, that a very strong case can be made that James Bond has very little to do with the business of intelligence. Bond's closest connection to intelligence is that he has been awkwardly tagged to MI6, a natural shift once the SOE ceased to exist and a hangover from Ian Fleming's wartime service with Naval Intelligence (Pearson, 2011). Furthermore, the fictional gadgets created for James Bond do also appear to have been developed by the US intelligence community from time to time (Fritzsche & Dürrbeck, 2020; McCrisken & Moran, 2018). In the later films Bond—unlike the cinematic creation of Jason Bourne—has an uncanny knack of being able to go 'off grid', something that seems almost as implausible as some of the key story lines, given the effectiveness of modern tracking technologies.

In the popular consciousness, Bond is the ultimate British Cold War warrior. The threat from SMERSH—an organisation that recruited from the USSR but was dedicated to trying to engineer war between the West and the Soviet Union—was all encompassing. The early focus on SMERSH can be read as a proxy for the general and pervasive fear of the USSR, which was further cultivated by politicians evoking the mantra of 'reds under the bed', something that would have been familiar to populations who had lived through the Second World War (Dodds, 2003). Our modern-day equivalents are Islamist terrorists, despotic regimes like North Korea, Iran and, to a lesser extent, Russia and China.

Within the contemporary international arena, and the threats that are transmitted down into the domestic realm, from Islamic terrorist plots, Russian imperialism, hybrid warfare or chemical agents, and North Korean hacking, the Bond films (and those like them) have provided a form of escapism and relief from the tension. The action-thriller spy genre has served to lift the gloom, which made the decision in 2020 to delay the new Bond film, *No Time to Die* (2021), because pandemic lockdowns in the US and the UK had reduced cinema revenues to zero for much of the year, something of an irony (Nicolau, 2020). The Bond films that have been released repositioned Britain from its post-imperial and post-war dwindling power status, to being visibly the centre of world events, something that recurs often in the popular imagination of the UK. What is more, British-made products were foregrounded in the films, such as Bond's wide array of cars from Aston Martin, Lotus and Jaguar. Even the use of a BMW 750iL in the 1997 *Tomorrow Never Dies* and a BMW Z8 in *The World is Not Enough*, was on message at the time due to BMW purchasing the dwindling British MG Rover Group, but with it the imminent and optimistic launch of an entirely redesigned Mini to be manufactured in Oxford.

The character of James Bond was and is an establishment figure. He is an establishment figure who sits uneasily with the establishment on occasion, but a Crown servant nevertheless, dedicated to his Queen and an irritant to most other forms of authority. Bond is much as Patrick Leigh Fermor was once described by his Housemaster: 'a dangerous mix of sophistication and recklessness' (Woodward, 2011). To this degree, the antithesis of Bond comes from Michael Caine's portrayal of Harry Palmer, a spy who suspects his own agency of foul play with leading scientists in the film version of Len Deighton's *The Ipcress File* (1965). Caine, with his working-class tenor, becomes the anti-establishment hero to Bond's inherently establishment figure.

One of the social utilities of the James Bond films was that they lightened the mood of post-war Britain, particularly during the incessant Christmas, Easter and bank holiday repeats on commercial television, and they spurred many imitations and fun parodies along the way. The perceived lightness of Bond ran hand in hand with the position of the inevitable 'Bond girl', there to service the films' hero as he pleased. The sexual politics of James Bond films have been much discussed, and they now fit into roughly the same frowned-upon and bygone category as 'wolf-whistling', the exploitative comedies of the 1970s and 1980s such as Benny Hill and the *Carry On* style comedy, and 'making a pass at someone' (Gerrard, 2020). Even into the late 1990s the Bond series was still portraying its female characters as essentially sexually available and one dimensional, including Denise Richard's receiving the memorably awful line as supposedly serious scientist Dr Christmas Jones, who is told: 'I thought Christmas only comes once a year'—a low point, even for this series.

The sexual politics of Bond have marginally improved as the series moved forward to the present day. Stronger female characters are beginning to be seen, some of them even able to avoid Bond's sexual advances, and the MI6 Director General, as described in the genre section of this chapter, is played by Judi Dench in what I described earlier as a confused mix of flirtatious matriarchy. The series also had retrograde attitudes towards homosexuality, although in keeping with the prevailing societal norms. Honor Blackman's character *Pussy Galore* was a lesbian whom Bond 'converts' to heterosexuality, something that thinkers like Germaine Greer have argued is the ultimate straight male fantasy. Jeremy Black argues that Fleming's ambivalence towards homosexuality comes from two sources. First, that he saw heterosexuality as normal and homosexuality as problematic; and second, that the homosexuality of Guy Burgess (a high-profile British intelligence defector) rendered all gay men inherently untrustworthy (Black, 2005). Thus, Bond is constantly confronted by adversaries who are gay. For example, Blofeld is protected by lesbians in *Diamonds are Forever* (1971), and in *From Russia With Love* (1963), gay intellectuals are highlighted as the enemies of progress. Young audiences of the 2020s are highly likely to view the sexual politics of James Bond with a mix of justifiable horror or a welcome rejection of 'woke' culture. Either way they do provide an accurate portrayal of mainstream societal values in the 1960s and 1970s, and the Bond franchise has proven to be a reasonable bell-weather of where 'middle-England' is at in terms of social conservatism, and a projection of a form of British values and framing rationale. The quite uncontroversial notion that a successor to the actor Daniel Craig might be female and/or black was met with curious levels of horror and opposition in some quarters, even though this should be—in the context of the politics of our time—a logical and progressive step (Daley-Ward, 2020).

The Bond franchise can be interpreted as a violent reaction to the sexual liberation of the 1960s, and to the sweep of progress politics ever since. Bond represents a particular model of heterosexuality, as the straight male hero figure, who all women want to be seduced by (Funnell & Dodds, 2016). The Bond films of the modern era, *Die Another Day* (2002) and *Casino Royale* (2006), observe this misogyny with an irreverent air, utilising another of the key Bond narrative devices of a slight tilt towards the camp, and signalling just enough distance from it to make it acceptable viewing for politically correct twenty-first century audiences. The continual reproduction of the notion of Britain as retaining imperial grandeur, of being a major player on the international stage, and of the inherent untrustworthiness of foreigners, retains a place in the heart of many British viewers, which may go some way to explain why the Suez crisis of 1956 did not end this delusional mythologising. The realities of post-Brexit Britain may end up doing this job instead (*Financial Times*, 2021).

What any of this tells us about intelligence is open to question. On one level the description of intelligence officers as being Bond-like is fanciful, but the Bond franchise has had a disproportionate impact upon other visual depictions of intelligence, where characters are able to operate individually in a way that—in the real world—would require a significant and active support structure. The unreality of Bond—the picture of unreason—does nothing to advance the public's knowledge of intelligence, but there again the realities of the interception of diplomatic and individual communications are unlikely to make for gripping cinema. The unreality is interesting for the extent to which it has captured analyses like these and for those of my colleagues in intelligence studies. We have given it far too much credit for the impact it has had on the public understanding of intelligence, where what we ought to be saying is that the reproduction of this unreality is a good case study in how our modern cultural economy can effectively reproduce simple tropes, and is a reflection of the preferences of the crowd, rather than resonating in any other way. Books from the Cold War era were far better at shining a light on intelligence methods than the cinematic output.

Immersive Entertainment: The Joy of Playing at Spies

Personal computers and games consoles have come a long way in the last thirty years. When my father bought the family's first console system, an Atari 2600, on which he and his friend Barry played protracted games of *Pong*, the games were mostly written by individuals and less frequently by teams of coders (Decuir, 1977). Early personal computers, such as the ZX Spectrum or Commodore 64, had 48kb and 64kb of 'random accessible memory' or RAM, whereas as a personal computer able to play good quality games now has 16 gigabytes of RAM in addition to any RAM that exists on the separate graphics card (Diver, M., 2019). Computing speed—the measure of how many calculations a computer can do within a set time period—has also seen an increase, from 3 MHz for the ZX Spectrum of 1986 to 3,000 MHz for a typical modern-day personal computer: a quantum of difference that is hard to fathom. Technical specifications have further diversified more recently as gaming consoles, which are not designed to carry out the generalist tasks of a personal computer, became more concerned with screen refresh rates, sound quality and the complexity of processes it can cope with. So, whilst early computers and consoles could be programmed by individuals, commercial video games today command multimillion pound and dollar budgets, and large teams of coders and graphic and video artists working over several years (Johnson, 2013).

Modern video games often seek to emphasise realism and immersion for their players, and across genres this has included the use of virtual reality headsets, 'force-feedback' steering wheel and pedal sets for motor racing simulations, and photo-realistic scenery and participants in war games such as *Battlefield I* (depicting the First World War), *Battlefield V* (depicting the Second World War) and the *Call of Duty* series which has tended to focus on contemporary operational theatres, where the playing experience is akin to being dropped into a cinematic portrayal of war (Ramsay, 2015). Virtual reality (outside of motor racing) and augmented reality, where gaming scenarios or imagery are overlaid on the real world, are in their relative infancy in the games market but promise to further enhance player immersion. Games premised around spying or espionage have struggled to match the development of immersion and real-world feel, in part because it is difficult to achieve and in part because it is reasonable to conclude it would be of limited entertainment value.

The number of intelligence or spy titles produced since 1980 has not kept pace with the number of conflict or war titles and they have—traditionally—been better suited to personal computer platforms, where the inclusion of a keyboard has been helpful in solving puzzles and engaging in dialogue with computer characters. The most populous category within intelligence video gaming is a version of the first-person shooter, something again akin to a James Bond-esque portrayal of a special forces trained individual moving around a computer-generated world, resolving issues mostly violently. There have been more subtle portrayals too, but these are a very small minority.

Within the intelligence sub-genre of video games, we do see some familiar characters and themes. In the thirty or so years of mainstream video gaming, James Bond has put his name to more than twenty titles, often tied into the cinema releases. Adults of a certain age, and this author is that age, lost many productive hours to the 1997 Nintendo 64 release of *GoldenEye 007*, which co-existed with the release of the film of the same name, and where a first-person narrative of a series of quests, which followed a classic shoot-and-kill format, was interspersed with the need to collect and use specialist equipment to progress the character through the game (Loyer, 2010). Quite unusually for the time, the player frequently needed to operate with stealth to avoid attracting the attention of computer-generated guards, and for the time it was released the game was a tour de force, and one we played extensively as undergraduates. Many of the titles associated with the Bond franchise have followed this first-person trajectory. The notable exceptions were the 1983 *James Bond 007*, which was a side-scrolling shooter due to the limitations of the technology, the 2000 release of *007 Racing*, which uses Bond's iconic cars to provide a driving game experience, and a text-based adventure *Shaken but Not Stirred* (1982), which also owed much to the limitations of memory and graphics of the time but which is also symbolic of a popular genre of games at the time that has subsequently died out.

There have been other linked franchises in the spy video game sub-genre. The *Mission Impossible* films have been accompanied by corresponding games, but all within the first-person shooter, puzzle approach. The games in the *Splinter Cell* series endorsed by Tom Clancy—author of noted espionage and military novels—are first person shooters, which are dominated by contrasting light and dark backgrounds that emphasise stealth and the skills of special forces operatives. These games have echoes in earlier PC titles such as *Death to Spies* (2007), which was a counterintelligence game in which the player's Soviet counterintelligence character had to identify and eliminate suspected Allied spies but without the benefit of the near ubiquitous thermal glasses of the *Splinter Cell* series. In *Death to Spies*, the player is a part of SMERSH, another echo to the Bond theme that runs heavily through this genre. The thirteen *Metal Gear* games, running from 1987 to the current day, are also stealth games in the Clancy mode, and they have a large gaming community and critical following. The *Metal Gear* series also focuses on an individual character performing great and brave deeds format, something that strongly resonates with spy cinema (Murray, 2018; Stamenković, Jaćević & Wildfeuer, 2017).

There is a sub-set of the spy video games genre that directly or indirectly evokes the sort of SOE history that—as noted earlier—underpinned Ian Fleming's work and that has become somewhat influential in our cultural understanding of intelligence. The 2009 *Death to Spies: Moment of Truth* sequel to *Death to Spies* is essentially a linear narrative of covert operations that are just run from a Soviet perspective. *The Saboteur* (also 2009), on the other hand, explicitly evoked the SOE and is a game with a farcical narrative of espionage, special operations and revenge. The narrative underpinning *The Saboteur* is so ridiculous that I would recommend ignoring it altogether and instead focus on the tasks the games presents.

Three outlier games—two of which are on sale, and one of which was abandoned by the publisher—were mould-breaking in their conception. The first of these outliers is the independent PC game, *SpyParty*, which has been gently iterated from its very limited release in 2009, and which is still being developed at the time of writing (Treanor *et al.*, 2015). *SpyParty* describes itself as 'a subtle game about human behaviour', which is a fair description of the game experience. My impression of *SpyParty* is that it has something of a boardgame ethic, cross-bred with the children's game of hide and seek. The playing action is tightly drawn and the outcomes are equally neat. It is a game played between two human players, with one of the players playing the 'spy', whilst the other player—more ominously—plays 'the sniper'. The spy player controls one of several pre-defined character avatars at a high-society cocktail party, in which the player vies to complete a number of time-limited missions whilst seeking to blend in with other computer-controlled characters. The player playing the sniper does not know who player one is, and instead has to observe all the characters in the room to work out who is the spy. The sniper player wins the contest if they correctly identify the spy and shoot them, or if the spy does not complete the tasks in time. Conversely, the spy player wins if the sniper shoots the wrong person, or if the spy completes their tasks in time. Whilst not a faithful recreation of a human intelligence or counterintelligence scenario, *SpyParty* does at least move away from the first-person shooter model. It also has the subtlety of the psychological underpinnings of human intelligence, which does have real-world echoes, and—up to the point where active shooting occurs—is both subtle and confined.

The second of these outlier games is *Orwell: Keeping an Eye on You* (2016), which is a pseudo-simulation where the player assumes the role of a tactical analyst, making assessments of a range of surveillance feeds using data-analytics software called Orwell. Unlike other spy genre computer games, the player makes their way through chapters of a story around a terrorist attack following the data, rather than in special forces mode. The game, and its successor *Orwell: Ignorance is Strength* (2018) which also channels the current concerns around so-called fake news, was developed by a small and independent German games studio and has been placed in the 'serious game' sub-genre by academics (Caserman *et al.*, 2020). The mass market appeal of video games sits in the crossover between military and intelligence outputs, whereas games that are closer to the nuance capable of being generated in the intelligence world are clearly less marketable affairs.

The last of these outlier games is an assumed to be abandoned title called *Agent*. This title is notable for the high-quality production team that was initially behind it, Rockstar Games, who have captured a large market share and critical acclaim with the two *Red Dead Redemption* games—set in the 'wild west'—and the *Grand Theft Auto* series, where the lead character is an active part of a car theft gang, but which have also contained some retrograde gender politics, particularly in the violence the player can on subject female characters, and the large number of video female sex workers the player can visit in the game (Gutiérrez, 2014; Smith & Moyer-Gusé, 2005). The game would have also been notable for its focus on the Cold War in the late 1970s—and Rockstar are noted for their beautifully drawn and immersive playing environments—to play the sort of strategic game that is the stuff of Le Carré's novels, transporting its 'players into the world of counter-intelligence, espionage and political assassinations' (Rockstar press release). As with *SpyParty*, this game did not seem to be the classic first-person shooter intelligence title, although that would have undoubtedly featured, but a more subtle and cinematic portrayal. It is not clear why the title was abandoned by Rockstar games, but it may be that the publisher had devoted so much resource to its second *Red Dead Redemption* game that it did not have the space to complete *Agent*. Rockstar was subject to some negative press around working conditions on the *Red Dead Redemption* game, where the writing team were said to have been overstretched, particularly in the latter stages of the game's production. This would chronologically fit with the dates where it is assumed *Agent* was abandoned (MacDonald, 2018).

Summary: Relatability and Immersion

The impact of the spy and spy thriller genre's cultural output should be stronger now than during the Cold War. The key to the spy genre's enduring success is its relatability and perceived connection to what the public thinks are identifiable truths or allusions to truths. Spy writers have been good at finding issues with contemporary relevance, some have been assisted in resonating with contemporary issues, and some of them have had operational experiences that significantly improve the accuracy of the portrayals they are making. These resonant facts chime with innate anxieties to produce the modern equivalent of morality plays: a safe space in which to contemplate questions of what is right and wrong, in the escapist setting of a cinema or a living room. But these safe spaces are carefully curated: they only allow the debate to occur within the received and accepted framing logics of the moral and operational superiority of the West, the moral vacuum of adversaries and those who are different, and the emphasis on strong and charismatic individual characters.

It should not be a surprise that the most successful spy genre films and programmes are either action pictures or psychological dramas: the spying is almost incidental to the bangs, crashes and chases. Consequently, the politics of spy films have often appealed to baser instincts and desires: foreigners are excitable, unreliable and venal, women are objects, and so on and so forth. This pattern has been nearly universally replicated in the video games market but not in novels, where the depictions have sometimes been subtle and astutely drawn.

In a hybrid media environment where consumers find ready and easy access to historical and re-historicised accounts, ready and pushed access to contemporary comment and political positioning, and access to a wealth of cultural inputs, the impact of these cultural industries is arguably more pronounced today than at any time since the end of the Second World War. The hybridised outputs, coupled with video on-demand services, have facilitated a consumption that continuously reproduces these established frames. Thus, not only is spy genre a reflection of the anxieties and ticks of society, and a means by which to shape perception, it is also increasingly a means for consumers to reinforce their perceptions and understandings of what intelligence is, what intelligence agencies and officers do and their notion of proportionality. The spy genre has itself become embedded in the swirling contestation of opinion as facts that appears to be the democratisation of knowledge production but is actually the consolidation of our Western empire of ideas.

References

Allen, R. (2003) 'Hitchcock and narrative suspense'. In R. Allen and M. Turvey (eds) *Camera Obscura, Camera Lucida: Essays in Honor of Annette Michelson* (pp. 163–182). Amsterdam: Amsterdam University Press.

Beevor, A. (2011) *Crete: The Battle and the Resistance*. London: John Murray.

Black, Jeremy (2005) *The Politics of James Bond: From Fleming's Novels to the Big Screen*. London: Bison Books.

Bradbury, R. (1990) 'Reading John le Carré'. In C. Bloom (ed.) *Spy Thrillers: From Buchan to le Carré* (pp. 130–139). London: Palgrave Macmillan.

Case, G. (2014) *Calling Dr Strangelove: The Anatomy and Influence of the Kubrick Masterpiece*. New York, NY: McFarland & Co.

Caserman, P., Hoffmann, K., Müller, P., Schaub, M., Straßburg, K., Wiemeyer, J., Bruder, R. and Göbel, S. (2020) 'Quality criteria for serious games: Serious part, game part, and balance'. *JMIR Serious Games* 8 (3), 1–14.

Corliss, R. (1970) 'Topaz: Review'. *Film Quarterly* 23 (3), 41–44.

Daley-Ward, Y. (2020) 'Women of the Year: Lashana Lynch on making history as the first black female 007'. *Harper's Bazaar*, 3 November.

Davis, W. (2015) *The Ariadne Objective: Patrick Leigh Fermor and the Underground War to Rescue Crete from the Nazis*. London: Random House.

Decuir, J. (programmer) (1977) *Video Olympics* [video game]. Atari Inc.

Diver, M. (2019) *Retro Gaming: A Byte-Sized History of Video Games—from Atari to Zelda*. London: LOM Art.

Diver, Tony (2019) 'John Le Carré has given spies a bad name, says ex-MI6 chief'. *The Daily Telegraph*, 28 September.

Dodds, K. (2003) 'Licensed to stereotype: Geopolitics, James Bond and the spectre of Balkanism'. *Geopolitics* 8 (2), 125–156.

Dover, R. (2009) 'From Vauxhall Cross, with love'. In R. Dover and M. Goodman (eds) *Spinning Intelligence* (pp.??–??). London: Hurst & Co.

Dynia, P. (1976) 'Alfred Hitchcock and the ghost of Thomas Hobbes'. *Cinema Journal* 15 (2), 27–41.

Fermor, Patrick Leigh (2014) *Abducting a General: The Kreipe Operation and SOE in Crete*. London: Hachette.

Financial Times (2021) 'Finding a new role for the UK in the world'. *Financial Times*. 4 January. Accessed 4 January 2021. https://www.ft.com/content/14557b60-13be-4ede-99ca-0a6893a94577

Foot, Michael R. D. (2011) *SOE: An Outline History of the Special Operations Executive 1940–46*. London: Random House.

Freeman, David (1999) *The Last Days of Alfred Hitchcock*. New York, NY: Overlook Press.

Fritzsche, A. and Dürrbeck, K. (2020) 'Technology before engineering: How James Bond films mediate between fiction and reality in the portrayal of innovation'. *Technovation* 92–93.

Funnell, L. and Dodds, K. (2016) *Geographies, Genders and Geopolitics of James Bond*. London: Springer.

Ganser, Daniele (2005) *NATO's Secret Armies: Operation GLADIO and Terrorism in Western Europe*. London: Routledge.

Gerrard, S. (2020) *From Blofeld to Moneypenny: Gender in James Bond*. Bingley: Emerald Publishing Ltd.

Gutiérrez, E. J. D. (2014) 'Video games and gender-based violence'. *Procedia—Social and Behavioral Sciences* 132, 58–64.

Johnson, J. (2020) 'Delegating strategic decision-making to machines: Dr. Strangelove redux?' *Journal of Strategic Studies* 45 (3), 1–39.

Johnson, R. S. (2013) 'Toward greater production diversity: Examining social boundaries at a video game studio'. *Games and Culture* 8 (3), 136–160.

Kapsis, R. E. (1988) 'Hitchcock in the James Bond Era'. *Studies in Popular Culture* 11 (1), 64–79.

Krämer, P. (2017) *Dr. Strangelove or: How I Learned to Stop Worrying and Love the Bomb*. London: Bloomsbury Publishing.

Laffey, M. and Weldes, J. (2008) 'Decolonizing the Cuban missile crisis'. *International Studies* Quarterl 52 (3), 555–577.

Le Carré, J. (2017) *The Pigeon Tunnel: Stories from My Life*. London: Penguin.

Lethier, P. (2001) *Argent secret: L'espion de l'affaire elf parle*. Paris: Albin Michel.

———— (2009) 'The clandestine clapperboard: Alfred Hitchcock's "Tales of the Cold War"'. In R. Dover and M. Goodman (eds) *Spinning Intelligence* (pp. ??–??) London: Hurst & Co.

———— (2010) 'The clandestine clapperboard: Popular cinema, espionage and intelligence'. PhD thesis, King's College London.

Loyer, E. (2010) 'Stories as instruments'. *Television & New Media* 11 (3), 180–196.

MacDonald, Keza (2018) 'Rockstar Games defends itself over working conditions claims'. *The Guardian.* 18 October. Accessed 13 November 2019. https://www.theguardian.com/games/2018/oct/18/rockstar-games-working-conditions-red-dead-redemption-2-rob-nelson

Martin, A. (2019) 'The challenge of narrative'. *Cinéaste* 44 (3), 22–27.

McCrisken, T. and Moran, C. (2018) 'James Bond, Ian Fleming and intelligence: Breaking down the boundary between the "real"and the "imagined"'. *Intelligence and National Security* 33 (6), 804–821.

Murray, S. (2018) 'Landscapes of Empire in Metal Gear Solid V: The Phantom Pain'. *Critical Inquiry* 45 (1), 168–198.

Nicolau, A. (2020) 'World's largest cinema chain says sales down more than 90%'. *Financial Times*, 2 November.

Pearson, J. (2011) *The Life of Ian Fleming.* London: A&C Black.

Ramsay, D. (2015) 'Brutal games: "Call of duty" and the cultural narrative of world war II'. *Cinema Journal* 54 (2), 94–113.

Silver, B. R. (1987) 'Woman as agent: The case of le Carre's "Little Drummer Girl"'. *Contemporary Literature* XXVIII (1), 14–40.

Smith, S. L. and Moyer-Gusé, E. (2005) 'Voluptuous vixens and macho males: A look at the portrayal of gender and sexuality in video games'. In T. Reichert and J. Lambias (eds) *Sex in Consumer Cultur: The Erotic Content of Media and Marketing* (pp. 51–63). London: Routledge.

Stamenković, D., Jaćević, M. and Wildfeuer. J. (2017) 'The persuasive aims of Metal Gear Solid: A discourse theoretical approach to the study of argumentation in video games'. *Discourse, Context & Media* 15 (1), 11–23.

Treanor, M., Zook, A., Eladhari, M. P., Togelius, J., Smith, G., Cook, M. and Smith, A. (2015) 'AI-based game design patterns'. Strathclyde University Repository. https://strathprints.strath.ac.uk/57219/1/Treanor_etal_FDG2015_AI_based_game_design_patterns.pdf

Vermaak, J. and Le Clue, N. (2020) 'Miss Moneypenny and the friend-zone: The indispensable and sexually unavailable "Bond girl"'. In S. Gerrard, *From Blofeld to Moneypenny: Gender in James Bond* (pp. 202–214). Bingley: Emerald Publishing Ltd.

Walker, M. (2004) '"Topaz" and Cold War politics'. *Hitchcock Annual* 13, 127–153.

Woodward, Richard (2011) 'Patrick Leigh Fermor, travel writer, dies at 96'. *The New York Times*, 11 June.

8

POPULAR CULTURE AND SPYING
A WINDOW INTO THE INTELLIGENCE WORLD

What You Need to Know...

Popular culture has been used by Anglosphere intelligence services to push information about their work and about threats they are dealing with. Agencies have used popular cultural outlets as a means by which to inform and seek forms of tacit permission for developments in tradecraft, like communications interception and enhanced measures in the global war on terror. These cultural depictions have also helped to shape how we see the world, how we view contested political spaces and what are reasonable responses. In short, they have provided the underpinning logics for how we encounter the world. They hae also been used by screenwriters and studios to help the public question key issues of our time and to spark public debate. The success of popular cultural accounts of intelligence and spying is in its resonance with shards of truth, with things the public think they recognise from the news. In this it shares much in common with the construction of conspiracy theories. There is a lot of overlap between the depiction of intelligence and how law enforcement and military activities are portrayed in their relevant cultural genres and in academic treatments of these professions. We are often forced to look at law enforcement dramas, in particular, for more accurate portrayals of intelligence tradecraft.

***

235

The spy genre, often described as the spy thriller genre, has been used to describe, illuminate and amplify issues of contemporary relevance for the last hundred years. Spy genre content has been used to examine recurrent themes around threats, betrayal, state power, and tragedy that have allowed a multitude of writers, authors and directors to provide their own unique treatment and insights on contested issues.

The depiction of intelligence in popular culture—be it through books, films, TV series, radio-plays, theatre productions or computer games—is a compelling mix of intrigue, power and implied or actualised violence. Popular cultural portrayals pick away at the tension between the individual and sovereign power. They also examine the tensions in individual choices or in the personal experience of surveillance or government repression. In general terms, Western spy fiction has helped to produce and (re)produce a political agenda that emphasises a form of individualism, creativity and subversion, certainly against the benign but deadening hand of the state. This fiction is not very fussy about what kind of state this might be, or which particular state it is. The political and framing role of spy fiction is in laying out the contours of a battle between 'us' and 'them' and in establishing what is and is not a proportionate response. These questions have also been the concern of a very small sub-set of international relations scholars working on defence, security and foreign policy (Daniel & Musgrave, 2017; Rowley & Weldes, 2012; Shepherd, 2012).

The tension between bold individual characters and powerful states, around who is the real enemy or competitor, or the tension between subversive groups and 'our' communities, will always be attractive to writers and to those who commission and broadcast popular cultural output. Such depictions might also appear useful to governments seeking to position and inform the public about issues or developments, although in relation to the euphemistically labelled practice of enhanced measures and the evocation of *24* by US military interviewees with the human rights lawyer Phillipe Sands, there is the potential for stark unintended consequences of popular culture on the operation of intelligence (Sands, 2008). Sands found that trainees at the US War College at Westpoint repeatedly noted that torture in *24* produced good intelligence; this provided them with evidence for its efficacy.

Lead character Jack Bauer's use of torture in *24* to provide critical and timely intelligence in order to create a positive operational effect closely aligned to the neoconservative side of the debate around the global war on terror, and the extent to which the US and its allies—endowed with moral superiority and a just cause— could bend international laws and norms to their outer edge (and beyond) in pursuit of these higher goals (Kearns & Young, 2018; Nikolaidis, 2011). Ron Suskind—in his forensic evaluation of the Bush Administration's response to jihadist terrorism—termed this the 1% doctrine, from a quote taken from Vice President Cheney: 'If there's a 1% chance that Pakistani scientists are helping al-Qaeda build or develop a nuclear weapon, we have to treat it as a certainty in terms of our response. It's not about our analysis... It's about our response' (Suskind, 2006). Suskind persuasively argued that it is the logic of the 1% doctrine that drove this heightened and often violent response to those suspected of membership of terrorist organisations.

The series *24* provided validation to neoconservatives that these aggressive approaches were appropriate and necessary because of what they delivered back to the agencies in intelligence. In partial contrast, Kathryn Bigelow's 2012 film, *Zero Dark Thirty*, established a more complicated and potentially difficult set of ethical dilemmas because it dramatised the hunt for Osama bin Laden, whilst being similarly accused of glamorising torture (Schlag, 2019). Bigelow is said to have received assistance from psychologists who had assisted the original in-the-field CIA programmes, but her intention was to show torture as an abhorrent practice, within the context of an episode lauded as a public success. The release of *Zero Dark Thirty* prompted the then Acting Director of the CIA to write to CIA staffers to say that the film:

> creates the strong impression that the enhanced interrogation techniques that were part of our former detention and interrogation program were the key to finding Bin Laden. That impression is false... multiple streams of intelligence led C.I.A.

analysts to conclude that Bin Laden was hiding in Abbottabad…
Some came from detainees subjected to enhanced techniques,
but there were many other sources as well… whether enhanced
interrogation techniques were the only timely and effective way
to obtain information from those detainees, as the film suggests,
is a matter of debate that cannot and never will be definitively
resolved. (Shane, 2012)

The case of the hunt for Osama bin Laden provides superficially
compelling evidence of a pattern of aggressive and norm-bending
US government behaviour. Indeed, given the neoliberal frame
of understanding that these cultural depictions work within,
extraordinary measures are a politically and morally legitimate
means of protecting our set of values from an existential threat.
Similar conceptual leaps have been applied to the incendiary
bombing of Dresden by the Royal Airforce in the Second World
War and the use of poison gas in the First World War. Temporarily
moving outside legal and moral codes of practice can be justified by
all sides in a war, even if they are often breaching international law.
The bin Laden case is potentially misleading, however, because bin
Laden—as a target—was of such a high value and of such strategic
importance that additional layers of executive involvement should
be expected: this is not everyday rule-breaking but exceptional.
Better illustrations can be found in the wider war on terror and the
US (and allies) behaviour towards Islamist suspects, such as the large
number of renditions (kidnappings) of suspects, and the detention
of suspects and irregulars in the Guantanamo Bay camp, which were
(and are) prolonged breaches of established norms during the war
on terror (Blakeley & Raphael, 2020).

It is known—from the 459-page executive summary of the 2012
US Senate Intelligence Committee's *Study of the Central Intelligence
Agency's Detention and Interrogation Program*, chaired by Senator
Feinstein—that there was systematic use of torture techniques,
including those the committee described as rape and kidnapping
(although officially described as rendition), throughout the duration
of the war on terror. It has taken academics like Ruth Blakeley and
Sam Raphael, in addition to activists in civil society organisations,

to conduct forensic studies of air traffic data and victim testimony through technically advanced methodologies to unpick the redactions in the official reporting to illuminate a large intelligence programme of official abuse, which Blakeley and Raphael describe as 'state terrorism' (Blakely, 2011; Blakeley & Raphael, 2020). The techniques used in these state programmes have been tacitly supported and re-enforced by popular cultural sources. The normalisation of this violence—which is historically contingent—is in great part due to the way it has been positioned in cultural outputs.

The Senate Intelligence Committee's work has been represented on the big screen by the 2019 film *The Report*, which focused on Daniel Jones, one of Senator Feinstein's staffers working to reveal— much as Blakeley and Raphael have done—the nature and frequency of the CIA's techniques and practices during this period. Strongly weighted for its American cinematic and Amazon Prime Video audience, the film advances the 'bad apple' thesis that elements of the CIA had gone far beyond their given remit in over-using these techniques and had misled their political masters along the way. There is some empirical evidence that might give weight to this account. It has been suggested that the psychologists who developed the enhanced measures programme were also at the forefront of validating that this programme had added value to the CIA's pool of intelligence and understanding of radical jihadist groups (Marks, 2018: Welch, 2017). This is the equivalent of a student marking their own homework and was deeply flawed as a result (Dyer, 2016). There was, however, considerable scepticism from experienced intelligence analysts, who doubted that the long-discredited approach to collection would suddenly yield these sorts of results. The Executive Summary of Feinstein's Committee report is long enough to dissuade most average readers from attempting it. The full report—at more than 6,000 pages—is enough to dissuade most experts, whereas the heavily curated and edited newspaper reports, and cinematic outputs, are of a length that all interested parties will be able to consume. So, when it comes to the public's (tacit) consent or view about what is proportionate or acceptable in attempting to contain, curtail and rollback terrorist actions, these have been strongly conditioned by popular cultural outputs.

Spy fiction is compelling when it manages to sit within a set of narratives that have the ring of truth about them. The position of intelligence officers and agencies as holders of hard-to-find truths, provides additional authority to their narratives. As a result, intelligence officers and agencies have the capacity to shape responses to threats and the ability to position issues in the minds of their audiences; similarly the cultural refraction of intelligence also has this capacity. The necessary secrecy around intelligence activities appears to be transgressed by popular culture, but in almost every situation that is not the case. The glamour of these fictionalised intelligence accounts helps to reinforce the narrative around the need to maintain the strict pathologies of secrecy. These fictional accounts also enforce the convenient narrative of the necessity to derogate away from individual human rights and liberties in the name of an identified collective good: as we will see during this chapter, spy dramas have normalised surveillance, have made it acceptable to fear 'the other' and made it acceptable to privilege the ends of protecting us from 'the other' over the ethics of precise tactics. It has done this by channelling popular feelings and insecurities and by showing that *our* good always procures hard-earned triumphs against *their* evil.

Regardless of one's political disposition, it is important to note—as has been rehearsed throughout this book—that the act of policing or disciplining behaviour through the use of secret intelligence services is not a value-neutral one. The politics of state intelligence are every bit as political as the politics of the terrorists or dissidents they seek to contain and defeat. In the Global North, we might all enjoy the benefits of living in liberal democracies, with mostly free trade and mostly free speech, and the freedom to choose a whole host of services and goods. But this political, social and economic system, that is premised upon openness, freedoms and choices, is not universal—even if for most of us it is our lived experience—and is not necessarily aspired to as being superior. Since the financial crash of 2008 and the rise of populist politics, the rejection of this form of social, economic and political liberalism has gained traction. But, even when cultural outlets have sought to represent the position of 'the other', they have done so within the established frame of understanding and tropes of our societies. This will be partly for commercial reasons but also because—as the intelligence services themselves found in planning for Iraq and the counterinsurgency that followed—it is difficult to truly put yourself in the shoes of the adversary or 'the other'.

The election of Donald Trump, the rise of Boris Johnson in the UK, and the contested and controversial victory for the leave campaign in the UK's 2016 EU referendum, are manifestations of the rejection of the post-Second World War political compact to instead privilege a mythical notion of past grandeur. This grandeur has been provided and reproduced by the James Bond series through the Cold War and has taken on a more modern role as a rejection of what has become viewed by some, like the actor Laurence Fox, as the rampant excesses of political correctness or 'woke' culture (Kay, 2020). This, too, is keenly observed and addressed by the Le Carré novel, *Agent Running in the Field* (2019). So, there is a basic reflexive point to be made that *our* politics are contested and that we should understand that our adversaries are, in ways we understandably do not like, challenging our politics and our social system. In return, we challenge their conception of politics when the government and its policing and intelligence agencies place them under surveillance or curtail their ability freely to associate; these are the disciplinary aspects of our way of politics, but we do not often see policing and intelligence in terms of disciplining ideology, and nor do intelligence officers, who tend to see their roles as non-political and objective (Omand, 2020). In that context, the nature, quality and plurality of inputs into the intelligence officer's mind, be they education, intelligence training, the views of those close to them, or indeed what they consume in their leisure time, are important to shaping the realities in which the officer operates.

Exploring the characters, the scenarios and the politics behind these cultural representations gives us insights into what might be called *real world politics*, and into the conditioning of society into certain political and philosophical positions. For example, one clear set of cultural messages involves creating a sense of all-encompassing threat, that at any moment in time the United States or the United Kingdom could be brought to its knees by terrorist atrocities. This apocalyptic fear plays on the notion that these terrorists seek to *end our way of life* and that we are engaged in a life-or-death struggle. Alternatively, the threats posed by Russian organised crime and laundered Russian money in London—something underplayed by the British authorities—has been brought into stark relief by the eight-part drama series *McMafia* (2018), which was based on a book of the same name by the investigative journalist Misha Glenny in 2009 (Glenny, 2009). The power of the drama was due to the resonance or traction with newsworthy events: investigative journalism had suggested that Russian politics and business play out violently on the streets of London, but at a time when Russia was also persistently being accused in the media and by politicians of interfering in British and American politics (Blake, 2019; The Intelligence and Security Committee of Parliament, 2020).

In recent times, the American and British governments have been convinced of the utility of popular media outlets in positioning their war against terrorism. Just as the British and German governments invested time in the Second World War in placing political propaganda within popular films, so Hollywood has enjoyed particularly close relations with both the Pentagon and the White House (Jenkins, 2016; Willmetts, 2016). After 9/11 the White House invested some time in cultivating US movie makers into representing the war on terror 'properly', sharing key ideas and concepts (Bennett, 2010; Dodds, 2008). The involvement—in an advisory capacity—of long-standing MI5 officers in the film *Four Lions* (2010) was interesting in as much as the leading, radicalised characters were shown to be vulnerable, ideologically illiterate, and three-dimensional. The film's writers—Chris Morris, Jesse Armstrong and Sam Bain—have a long track record of brutal, but highly intelligent and astute comedy, and *Four Lions* is a darkly comic film that does more to provide the audience with a nuanced sense of radicalisation than almost any other mainstream film (Brassett & Sutton, 2017). Most other cinematic portrayals have struggled to break away from the central conceit of the global war on terrorism being a clash of civilisations, which implies that it will be impossible for secular or Christian communities to live alongside Muslim communities. What that implies for societal cohesion and public policy is somewhat bleak, and the failure (in public relations terms at least) of the UK's counter radicalisation programmes is emblematic of how such entrenched stances can produce counterproductive results (Qurashi, 2018).

The cooperation between intelligence agencies and film studios has generated a curious mix of a corporate film industry with a public service broadcasting strand that focuses on terrorism and interstate conflicts as a new place to play out its vulnerabilities and to create mythologised heroes and a deeply symbolic fight between good and evil. An early example of this cooperation between government agencies and studios is the drama *The FBI,* which ran from the mid-1960s to the mid-1970s, and which received advice from the FBI Director J. Edgar Hoover until his death in 1972. After the 9/11 attacks, President Bush's political counsellor Karl Rove met with the Motion Picture Association of America and various film producers to see if he could persuade them to present the war on terror in a particular way (Stockwell, 2005). Rove was allegedly keen to ensure that the movie houses did not present the global war on terror as a Samuel Huntingdon-esque 'clash of civilisations'. In this aim, and if it is true, Rove clearly failed: most studios depicted the global war on terror precisely as a clash between competing civilisations, which was—as it turns out—not unhelpful to the Bush Administration in seeking to make the public case for ratcheting up terrorism legislation.

Governments have not widely advertised their involvement in the production of this content, and studios have similarly been coy. And whilst this is not indicative of conspiracy, it is strongly suggestive of a desire to manufacture a message quietly, and indeed manufacture the cultural inputs being enjoyed by the public. There have yet to be any long-term studies—and the control sample would be almost impossible to construct—of how this form of cultural output has shaped the political views of those who have consumed them. Political marketeers use rough proxies to draw a correlation for effectiveness. The homogenising impact of these cultural artefacts in describing security forces bravely trying to prevent sociopathic and psychopathic extremists from doing us harm has been to police the boundaries of the debates on this subject and to lay out an internally coherent picture of the fight against militant radicals.

Compelling Narratives: Ticking Time Bombs

The 'ticking time bomb' plot device, the existential emergency, is a device used constantly in popular representations of intelligence activity. The idea that a Jack Bauer from *24* or an Adam Carter from *Spooks* would have allowed the 'CREVICE' plotters in southern England, bent in Spring 2004 on blowing up a large British shopping centre and nightclub, to develop their plot and reveal so much of their network would be unthinkable (Horne & Horgan, 2012). Jack would have tortured and/or killed them earlier than the real-life security officials intervened, resulting in the plot very nearly, but not quite, succeeding; and Adam would have used perfect satellite imagery, communications intercepts and surveillance to rein them in at the very last moment, his powers of detention a direct distortion of MI5's requirement for police help in these circumstances.

The tension between a law enforcement mentality of early intervention, collect evidence and charge where appropriate, and an intelligence mindset of allow the plot to develop as far as possible to reveal as much of the conspiracy as possible, is both illuminated and confused by the ticking timebomb plot device. In the real world, the CREVICE plot was allegedly somewhat hastily disrupted when the CIA allegedly threatened to pre-emptively bring the network down if MI5 did not do so immediately. If true, this is surely worthy of being dramatised itself, and raises questions about how and why the CIA were conducting active operations on UK soil. These forms of allied intelligence effort were also present in the Brussels bombing in March 2016, where it is said that UK and US intelligence provided live feed and movement data on the perpetrators to the struggling Belgian authorities. Belgian security services were finding it difficult to track and trace perpetrators, who were behaving in such a way as to attract attention and to cause a televised standoff with authorities. These sorts of tensions make for potentially good drama and have been played out in the BBC's small-screen series *The State Within* (2006), and Armando Iannucci's (2009) *In The Loop*. In the case of the latter, this presented a big-screen satire of inharmonious US–UK diplomatic politics, drawn using established and unfair nationality-based tropes of the over-bearing and boorish Americans, and pasty, slippery and too-clever-by-half Brits. The election of Donald Trump in 2016, and indeed the ascent of Boris Johnson in the UK, diminished the need to provide fictionalised, or indeed satirical, treatments of modern politics. The news—unfortunately—delivers daily scenarios that most satirists would struggle to conjure.

The importance of the 'ticking time-bomb' plot device, and the evocation that this is somehow representative of how intelligence operations work, produce a conditioning effect on the viewers and a trickle-up effect on policy makers; what one might call a fog of perception, echoing the classic military notion of the fog of war. It helps to condition and to shape what Slavoj Zizek describes as objective violence—that which secures the state and certain modes of trade—while portraying the violence of adversaries as exceptional and shocking: to use his terminology, 'subjective violence' (Zizek, 2009).

24 rightly attracted opprobrium from liberal quarters for the easy way it slipped into scenes of torture without sound justifications for doing so, either artistically or in terms of the operational art it sought to show. In these depictions there is very little place for Alan Dershowitz's judicially justified torture—decisions are portrayed as coming down to an individual officer making an immediate decision, and only very little in the way of their being obvious lines of accountability (Dershowitz, 2014; Wisnewski, 2008).

In contrast to the US approach, British depictions of torture often involve violence being meted out by adversaries, including foreign nationals and private security officers. For the most part, enhanced measures carried out by British officers are done reluctantly and are carefully discussed by ad hoc committees of senior intelligence officers. This portrayed difference between the US and UK is signalled as being in the American case everything is subordinate to the national interest, with charismatic officers making immediate decisions. In the UK, derogations of human rights are shown to be agonised over and possibly resulting in further attacks from radicalised enemies. Within the CIA's practice of extraordinary rendition, of kidnapping suspects, the agency seemingly had few brakes on its activity, and in self-reporting intelligence successes was able to expand operations beyond the limits of its prison real estate. Cases taken against the

British government have been highly suggestive of British intelligence officers being present during the torture of American prisoners and/or supplying questions to be asked, whilst not taking part in the physical acts of torture themselves (Blakeley & Raphael, 2020). Similarly, the US rendition flights used UK airspace and refuelling when these aircraft did not contain prisoners but did not refuel in the UK when prisoners were on board, again suggesting that the UK was content to receive intelligence product sourced in this way but wished to maintain levels of plausible deniability (Bellaby, 2018). By design or by accident, art had imitated life.

The ticking-time bomb plot device has allowed dramatists and the viewing public to hold up dearly held values to the light. Depictions of national security problems tend to portray protagonists in terms of being good or evil, with very little space for nuance. In doing so a choice is provided to the audience about who is 'us' and who is 'them', and what membership of either group suggests, and how the relationships between those two groups should develop. In particular, and this has been a shifting picture over the last twenty years, the extent to which we should accept or tolerate aspects of 'them' in our societies, and consequently what actions are proportionate to take against those groups. The universalised norm of the prohibition of torture has existed in international law since 1948 and the Universal Declaration of Human Rights, which declared in Article 5: 'No one shall be subjected to torture or to cruel, inhuman or degrading treatment or punishment.' Prior to the 1948 declaration the prohibition on torture had been upheld via *jus cogens* (a lawyer-ish way of saying customary international law), which takes precedent over other forms of law, meaning that it is not limited to a particular jurisdiction and is to be universally applied. The Geneva Conventions, covering conduct during war, places a ban upon 'violence of life and person, in particular murder of all kinds, mutilation, cruel treatment and torture... [and] outrages upon personal dignity, in particular humiliating and degrading treatment'. Of particular relevance to intelligence operations is the prohibition on the use of force to obtain information (Article 31 of the Fourth Geneva Convention), and the US has itself in the 1999 *Initial Report of the United States of America to the UN Committee Against Torture* confirmed the illegality of torture and the extraterritoriality of punishment regarding the use of torture techniques. The exceptionalism of the global war on terror, and the impact it had upon Western thinking, is demonstrated by US Vice President Cheney's 2001 declaration that:

> We also have to work sort of the dark side, if you will. ... A lot of what needs to be done here will have to be done quietly, without any discussions, using sources and methods that are available to our intelligence agencies if we're going to be successful. That's the world these folks operate in. And so it's going to be vital for us to use any means at our disposal... It is a mean, nasty, dangerous, dirty business out there, and we have to operate in that arena. (*The Washington Post*, 2001)

The ticking time-bomb rationality, so often used in cultural depictions of intelligence, has allowed those in the West to frequently part with our stated core values, supposedly in the name of protecting them. Do such moments fundamentally undermine the liberalism they seek to protect? There is a strong argument to say they do, moving us closer to the illiberalism that Western states have sought to oppose, and depriving the West of the critical moral gap between its actions and those of its adversaries. This view privileges the inherent moral superiority of North America and Western Europe or accepts that moral superiority is a high price to pay against real-world impacts. The alternative view is that by accepting casualties and opposing our adversaries within the boundaries of international law and human rights frameworks, we maintain a higher moral plain and ultimately undermine our adversary's moral and political claims.

Measures that seem to contradict our core values have been used across many times of existential threat. The firebombing of Dresden in February 1945, and the decision to go to war against Iraq in 2003, were episodes when core British values were put to one side in the name of security expediency. From a cultural perspective, the mainstreaming of certain core messages—of what the state is fighting for, and how we should fight for it—is important. The intangible is how these signals filter around the polity, percolating through the public, the political classes, the military, the security sector and the news media in the 'fog of perception'. The impression often given of intelligence officers and government elites being entirely immune to these kinds of cultural messages falls at the first hint of reflexive thought. Intelligence does not operate in a vacuum and officers are not immune from the created realities of media invention. So, while it is useful for the CIA to meet with and advise the producers of *24* on story lines, eventually the new reality they create—through *24* and other broadcast media—and the public acceptance of it, constrains policy makers and politicians into certain ways of working. If torture works for a compelling character in a programme or film, the argument might go, why is it not being used by counterterrorism professionals?

The ticking time bomb as a hook upon which to explore intelligence and culture, highlights some stark realities of the combination of fiction and reality. But the realities of the vast majority of intelligence work do not relate to such stark scenarios and can be related more closely to the mundane and even the banal. One film that does show this side of intelligence activity is the award-winning film *The Lives of Others* (2006), which focuses on an intricate portrayal of the collection of intelligence in communist East Germany during the Cold War: it is a highly effective demonstration of the importance of empathy in human intelligence (Diamond, 2008). A focus on supply lines, support networks and financing routes (like narcotics and charities) provides a far bigger intelligence target to hit; it also provides a far wider opportunity to wrap up whole networks, rather than just the individual fanatic willing to sacrifice him or herself. So, while real-world intelligence largely focuses upon the network-centric view, the focus of popular culture is nearly always on the individual fanatic or small group of fanatics, which skews the public perception of what intelligence officers spend their days doing, and indeed how they should do it.

Tradecraft and the Big Screen: From Handbooks to Handwringing

One area of popular culture that is largely immune from the attentions of writers, producers and directors is the humble intelligence analyst and, more particularly, the sort of character who works on strategic intelligence. For the most part, analysts—when they are portrayed—

are depicted as decidedly bookish, often with autistic spectrum disorders, and peripheral to the story. The business of analysis or assessments is often conflated with tactical analysis: the characters of Chloe in *24,* Colin in *Spooks* and Susan Cooper in *Spy* (2015) are tactical operators, essentially guiding their field operatives: Colin has the poor fortune to get himself killed in a scenario that would be difficult to imagine in the real world. The early Jack Ryan film, *The Sum of All Fears* (2002), has the lead protagonist as CIA analyst, who then takes on a far more developed field role. But these tactical roles are the mainstay of what counts as analysis in popular culture, and perhaps the trade does lack something in the way of entertaining angles. It is, however, a vital part of the business of intelligence.

The recruitment of agents, of those to provide information or to commit treason against their countries or causes, has the necessary ingredients for dramatic construction. University lecturers teach that human intelligence (HUMINT) is often a patient and lengthy process. Practitioners often concur, but also throw in the experience where contingency led to the development of opportunistic informant relationships, often described as community contacts or confidential sources. In popular culture, there is often seldom time to allow for nuanced and careful development of a recruitment story, nor the time to work through what the three-dimensional motivation of an informant might be. So, we see Florence Pugh's Charlie in *The Little Drummer Girl* (2018) being part seduced and part convinced into giving purpose to her life in her recruitment. Her lack of conviction in the cause she has been recruited to forms part of the reason behind her disaffection during the series. In *Atomic Blonde* (2017), Charlize Theron's cartoonish and violent film about multiple levels of betrayal in Cold War Germany, all the leading characters use sex, drugs and money to recruit their agents.

By contrast, the exceptional five-seasons-long US drama series *The Wire* (2002–8) is particularly strong when it deals with the recruitment and running of an informant. The character of Bubbles, based on a real-life police informant, cooperates with the police initially as a means to exact revenge for his friend who was badly beaten up by one of the drugs gang (Henning, 2014). The peripheral Bubbles storyline is interesting because it shows the quality of human intelligence that is possible from what appears to be a shambolic source, and the way in which a source can be carefully retained with compassion and small remittances. The depiction of Bubbles is far closer to real-world informant running than the sort of trophy conversions seen in mainstream popular culture (Twomey, 2020). Within the mainstream, the many reasons why informants get involved in intelligence work, and what sustains them in the work, sometimes for decades, is almost entirely absent from the popular cultural repertoire, which is a missed opportunity as it leaves a large gap in the public's understanding and leaves most people assuming that officers and agents are not like them, when nothing could be further from the truth.

Interrogations are commonplace within the popular cultural depictions of intelligence. They range widely from those involving torture or near torture, through to those that resemble police interviews and to more *gentil* forms that seem more akin to conversations. Intelligence interviews are distinct from law enforcement interviews. The purpose of the law enforcement interview is to collect evidence with the intent of forming a case that will be prosecuted in court. An intelligence interview—where such a formal thing happens at all—might end up in court, but that is unlikely to be the purpose of the interview or conversation. Here the purpose is more likely to be to try to acquire a greater level of understanding of the context, of the protagonists, and perhaps even to try and recruit the interviewee in some form or another. The research literature and the evidence from practitioners is that calm, non-coercive interview techniques are more effective ways of drawing out information from an interviewee than the coercive methods more commonly seen in cinematic and televisual depictions of the craft. Indeed, the research tells us that coercive and violent techniques encourage an informant to say anything to end the experience, which, if the aim is to secure usable information, is hopeless, and such techniques destroy the trust between an interrogator and informant that is essential to their ongoing relationship (Alison & Alison, 2017). An excellent example of patient interrogation was published by Ian Leslie in *The Guardian* newspaper in 2014, which was a description of an interrogation of a suspected Islamist terrorist (given an assumed name of Diola in the article), who was believed to be plotting to kill a member of the armed forces or police officer in London:

> Diola: 'Tell me why I should tell you. What is the reason behind you asking me this question?'
>
> Interviewer: 'I am asking you these questions because I need to investigate what has happened and know what your role was in these events.'
>
> Diola: 'No, that's your job—not your reason. I'm asking you why it matters to you.'
>
> The interviewer, who has remained heroically calm in the face of Diola's verbal barrage, is not able to move the encounter out of stalemate, and eventually his bosses replace him. When the new interviewer takes a seat, Diola repeats his promise to talk 'openly and honestly' to the right person, and resumes his inquisitorial stance. 'Why are you asking me these questions?' he says. 'Think carefully about your reasons.'
>
> The new interviewer does not answer directly, but something about his opening speech triggers a change in Diola's demeanour. 'On the day we arrested you,' he began, 'I believe that you had the intention of killing a British soldier or police officer. I don't know the details of what happened, why you may have felt it needed to happen, or what you wanted to achieve by doing this. Only you know these things Diola. If you are willing, you'll tell me, and if you're not, you won't. I can't force you to tell me—I don't want to force you. I'd like you to help me understand. Would you tell me about what happened?' The interviewer opens up his notebook, and shows Diola the empty pages. 'You see? I don't even have a list of questions.'
>
> 'That is beautiful,' Diola says. 'Because you have treated me with consideration and respect, yes I will tell you now. But only to help you understand what is really happening in this country.' (Leslie, 2017)

The difference in the purpose of the interview, the intended end-use, if you will, strongly impacts upon the conduct of the interview. For one, the intelligence interviews do not have to be produced in court, and there are many examples where the detail of interactions is prevented from entering court. Therefore, the shape of the conversation does not have to remain within the tightly controlled boundaries that law enforcement interviews do. There is greater scope to work through the motivations of the interviewee, rather than to try and press for evidential leads, and indeed to offer incentives to interviewees that would be deemed improper in a law enforcement interview. For the majority of intelligence operations, the interview or interrogation is an anathema.

The purpose of intelligence is to identify, contain and roll back threat, placing a well-timed intervention to dissuade or disrupt adversary activity. For government intelligence agencies, this will often mean that there is no actual contact with the target at all— intelligence being gathered remotely or via informants. Only if the issue comes to be prosecuted will law enforcement officers, with powers of arrest, come into play. The film *The Lives of Others* (2006) and the novel *A Legacy of Spies* (2017) both show an intricate and tense portrayal of interrogations, where the asymmetry of knowledge between the interrogator and the interviewee forms much of the dramatic tension. In *The Lives of Others*, the interrogator has copious quantities of covertly collected information to hand, and the discomfort of the interviewee is the creeping realisation of the quantity and quality of that information, something that is only confirmed at the end of the film when the target seeks out his Stasi files after the fall of the Berlin Wall as many have done since (Garton-Ash, 2010).

In *A Legacy of Spies*, the asymmetry between the MI5 lawyer and the key protagonist, the retired intelligence officer Peter Guillam, is more nuanced and simmering: Guillam knows the operational detail inside and out, whilst the lawyer gently oscillates between contemplating protection and revelation (Le Carré, 2017; Snyder, 2020). Such carefully drawn psychological portrayals stand in stark contrast to those we can see, for example, in the remake of James Bond's *Casino Royale* (2006), where the interrogation of James Bond by his nemesis Le Chiffre, played by Mads Mikkelsen, is seen to repeatedly attack James with a belt, that manages to eye-wateringly and repeatedly miss both his legs. True to life, perhaps, Le Chiffre's violence does not yield good intelligence. Similarly, in *Zero Dark Thirty* (2012) the interrogations are graphic and harrowing. Interviewees are subjected to repeated torture, the scenes made all the worse by the realisation that the film is based on real-life events. These cinematic portrayals of brutality, which are closer to the experiences of those interrogated by the Americans in the global war on terror, by the Syrian government during the civil war, and routinely by the Chinese government, say much about the permissive role of revenge and retribution in interrogations, which is either due to an ambivalence to collecting usable intelligence or a desire to apply harsh punishments to those who dare to oppose the side of the interrogator. This essentially colonist power imbalance continues to be played out on screen and across the world.

The Panopticon: Electronic Surveillance

The boundless potential of government communications interception and surveillance has been a reliable source of content for spy dramas, only surpassed by the disturbing revealed reality of the NSA's dragnet surveillance programmes, revealed by the whistleblower Edward Snowden. In terms of cinematic portrayals of these surveillance capabilities, the 1998 film *Enemy of the State* seems eerily prescient of what would subsequently be revealed about the NSA. In this film, the NSA is seen to be able to intercept telephone and internet traffic at will (a foretelling of the PRISM and Boundless Informant programmes). Whilst there is no evidence that the NSA cooperated or advised the producers of *Enemy of the State*, or the 2009 film *Echelon Conspiracy*, which takes its name from the Five Eyes signals sharing programme also called Echelon (also referenced in *The Bourne Ultimatum*), these films establish a mainstream cultural punctuation point that revealed the ability of the US and British governments to intercept communications data and to analyse the enormous datasets associated with dragnet programmes (Aldrich, 2010; Bamford, 2008). More realistic depictions of the day-to-day interception of communications come from law enforcement dramas, such as the American police intelligence drama *The Wire* (2002–8) and the French drama *Spiral* (the 2019 season in particular), where the business of securing authority to intercept calls and location data, and the background work required to locate a telephone to intercept, is part of the rich seam of the drama and indeed of the day-to-day existence of law enforcement intelligence officers.

The fanciful notion that an intelligence agency could use the microphones in mobile phones to act as bugs, saving them the trouble of using what Le Carré liked to call 'the burglars' to install listening devices in a home, was pre-trialled by the 2006 film *The Listening*. In this film an NSA whistleblower reveals the operation of Tumbleweed, which is a programme of mass surveillance and interference with landline and mobile telephony. The operational code name might not have been correct (it was CAPTIVATEDAUDIENCE), but the underlying details were (Zetter, 2014). Given the exposure the Snowden scandal received, it is surprising that the public still have a slight understanding of the technical potential around interception and what agencies can achieve through analysing the large datasets they create. Big data is not particularly televisual or cinematic, and the only real attempt to address the potential of these technologies has come in the form of documentaries and docudramas, which notably include Alex Gibney's profile of WikiLeaks, *We Steal Secrets* (2013), and Oliver Stone's biopic of Edward Snowden, titled *Snowden* (2016), which have sought to address wider issues around surveillance. More recently, the Netflix funded documentary *The Social Dilemma* (2020) provided a hard-hitting exposé of how and why the large internet platforms store, analyse and shape all our behaviours, joining up the behaviours of private platforms and government actors.

The Eyes from the Sky: IMINT

Whilst the portrayal of cyber operations has fallen someway short of the sorts of capabilities revealed by Edward Snowden, the portrayal of IMINT in popular culture is weak and over-specified. For practitioners, the development of IMINT has been vast since the halcyon days of the Cuban Missile Crisis in 1962 where the public first became familiar with the concept of grainy photographs taken from high-altitude cameras mounted on U2 aircraft. In this era the quality of IMINT was highly dependent on the ability to repeatedly overfly the target in these slow-moving aircraft. In this context the results achieved were impressive. As we move towards the present day, imagery is still collected via air-mounted camera platforms, be they high-altitude platforms as in the 1960s or unmanned aerial vehicle platforms (UAVs), which can remain in the air for up to seventy hours at a time. Imagery is also collected via satellites, and consumers have become used to this form of photography via the Google Maps service, that has almost entirely replaced traditional mapping in the Western world. The ubiquity of closed-circuit television (CCTV), of sophisticated cameras on mobile telephones and the rise of dashcams mounted on car dashboards, has increased the pool of imagery available to intelligence agencies, be it via open source scraping—and again Bellingcat is a good example of how this is used in the open source realm, and the documentary *We Live in Public* (2009) provides interesting insights leveraged via a cinematic art project and social experiment to evaluate the impact of this constant consumerist surveillance—or by direct interception (Higgins, 2021).

Satellite imagery, which is still dependent upon multiple overflights, has often been erroneously depicted in popular culture as being a highly mobile platform capable of hovering over targets for extended periods of time. The notion of 'moving the satellite', as fictional characters are often seen demanding, is fanciful in the real world: chance would be a fine thing. The success of this platform as a source of intelligence depends upon the number of satellites available to the collector and—somewhat prosaically—upon clear skies. In cinematic portrayals, such as the *Bourne* series of films (2002–16), there was a concerning absence of reality in the portrayals. The rapid utilisation of satellites for positioning, communications and ubiquitous and immediate crystal clear imagery, all controlled from a single control hub, all suggested a set of capabilities that is unrealistic. The conceit of these portrayals is a trade-off for the compelling narratives that underpin them but a base line for the public understanding of intelligence. The Indian film *Parmanu: The Story of Pokhran* (2018) inverts the mainstream depiction of satellites in intelligence, showing the Indian nuclear programme being developed in the blind spots of US satellite coverage, a clever twist on the sense of the all-seeing American eye, but an acknowledgement of the nature of this international relationship.

The use of UAVs as the technology of choice in extra-judicial killing (or targeted assassinations if you prefer) by the American military and

CIA during the Obama era, and by other nations—notably Turkey—has bridged the gap between surveillance and offensive weaponry, a gap that had existed between exceptionally slow- and fast-moving spy planes such as the U2 and SR-71 Blackbird, and offensive platforms acting upon the intelligence. According to the defence and security research company *Janes*, there are approximately 80,000 surveillance UAVs and only 2,000 offensive UAV platforms currently operating globally (Sabbagh, 2019). The cinematic portrayal would suggest that all UAVs had both surveillance and offensive capabilities on them, dramatically changing the character of these deployed platforms and increasing the fear of those seeing them in the skies above them. The political thriller *Eye in Sky* (2015) is emblematic of a small tranche of films that have sought to highlight the capabilities provided by UAVs, whilst also highlighting the moral and ethical dilemmas around their use. The 2014 film *Good Kill* pivots around the ethical weight borne by remote pilots engaging in both surveillance and offensive operations with their UAVs, with the lead character—played by Ethan Hawke—experiencing a breakdown because of his participation. The drone, as a dramatic device, has spurred several dystopian cinematic portrayals, feeding a line of public thought about the oppressive quality of the 'all-seeing-eye'. *The Purge: Election Year* (2016) and *The Slaughterbots* (2017), as examples, place the UAV as a tool of oppression, both monitoring populations for subversive behaviours and attacking those it concludes have transgressed. The rise of the dystopian UAV film has coincided with the reduced cost of consumer drones, and a commensurate rise in the numbers of people complaining about drones being used for prurient purposes or to cause disruption at major transport hubs (Shackle, 2020). Our relationship with UAVs is developing in parallel to somewhat slow and fitful attempts by governments to regulate these technologies.

Popular Culture and Intelligence: Partial Glimpses into a Secret World

Enjoying the popular cultural depictions of intelligence, be it in the cinema, on the television, through the radio or audiobooks, on our personal computers or games consoles, or via a good, old-fashioned printed book, we can be transported into alternative realities that offer the promise of insights into closed worlds. The issues that intelligence agencies, and therefore intelligence officers, worry about make for good drama. The jeopardy of war or terrorism is purpose built for dramatic interpretations and re-creation, whilst the interpersonal morality plays of officers and agents, traitors and idealists are themes repeated down through the ages. What is often missing in these depictions is an interrogation of the overarching context. So much of this context is assumed, and that these cultural artefacts work for us shows the conditioning and reproductive effect of popular culture upon us.

The depictions of intelligence tradecraft in popular culture offer partial coverage, and do not offer a great deal in the way of reality. What they do offer, however, is a spectrum of possibilities all the way from mindless entertainment up to a way of rehearsing or playing with issues that sit round substantive contemporary issues—like the application of state force, or how much intrusion into someone's private life is proportionate and justified. Where the popular cultural response to intelligence has changed over the last ten years is in the number of critical engagements with issues like profiling, technology, surveillance and whistleblowing, that have been distributed widely and enjoyed commercial success. This tells us a great deal about the evolving relationship between the public and intelligence services during this time, where the public's general mistrust of intelligence agencies following the Iraq War debacle in 2003 evolved further through the Cablegate release of diplomatic communications (Pieterse, 2012). This mistrust was compounded by Edward Snowden's revelations about dragnet surveillance within the Five Eyes group of nations (Greenwald, 2014; Snowden, 2019). Snowden had the unintended effect of undermining public trust in government intelligence, when one of his enduring campaigning points had been to highlight the daily and indiscriminate collection of personal data by private data brokerages and social media platforms, which have seen no commensurate drop-off in usage (Ruby, Goggin & Keane, 2017). Public support for intrusive surveillance has ebbed and flowed with anxiety about the prospect of more terrorist attacks across Europe, in part connected to the large numbers of migrants heading out of the Syrian civil war and towards Europe, which have been conflated in the media as a combined threat. The vacillations about terrorism and counterterrorism, and foreign espionage on our shores, pitched against the seemingly half-hearted and under-resourced attempts to counter this, have been expressed through popular cultural sources. Similarly, the decision of the British government in November 2019 to withhold the Intelligence and Security Committee's report into Russian interference in UK politics prior to the general election, when it was commonly felt that the governing Conservative Party would come in for serious criticism, added yet more public derision and mistrust (Corera, 2019). The report, eventually released in the summer of 2020, was heavily edited and suggested that the intelligence agencies had not looked for foreign interference and therefore had not found any (Intelligence and Security Committee of Parliament, 2020). This was another masterclass in the British establishment's desire to avoid difficult questions and even more difficult conclusions (Defty, 2020).

Popular cultural artefacts have a real-world impact on those consuming them. For a majority of the public, cinematic and televisual depictions of intelligence might be its only reference point to intelligence tradecraft. The nuance of the intelligence process, of analysis and assessment as a trade at all, what amounts to lawful and unlawful actions and what is proportionate and appropriate, are barely understood by the public, and indeed by students prior to them sitting specialist modules. So, the knowledge gleaned from books, films and television programmes is a form of docudrama, that has a privileged place in positioning the agencies, officers, the moral code and framing logics of our politics for the general public and as a version of the truth about the business of intelligence.

The education of the public, if that is what it is, about intelligence happens in the round. The role of newspapers, of popular contemporary history, and of compelling accounts of intelligence activity, such as Tom Marcus' two autobiographical books *Soldier Spy* (2017) and *I Spy* (2019), form this education in the round (Marcus, 2019). For analogies we should look to James Der Derian's MIME-NET and Andrew Chadwick's hybrid media system to understand how these disparate but reinforcing threats serve to create a strong and cohesive whole: they constantly create new realities in which policy makers and intelligence officers work, and the public responds. Phillipe Sands' book on torture (Sands, 2008), produced an alarming account of how far the imagined reality can influence the real world, whilst Glenn Greenwald's book on Snowden, and his autobiographical effort, illuminated much of the new reality in which the public exists but had not realised until recently (Greenwald, 2014; Snowden, 2019).

Popular culture is but one of many ways into the subject of intelligence agencies and the business of intelligence, but it forms the most persuasive, and often the most immediate and relatable version. Programmes focusing on events or issues that resonate for audiences on big-screen televisions draw the audience in, asking them to make emotional rather than rational decisions about events. We see torture becoming a rational form of intelligence collection when placed against a ticking time-bomb scenario. Intrusive surveillance, even dragnet surveillance, can seem proportionate and reasonable when placed in this dramatic context, particularly when the depiction of the software and techniques shows a fluid ubiquity to being able to pull out the right piece of information on demand. Similarly, intelligence officers are nearly always shown to be charismatically flawed, rather than—as we see from Edward Snowden's account—people who occasionally lapse into prurience, spying on former partners, or seeing how many webcams can be tapped for lurid footage (Ackerman & Ball, 2014). It is fortunate for both government and private company bulk collectors that the outlets that dominate the narrative around this are still seen as co-existing with activists and more fringe concerns, when these public policy questions should be front and centre of public discourse.

There should be a critical eye cast over an industry that has established and reinforced political and social norms and clichés ad nauseum. Our eye should become more critical when we tie the political and normative messages these outputs present with the enhanced distribution networks that are offered through subscription and direct payment streaming services, and—less legally—through torrented sharing: niche productions can find a more ready audience than in 2009. But we should also note that in the last ten years these classic intelligence tropes have been challenged by content that has questioned authority (notably *Eye in Sky*, 2015, or the film *Official Secrets*, 2019), or that has shown more complex and empathetic portrayals of intelligence officers, and indeed enemies (for example, the BBC drama series *Page Eight*, 2011 or *The Little Drummer Girl*, 2018), or that has sought to show the interaction of private actors in the intelligence realm (for example, the *Kingsman* films of 2015 and 2017, the TV mini-series *The Night Manager* of 2016, or the 2009 film *Duplicity*). In classic intelligence genre work, intelligence officers show 'gut-feeling' over analytical precision and this is nearly always successful. Similarly, they are acutely individualistic and often carrying a single, defining personality flaw. Their senior officers are nearly always politically involved, whilst ignoring compromised politicians—two things that are neither accurate nor positive signals about the nature of government intelligence. Furthermore, agents or informants are generally to be mistrusted, and moles and double agents invariably end up dead. The difficulty of running agents or working undercover seems to be most effectively delivered in contemporary historical dramas such as *The Americans* (2013–18), and *Deutschland 83* (2015). Fictionalised foreigners, particularly those from the Middle East or Asia, are particularly excitable and volatile. Politicians are driven exclusively by electoral advantage and ill-thought-out schemes—although reality may have followed art in this respect—whilst the enemy is invariably without scruple, pursuing a political agenda one would be hard-pressed to find in any sanatorium. The technologies involved in state espionage are always flawless, witness satellites always positioned in the right place, at the right time, rather than requiring multiple over-flight image runs. Imagery and signals intelligence are always in perfect view, giving clear sight to the analysts, who can bring incredibly disparate pieces of information together at lightning speed into cogent and actionable intelligence. The only time the British Joint Intelligence Committee is mentioned is when it suddenly acquires rogue tendencies in the long-running TV series *Spooks*. Realistic looking counterintelligence activity is largely confined to law enforcement dramas, such as *Luther* (2010–19) and *Line of Duty* (2012–21), in addition to the television and cinematic portrayal of *Tinker Tailor Soldier Spy* (1979 and 2011), whilst the best depictions of the interception of communications come in the tense TV series *The Wire* (2002–8) and the French police drama *Engrenages* (which I translate as the English word *gears* but which is translated by the distributors as *Spiral* in the UK) (2005–20).

Ultimately what purpose does spy entertainment serve? It is not a public information service, so it does not seek to directly inform, although it has sought (and achieved) to shape our encounters with security issues and the place of the Anglosphere in the world. The entertainment industry is part of a complex mix of inputs that include education, background and experience, through which we understand this important area of government life. And it is government life, because popular cultural portrayals are far more closely targeted towards government intelligence and far less so on private intelligence. So, these films, games, books and programmes are part of a 'fog of perception' that reinforces particular ways of thinking about the world, about power, surveillance, gender and race, and issues of war, terrorism, migration and so on. From the path dependencies these outputs create, our officials and politicians find themselves with less politically realistic scope to de-securitise their responses. The reality of this can be seen through the various counter-radicalisation programmes in the US and UK, which set out to carry out counterterrorism work differently but which ended up being viewed as having been co-opted by those who felt persecuted by these programmes and by some of those working within them. If we collectively treat this form of entertainment as a diversion from reality, showing emblematic fragments of intelligence activity, then we are unlikely to be seduced by its counterproductive charms, overreading it as a version of the real world. These cultural artefacts do confirm the logical underpinnings of a neoliberal way of the world, that is our dominant frame of understanding. From that point of view they not only represent the way our world works, but they help to perpetuate it.

References

Ackerman, S. and Ball, J. (2014) 'Optic nerve: Millions of Yahoo webcam images intercepted by GCHQ'. *The Guardian*, 28 February.

Aldrich, Richard (2010) *GCHQ: The Uncensored Story of Britain's Most Secret Intelligence Agency.* London: HarperCollins.

Alison, Emily and Alison, Laurence (2017) 'Revenge versus rapport: Interrogation, terrorism, and torture'. *American Psychologist* 72 (3), 266–277.

Bamford, James (2008) *The Shadow Factory: The Ultra-Secret NSA from 9/11 to the Eavesdropping on America.* New York, NY: Doubleday.

Bellaby, R. W. (2018) 'Extraordinary rendition: Expanding the circle of blame in international politics'. *The International Journal of Human Rights* 22 (4), 574–602.

Bennett, B. (2010) 'Framing terror: Cinema, docudrama and the "War on Terror"'. *Studies in Documentary Film* 24 (3), 09–225.

Blake, H. (2019) *From Russia with Blood: The Kremlin's Ruthless Assassination Program and Vladimir Putin's Secret War on the West.* London: Mulholland Press.

Blakeley, Ruth (2011) *State Terrorism and Neoliberalism.* London: Routledge.

Blakeley, Ruth and Raphael, Sam (2020) 'Accountability, denial and the future-proofing of British torture'. *International Affairs* 96 (3), 691–709.

Brassett, J. and Sutton, A. (2017) 'British satire, everyday politics: Chris Morris, Armando Iannucci and Charlie Brooker'. *The British Journal of Politics and International Relations* 19 (2), 245–262.

Corera, G. (2019) 'General election 2019: The mystery of the Russia report'. *BBC News*, 10 November. Accessed 11 November 2019. https://www.bbc.co.uk/news/uk-50366956

Daniel, J. F. and Musgrave, P. (2017) 'Synthetic experiences: How popular culture matters for images of international relations'. *International Studies Quarterly* 61 (3), 503–516.

Defty, A. (2020) 'The delayed publication of the Russia Report demonstrates why reform is needed to preserve the Intelligence and Security Committee's independence'. British Politics and Policy at the LSE [Blog]. 13 August. Accessed January 31, 2021. http://eprints.lse.ac.uk/106030/

Dershowitz, A. M. (2014) 'Reply: Torture without visibility and accountability is worse than with it'. *University of Pennsylvania Journal of Constitutional Law.* 326.

Diamond, D. (2008) 'Empathy and identification in von Donnersmarck's *The Lives of Others*'. *Journal of the American Psychoanalytic Association* 56 (3), 811–832.

Dodds, K. (2008) 'Hollywood and the popular geopolitics of the War on Terror'. *Third World Quarterly* 29 (8), 1621–1637.

Dyer, Owen (2016) 'Prosecution of US psychologists who ran CIA torture program moves a step closer'. *British Medical Journal*, 28 April 28, 353.

Garton-Ash, T. (2010) *The File: A Personal History*. New York, NY: Vintage.

Glenny, M. (2009) *McMafia: Seriously Organised Crime*. London: Vintage.

Greenwald, G. (2014) *No Place to Hide: Edward Snowden, the NSA, and the US Surveillance State*. New York, NY: Macmillan.

Henning, K. (2014) 'Teaching fiction? The Wire as a pedagogical tool in the examination of punishment theory'. *Journal of Legal Education* 64 (1), 120–122.

Higgins, E. (2021) *We Are Bellingcat: An Intelligence Agency for the People*. London: Bloomsbury.

Horne, C. and Horgan, J. (2012) 'Methodological triangulation in the analysis of terrorist networks'. *Studies in Conflict & Terrorism* 35 (2), 182–192.

Intelligence and Security Committee of Parliament (2020) *Russia*. London: UK Parliament.

Jenkins, T. (2016) *The CIA in Hollywood: How the Agency Shapes Film and Television*. Austin, TX: University of Texas Press.

Kay, J. B. (2020) 'Out of place: Women as linguistic interlopers in mediated political speech'. In J. B. Lay, *Gender, Media and Voice* (pp. 149–169). London: Palgrave Macmillan.

Kearns, E. M. and Young, J. K. (2018) '"If torture is wrong, what about 24?" Torture and the Hollywood effect'. *Crime & Delinquency* 64 (12), 1568–1589.

Le Carré, J. (2017) *A Legacy of Spies: A Novel*. London: Penguin.

Leslie, Ian (2017) 'The scientists persuading terrorists to spill their secrets'. *The Guardian*, 13 October.

Marcus, Tom (2019) *I Spy: My Life in MI5*. London: Macmillan.

Marks, D. F. (2018) 'American psychologists, the Central Intelligence Agency, and enhanced interrogation'. *Health Psychology Open* 5 (2), 1–2.

Nikolaidis, A. (2011) 'Televising counter terrorism: Torture, denial, and exception in the case of 24'. *Continuum: Journal of Media & Cultural Studies* 25 (2), 213–225.

Omand, D. (2020) *How Spies Think*. London: Penguin.

Pieterse, J. N. (2012) 'Leaking superpower: WikiLeaks and the contradictions of democracy'. *Third World Quarterly* 33 (10), 1909–1924.

Qurashi, F. (2018) 'The Prevent strategy and the UK "war on terror": Embedding infrastructures of surveillance in Muslim communities'. *Palgrave Communications* 4 (17), 1–13.

Rowley, C. and Weldes, J. (2012) 'The evolution of international security studies and the everyday: Suggestions from the Buffyverse'. *Security Dialogue* 43 (6), 513–530.

Ruby, F., Goggin, G. and Keane, J. (2017) '"Comparative Silence" still? Journalism, academia, and the Five Eyes of Edward Snowden'. *Digital Journalism* 5 (3), 353–367.

Sabbagh, Dan (2019) 'Killer drones: How many are there and who do they target?' *The Guardian*, 18 November. Accessed 27 November 2019. https://www.theguardian.com/news/2019/nov/18/killer-drones-how-many-uav-predator-reaper

Sands, P. (2008) 'Torture team: The responsibility of lawyers for abusive interrogation'. *Melbourne Journal of International Law* 9 (2), 365–390.

Schlag, G. (2019) 'Representing torture in *Zero Dark Thirty* (2012): Popular culture as a site of norm contestation'. *Media,War & Conflict* 14 (2), 1–17.

Shackle, S. (2020) 'The mystery of the Gatwick drone'. *The Guardian*, 1 December.

Shane, Scott (2012) 'Acting C.I.A. chief critical of film "Zero Dark Thirty"'. *The New York Times*, 22 December.

Shepherd, L. (2012) *Gender, Violence and Popular Culture: Telling Stories.* Abingdon: Routledge.

Snowden, E. (2019) *Permanent Record.* New York, NY: Pan Macmillan.

Snyder, R. L. (2020) 'Secret cold warriors: John le Carré's A Legacy of Spies'. *Orbis Litterarum* 75 (1), 15–23.

Stockwell, S. (2005) 'The manufacture of world order: The security services and the movie industry'. *M/C Journal* 7 (6), 1–8.

Suskind, R. (2006) *One Percent Doctrine: Deep Inside America's Pursuit of Its Enemies Since 9/11.* New York, NY: Simon & Schuster.

The Intelligence and Security Committee of Parliament (2020) *Russia Report.* London: HMSO.

The Washington Post (2001) 'Interview with Dick Cheney'. *The Washington Post.* 16 September. Accessed 12 November 2019. https://www.washingtonpost.com/wp-srv/nation/specials/attacked/transcripts/cheney091601.html

Twomey, R. (2020) 'Superheros, Dickens, and uncertain endings: *The Wire*'s authentic characters'. In R. Twomey, *Examining the Wire* (pp. 59–94). London: Palgrave.

US Department of State (2001–9) *Initial Report of the United States of America to the UN Committee Against Torture.* https://2001-2009.state.gov/g/drl/rls/index.htm, accessed 17 November 2022.

US Senate Select Committee on Intelligence (SSCI) (2014) *Study of the Central Intelligence Agency's Detention and Interrogation Program.* https://

www.intelligence.senate.gov/sites/default/files/publications/CRPT-113srpt288.pdf, accessed 17 May 2022.

Welch, M. (2017) 'Doing special things to special people in special places: Psychologists in the CIA torture program'. *The Prison Journal* 97 (6), 729–749. https://2001-2009.state.gov/g/drl/rls/index.htm (accessed 18 May 2022).

Willmetts, S. (2016) *In Secrecy's Shadow: The OSS and CIA in Hollywood Cinema 1941–1979*. Edinburgh: Edinburgh University Press.

Wisnewski, J. J. (2008) 'Unwarranted torture warrants: A critique of the Dershowitz proposal'. *Journal of Social Philosophy* 39 (2), 308–321.

Zetter, K. (2014) 'How to keep the NSA from spying through your webcam'. *Wired*, 14 March.

Zizek, Slavoj (2009) *Violence*. New York, NY: Profile Books.

9

FUTURE TECHNOLOGICAL ADVANCES AND THEIR IMPACT ON INTELLIGENCE

What You Need to Know...

Intelligence will continue to be a technology business. It will continue to develop tradecraft and technologies premised on existing technologies, seeking to gain advantage from expanding the possibilities that exist within current platforms. These include in AI, in speech recognition and facial tracking, and in communications intelligence. Government agencies will also continue to support technologists in developing strategically significant innovations like quantum computing, genomics for surveillance and investigations, and a wider array of deployable surveillance devices such as ground drones. As happened with Web 2.0, governments and agencies are currently developing technologies more rapidly than they are developing and refining the use cases, the ethics around usage and the possible societal implications of these technologies. The importance of these technologies is partly the additional investigative traction they provide, but also that they reduce the scope for dissent and alternative values, political discourse and narrative. These future technologies have the potential to change further our relationship with the state and the balance in our relationship with computerised technologies.

***

Intelligence has become a technology business. All capable intelligence nations have a strong presence in technical intelligence, be it through interception, surveillance, processing raw data or analysis. Earlier chapters explored the crossover between popular cultural depictions of surveillance and the real-world capacity of intelligence agencies. One of the starkest examples I provided was where some US agencies—in the case of the film *Enemy of the State*—considered legal action against the producers, so convinced were they that they had been assisted by insider leaks.

The technology to intercept communications, to track whereabouts, and to assess personal preferences and judge the real-world social networks an individual operates within, is impressive. The common response of politicians seeking to justify the use of ever more capable technology and techniques is that in the wrong hands these technologies would be concerning. But in their hands, the technologies enhance the security of the nation and the security of us humble citizens within it. As we have seen with the recent debates around the (erroneous) use of NSO's Pegasus platform to spy on activists and journalists, the space for political dissent has narrowed with the development, improvement and roll-out of intrusive technologies (Gurijala, 2021). I often take the examples of the universal enfranchisement movement in the UK (known commonly as the Suffragettes) and the anti-apartheid movement in South Africa to discuss with my students what would be the likelihood of either of these universally acknowledged positive political and social developments occurring in today's surveillance societies. Examples from even the most recent 2022 Winter Olympics demonstrate how a capable government—in this case China—can amplify the control of its own messages, whilst suppressing the messages of critics: an example of message manipulation and population control (Myers, Mozur & Kao, 2022). The conclusion the classes often reach is that it would be far more difficult for these groups to achieve the same today. That should give us pause for thought: it is dangerous to think that we have reached the end of human development.

In the light of this Suffragette and anti-apartheid thought experiment, is it the case that the real safeguards we have against the misuse of such technologies by intelligence agencies are their lack of resources (be it personnel or money), or the effectiveness of the regulatory environment they work within? If we accept that this is the case, and I would add the necessity for us to remain living in political systems that accept plurality, then the development of automated systems—which removes some of the human decision component and the necessity for large pools of human resource—should be of concern. That would place a greater emphasis on political systems accepting plurality and on accepting strong regulatory oversight, two things that have been notably challenged in the United States and the UK since 2016. As has been argued throughout this book, it is not necessary for intelligence officers to be conscious of their role in the political or ideological contest: the structural conditioning of their training, their structures and contexts provides the consistency of framework to operate effectively.

This chapter provides a horizon scan of how the technological developments we are seeing today, and which are in their infancy, will challenge and often facilitate intelligence activity in the future. The chapter explores this with regard to the strategic level of international politics, at how intelligence and criminal investigations will be impacted, on technological developments with computing, processing, sensors, on the evolution of decentralised finance and privacy technologies, and the metaverse as a significant development in the internet. The established literature tends to view these developments purely as value-neutral technological developments. As the work of Sana Rahim shows us, the value-neutrality of science and engineering is actually highly political, and so it is in the realms in this chapter (Rahim, 2021). The development of the metaverse is the most obviously political, as it seeks to augment the analogue world we live in with a virtual reality overlay—the replication and development of political and social norms will be striking in these virtual realities. The more obviously technical developments are not overtly political but they do serve to reinforce the political vision and system that is deploying them. We applaud ourselves when intelligence capabilities are used in defence of a system we admire, and we decry it when it is one we fear or oppose. Collectively, we should be more reflective about this.

Strategic Concerns

The Russian war of aggression against Ukraine that began in February 2022 (still ongoing at the time of writing) highlights the opportunities and challenges of the network-enabled international economic and information system. The Ukrainian military and government were strongly ahead of the Russians in their information campaign in the early weeks of the war. President Zelensky's daily vlog, the content produced by embedded journalists (some of whom sadly paid with their lives) and a legion of citizen journalists uploading footage, along with collaboration with open source intelligence verifiers, like Bellingcat and @OSINT_Eye_ on Twitter, verified timestamps and geo-locations to provide measures of accuracy on the footage coming out of the theatre of operations. Unlike the Nuremberg Trials at the end of the Second World War, the war crimes being committed in Ukraine will not need to be solely evidenced from survivor testimony. The evidence used in any potential war crimes trials will come from images and videos captured on mobile phones, on CCTV, and stored in the cloud or posted on social media and given an indelible record in cyberspace (Chouliaraki, 2015; Karstedt, 2010).

The war against Ukraine is clearly a military conflict. At its barest it is a conflict for territory and control. But it is also an economic and information conflict, too. The strength and immediacy of the economic sanctions placed upon Russia, upon key figures in Russia and upon Russian interests outside its borders came as a surprise to the politicians involved, as it did to commentators and academics, even if some were sceptical about the impact the sanctions would have (BBC, 2022; Popov, 2022). This surprising level of post-Cold War cohesion amounted to a reinforcement of maligned and undermined norms around self-determination, freedom and choice: the norms that had been allowed to be eroded through the weak response to Russian influence and disruption operations across the whole of the North Atlantic area. In the UK, for example, the National Crime Agency (often described as the UK's FBI) was provided with dedicated resource and it pooled resources with full members of the UK intelligence community to create a Kleptocracy Unit to work on disrupting the proceeds of crime being allegedly laundered through London, albeit not one receiving additional funds (Hinds, 2022; Mendick, 2022; Pickard, 2022). This is in stark contrast to the scant attention the NCA received in the government's *Integrated Review of Security and Defence*, just two years earlier (Levi, 2021). The UK government's promise to reform the registers covering the ownership of land and businesses had been called for by anti-corruption campaigners but had been stalled for more than five years. In the eventuality it required the strategic shock of Russia's invasion of Ukraine and the foreign policy imperative of restricting the movement of Russian wealth to persuade the UK government to act on this (Cooley, Heathershaw & Sharman, 2018). Critics of the British government's role in dealing with corrupt finances, such as Oliver Bullough, doubt these changes will be impactful (Bullough, 2022). Irrespective of the British government's effectiveness in enforcement, which seems contested, the reinforcement of liberal political values has—at the time of writing—taken on a whole-of-government and whole-of-society dimension. This is a war-like disposition and makes the Euro—Atlantic area's response to Russian aggression not only a war of production in terms of arms transfers, but also a war of economic attrition, particularly towards commodities and energy, and a conflict of ideas, ideology and framing logics.

In the cyber-realm and information campaign, commentators, including myself, pointed to the considerable successes the Russian military have enjoyed in the last decade against Western targets as a sign of what was likely to follow, prior to the Ukraine military campaign (Dover, 2022; Nayar, 2021; Oxford Analytica, 2022b). My assessment was that targets would be found in core infrastructure, on government websites, and in disinformation campaigns that gained traction, to really test the cohesion and morale of Western societies. At the time of writing, the Russian cyber-machine has spent more of its time defending against cyber intrusions by Ukrainian assets, a volunteer force from Anonymous, and—one assumes—from Western technical intelligence assets attacking Russian installations. Notably, the Russian Defence Ministry website was attacked once to extract the names and addresses of those serving in the Ukrainian invasion campaign, and the defence ministry and state television were attacked to show footage of the campaign and its impact upon Ukrainian citizens, in direct contrast to the disinformation being broadcast by the Russian government in its denial that these military operations were occurring (Chrinios, 2022; Pitrelli, 2022). Informed analysts still predict that as the Russian campaign continues to suffer unexpected difficulties, the military will escalate its cyber-attacks on Ukrainian and Western targets, including those of core infrastructure (Halpern, 2022).

The importance of the control and nature of information in war has been ably demonstrated by the first month of conflict in Ukraine (Pomerantsev, 2021). The decision by Facebook and Twitter to allow calls for violence against Russian military targets and being openly partisan is—in part—a business decision to avoid the negative publicity of running Russian disinformation to support what—for them—is the tiny Russian market for their services (Vengattil & Culliford, 2022). The information domain also sees the suppression of the free press in Russia as partly a demonstration of potentially how vulnerable Putin is to a popular domestic backlash against his war and as partly an opportune moment for him to start to reinforce the necessary apparatus around his increasingly authoritarian regime (US State Department, 2022). The decision of the EU to remove the broadcaster *RT* from satellite feeds into mainland Europe (and by consequence the UK) is itself a complex ethical matter and a decision to adopt an illiberal stance against freedom of speech, on the grounds of countering disinformation (Kayali, 2022). The reality is, however, that, in the UK, *RT* was watched by an estimated 15,000 viewers a day, whilst most of its viewers were actually sourced via its YouTube landing page (Crilley & Chatterje-Doody, 2020). The advantages, to the West, of retaining a number of journalists able to report from Russia far outweigh the advantages of shutting off *RT* from those who are already pre-disposed to receiving pro-Putin newsfeeds (Waterson, 2022). A number of populist European figures, who had in years past expressed their (sometimes qualified) admiration for Putin, found themselves belatedly on the wrong side of history as European sentiment turned so starkly against Russia and against anyone not directly opposed to Putin and his invasion (Horowitz, 2022; *The Guardian*, 2022). The prior political and media complacency in defending liberal values of the previous decade seemed to crystallise into a strong response immediately after the Russian invasion on the 24 February 2022.

Prior to Russia's invasion of Ukraine, the strategic impact of technology on international relations and intelligence as a facet of international relations had been centred on the information and influence domain, the acquisition (by fair means or foul) of intellectual property, and the vulnerability of the undersea data cables that form the internet's plumbing (Karatzogianni & Aldrich, 2020). Whilst the strong debate around, and then exclusion of, the Chinese firm Huawei from US government contracts in 2019, and reaffirmed in 2020, focused on the vulnerability to China's technical intelligence efforts, the COVID-19 pandemic shifted attention onto fundamental supply issues (Dunn & Leibovici, 2021). The controversy around Huawei stemmed from the perception that it was owned by the Chinese government and furthermore took instruction from government agencies (Inkster, 2019). The moves to ban Huawei could also be interpreted as part of the competition around 'who owns and runs the internet' (Haggart, Tusikov & Scholte, 2021). The US successfully excluding Huawei from the Euro–Atlantic area paves the way for the Five Eyes group of nations to retain its dominance in surveillance of internet traffic and usage (Tang, 2020). Control, interception, storage and analysis of communications data is a key twenty-first century battleground, representing not only military priorities but the reinforcement of political and social norms as it curtails the actions of competitors.

The disrupted supply of computer chips in 2021 and 2022, caused by the outsized demand for home computing during the COVID-19 lockdowns, has provided a renewed focus on the future of the strategically important island of Taiwan, upon which China has a territorial claim. This issue tests our collective response to the challenges of globalisation in the face of hostile powers, such as China and Russia. Such is the importance of the Taiwan Semiconductor Manufacturing Co.'s facilities to the global supply of electronics that military analysts have considered the prospect that a threat to destroy them might serve to dissuade a Chinese military invasion to repatriate the territory (McKinney & Harris, 2021). In a response to McKinney and Harris, Eric Chan countered that expatriating

Taiwanese chip expertise to the United States or blockading Taiwan would be a more effective course of action, given the dangers to the global economy of disrupting the production of electronics (Chan, 2022). The notion of economic war, which has been evoked by the US, the EU and Russia over the situation in Ukraine, has these wider resonances, particularly when it comes to strategically important and contested locations like Taiwan and the political and economic fallout of military operations there. Whether the Five Eyes nations have the strategic intelligence expertise to assess these threats and to support government decision making to respond to them is open to question. The frailty of the globalised economic system seems, post the 2008 economic crisis, during the opening phases of the COVID-19 pandemic and now during the Ukrainian conflict, beyond doubt. The role of Western intelligence will be to help their governments navigate and mitigate these frailties.

Future Intelligence Investigations

Edward Snowden's revelations in 2013 demonstrated how far ahead of regulations and the law intelligence officers and law enforcers can get with technological improvements (Johnson *et al.*, 2014). As a result, investigatory powers—the lawful measures to impinge upon an individual's privacy and other rights—take on an even greater importance. The regulations over investigations are difficult to keep relevant in an era of technological and tradecraft advancements. Investigatory powers, as a discreet area of public policy, also sits in the middle of strong competing interests from information regulators, competition regulators and those seeking to mitigate online harms. Trying to find a common way that does not negatively impact on the work of these other interests and agencies has proved to be a complex balance for policy officials to attempt to strike.

The pooling and sharing of large amounts of data has similarly proved to be contentious, with Brexit producing the unedifying situation of the National Crime Agency being found to have unlawfully copied and retained data from the Europol databases as a means to avoid a cliff edge of deprived access on the day after the UK's exit from the EU (Shellaker, 2021). On the continent itself,

Europol had to be granted additional time to put its data warehouses in order in 2021, as it also grappled and struggled with the effects of privacy legislation (Europol, 2022).

From the point of view of law enforcement officers, the restrictions on what they can achieve through online investigations run at significant cross purposes with the public perception. Whilst any ordinary citizen can use search engines to scour the web, or search within social media platforms for information about a colleague, a friend or a new acquaintance, an official needs to secure permission to do so, and must be able to provide a rationale as to what they are looking for, what they expect to find, and how it will assist the investigation of a crime or other kind of threat (Crown Prosecution Service, 2020). Paradoxically, then, an inquisitive citizen can achieve more (without permission) than a law enforcement officer using basic web-tools. This asymmetry of power is, of course, there to provide a bulwark against law enforcement dragnets and to provide a thin notion of privacy in the internet age. Government officials are quick to point out that an individual's privacy is better protected from intelligence or law enforcement intrusion than it is from the intrusion of private interests or private platforms. As noted earlier, Russia's war against Ukraine, which began in February 2022, also highlighted the power of organised open source intelligence organisations that used sophisticated open source techniques to attack a problem. Even more interestingly, they publish their techniques—their tradecraft, if you prefer—openly online, allowing anyone to see what they can find (Bellingcat, 2022).

Moving away from tradecraft and into embryonic technologies, one area of potential exploration for future investigators is genomic sequencing. Fully sequenced genomes are far more extensive than the so-called 'short-tandem-repeat' analyses used for profiling offender DNA (UK Government Office for Science, 2022). The UK government's report on genomic sequences notes:

> There are correlations between certain genes and characteristics that can influence criminal behaviour. Alleles of the MAOA (Monoamine Oxidase A) gene have been linked to aggressive behaviour. Substance Abuse Disorders (SUD) have been linked

to specific genes, with a tendency to abuse substances having high heritability. (UK Government Office for Science, 2022, p. 142)

Such a conclusion would lend itself to the kind of predictive policing where an individual would not need to have committed an offence to come under suspicion.

The Office for Science authors provide very strong cautions about the future ethical challenges in this area and even suggest that future government investigators should be prohibited from accessing genomic data, to avoid creating social harms. In this regard, the report is quite unusual for an official scoping paper about future technologies. Such reports very rarely foreground considerations about proportionality ahead of any potential use cases and the development of an experimental evidence base: this is how many of the technologies and techniques that were revealed by Snowden came into use. In this case it may be that the additional reach of genomic data has provided an unusual amount of concern and thus encouraged the Office for Science to apply a strong precautionary principle. The enforcement of political and social norms through the combined action of intelligence and law enforcement may well be far easier with the sort of biological reach that is available, firstly in being able to identify offenders or those dissenting, and similarly being able to predict genetically who is more likely to dissent.

The rapid development of drone technologies has created additional overflying surveillance in our skies. Often these are privately operated drones being used for recreational purposes. The impact of military drones has been felt in the Afghan conflict, and more recently in the Ukrainian theatre of war, too. In terms of future use cases, there have been various developments of robot infantry (that has been much contested in the military realm around whether they are permitted to kill autonomously) but, in the law enforcement and intelligence space, the use of robot dogs has become an emerging feature of the United States' attempts to secure its southern borders. These technologies have been attractive to US border agents due to the dangers there are for personnel in these contested spaces and that the environment is so inhospitable to living dogs. Robot dogs are, in these circumstances, ground drones that supplement the insights provided by aerial drones (Department of Homeland Security, 2022). These ground-level drones are certainly not aesthetically pleasing, as they look dog-like enough to be recognisable but do not look as friendly as canines.

The presence of robot dogs on the streets changes something tangible in the relationship between society and government agencies. The animal-like qualities of a robotised canine are tangibly different to the static surveillance of CCTV or the mechanised qualities of small drones. The hybridisation of robot dogs resonates more with dystopian fiction like the 2011 novel *Robopocalypse,* than it does with a reasonable public policy response (Wilson, 2011). There are drone technologies that seek to address the tension between robots and humans, in particular to create synthetic biology. The University of Bristol has developed something it describes as the 'liquid-amplified zipping actuator', which is a technical way of describing an artificial muscle that creates its flapping wing without a motor of gearing. The developers argue that this helps them reduce the weight, cost and complexity of surveillance drones, and presumably also reduces the extent to which population observation is being carried out by devices that are obviously robotic (Helps *et al.*, 2022).

Privacy and Cryptocurrency

The loose collective of public interest hackers, known as Anonymous, made this prescient observation about identity and privacy:

> Identity. One of our most precious possessions. You believe we all have one, but you are sadly mistaken. Identity belongs only to those who are important. Those who have earned it by struggle and blood. Those who matter. You my friend, do not. Identity is a fragile and weak thing. It can be stolen or replaced. Even forgotten. Identity is a pointless thing for people like us. So why not let go of it and become Anonymous? (Deseriis, 2015, p. 165)

The comfortable assumptions about identity that existed before the internet age—that one's identity was straightforwardly established and that there was space for private exchanges—began to be tested by contested revelations that intelligence services routinely intercepted communications (Campbell, 1988; Machon, 2005). In the early 2000s very little mainstream concern was expressed about intrusions into privacy from governments or from internet platforms. The revelations by Edward Snowden, and those surrounding Spy Cops and the alleged use of identities stolen from dead babies, up to the most recent investigative journalism into the Pegasus intrusions, have brought the subject into sharp relief, with their being a strong market segment for stronger privacy technologies (Lewis & Evans, 2013). The growing media interest in NSO's iPhone Pegasus exploit has increased the attention on some of their competitors, such as QuaDream, and on firms who have been accused of trying to buy intrusive access to European communications networks (Bing & Satter, 2022; Timberg, 2022). The space and the scope for individuals to enjoy private communications, or space to develop their thoughts, have been curtailed. The growing incidence of identity theft, and developments in technologies where one's avatar identity might be as valuable as one's analogue identity, also suggest that intelligence officers will have a great deal of complexity to contend with, but also a good number of additional opportunities as well.

Instant messaging technologies (WhatsApp, Lane, Telegram and Signal) have attracted negative commentaries where they have been used to spread hate speech and similarly been used in the criminal exploitation of individuals (Quinn, 2021). In response to the workarounds used to services that autodelete messages, which has further enabled the generation of explicit content, some of the more popular messaging services are moving to a system where users will be notified when disappearing messages are screenshotted in their end-to-end encrypted conversations (Perez, 2022a). An alert of this kind is likely to be incorporated into WhatsApp (the messaging app with the largest user base), significantly reducing the likelihood of it being used in criminal enterprise and other types of abuse.

Western governments have bemoaned the role that even commercial encryption is having on complicating and slowing the work of investigators and intelligence officers (Veen & Boeke, 2021). Consequently, there have been some misguided proposals and attempts to outlaw encryption, something that would undermine some important networked communication technologies such as banking and secure communications (Ball, 2022). In an influential public blog, two GCHQ officials proposed six principles governing exceptional intrusion into communications (Levy & Robindon, 2018). These principles were:

(1) intrusion into end-to-end encrypted communication should be exceptional;
(2) intelligence tradecraft will evolve to meet the technological changes, and service providers should not build in measures to trip lawful access when there is no benefit to customers;
(3) investigators should not expect access one hundred percent of the time;
(4) there should be no unfettered official access;
(5) measures should not negatively impact on the trust between the public and their service providers; and
(6) there should be transparency about what the government intercepts and why.

Such principles echo those of Sir David Omand, with his stricture that intrusive intelligence efforts should always be a last resort, proportionate, targeted and appropriate (Omand, 2010).

As the privacy debate continues to evolve, the plans of developers like DuckDuckGo to move into the desktop browser business are likely to draw users away from Google and Microsoft browsers, which are not seen as being privacy focused (Weinberg, 2021). The presence of an encrypted desktop browser—in addition to TOR, which only has negative connotations associated with dark-web markets—is likely to cause mainstream browser providers like Google to pivot towards privacy-centric versions of their products, too (Jardine, Lindner & Owenson, 2020). As a growing disruptor in internet browsing, DuckDuckGo has linked its products in email protection, app tracking and privacy browser. If DuckDuckGo succeeds in taking a reasonable proportion of users, we might reason that that this will spur investors in other companies to demand the same from them. It may also trigger further privacy evolutions in Windows' and Apple's operating system, protecting individual privacy whilst potentially hindering intelligence officers in their investigative work.

Whilst there clearly is some interest in privacy and anonymity technologies, it is likely to require a strategic-level shock to generate a mainstream appetite for decentralised internet networks such as that developed by San Francisco-based Pollen Mobile (https://www. pollenmobile.io/) (Korosec & Matney, 2022). In Pollen's model, there is a decentralised data-only mobile network of 'flowers' (radio towers), 'bumblebees' (connectivity validators) and 'hummingbirds' (phones), which tries to incentivise private operators to install radio towers ('flowers') costing between $1,000 and $10,000, with the promise of PollenCoin cryptocurrency as a reward for the quality and quantity of data these towers transmit. There are a lot of moving parts in this disruptive internet model, but it would provide a privacy offer to local communities and require technical intelligence to get physically closer to these networks to be able to intercept them. The anonymity projects that have been typified by decentralised finance are applicable in other contexts and the architecture of the internet is an obvious vulnerability for those advocating for meaningful privacy.

In the cryptocurrency or decentralised finance (DeFi) sector (that is virtual currency, underpinned by blockchain ledgers—the ledger being revalidated across all computers hosting it), adoption has reached the stage of it permeating into popular consciousness, even if the numbers holding cryptocurrency investments have been relatively small. Cryptocurrencies offer the promise of anonymous ownership and have been widely adopted by criminals seeking to place their funds out of the reach of investigators and tax authorities (Kethineni & Cao, 2020). There have been efforts made to de-anonymise ledgers, and some successes to this end, too (Gaihre, Pandey & Liu, 2019). Crypto-mixers (where coins are repeatedly exchanged to disguise their end beneficiary) are growing in popularity for those seeking to hide their assets (Stevens, 2022). Consequently, law enforcement intelligence agencies are seeking ways to defeat the utility and usage of mixers.

The continued growth of decentralised finance is premised upon several factors. The first is the exceptional returns realised by early adopters of Bitcoin (in particular). The second is the perception of government over-reach into people's finances. The Canadian government freezing the assets of protesting truck drivers is an example cited by DeFi proponents (Oxford Analytica, 2022a). Similarly, Ukrainians seeking a place to park their assets whilst the war continues, and Russians seeking to get around banking sanctions, are similarly driving adoption and price, as drug cartels and organised crime interests did in the early evolution of Bitcoin (De, 2022). There is also a respectability threshold being crossed: when companies like PayPal provide a limited cryptocurrency offer, it convinces retail investors it is a legitimate store of value, and potentially expands the usage of certain coins with a social shopping offer (Baur & Dimpfl, 2021). The encrypted messaging service, Signal, is also working to integrate cryptocurrency into its platform, to some resistance from those who think it will be a magnet to organised crime and then attract regulators to examine Signal as a communications platform (Newton, 2022). PayPal has announced its intention to launch a so-called stablecoin pegged to the US dollar, in other words a virtual dollar, a more reliable way of engaging in foreign exchange; the Bank of England is also developing what most describe as the 'Brit Coin', an official and yet similar proposition. Stablecoins do not, however, offer the privacy features of fully fledged cryptocurrencies.

Internet of Things: Smart Cities and Homes

The Internet of Things—spaces connected by sensors and network communications—has been relatively mainstream since 2012 (Kumar, Tiwari & Zymbler, 2019). Most modern homes in the Euro–Atlantic area will have some form of 'smart' device, even if this is limited to a smart meter to measure a home's use of electricity and gas. One of the barriers to the wider spread adoption of Internet of Things devices has been the absence of common standards and cross-platform integration. This is finally being addressed by Amazon, Apple, Google and Samsung (as the leading developers of smart devices) through an initiative called Matter, which was a headline event at the 2022 Consumer Electronics Show (Tuohy, 2022). The adoption of a common standard should have the effect of broadening the development of other smart items, but also make it simpler for technical intelligence to build long-lasting and impactful data extraction tools for digital forensics and other kinds of intelligence work. Such efforts are being mirrored by Google's plans for the Android ecosystem that will allow Chromebook users to sync chat and, via Bluetooth, to further sync wearables (smart watches, exercise devices), computers and televisions and so on into one cloud space (Kay, 2022). In a very similar way to the standardisation of the Internet of Things, these developments in Apple and now in Android make the life of investigators far easier.

For its part, Amazon's Sidewalk platform, when matched with its own 5G service, shows an intention to have sensors and therefore data aggregation over estate-sized spaces, whilst IBM continues to deploy sensors across larger conurbations (Bermbach *et al.*, 2021). All told, these offer those with investigatory powers an expanded horizon of information from which to scan for threats in the future.

Artificial Intelligence

Artificial intelligence (AI), more accurately described as machine learning, has promised much in terms of being able to intelligently and adaptively analyse large datasets in place of human analysts. For some, AI raises the prospect of a *Minority Report* dystopia, where a computer system would be capable of predicting a propensity for criminality before any offence had been committed and to take action against them (see the brief discussion about genomics earlier in this chapter) (Spielberg, 2002). For others, AI is a growth area that has yet to come to any kind of meaningful fruition, and has—instead— heralded the warehousing of data for future intelligence use.

The main use case for AI in the intelligence world is in the sophisticated assessment of large datasets: in essence to produce trend analysis that demonstrates outlier behaviour that pre-signals a threat or demonstrates a strategically important development. The obvious vulnerability from this is that initial coding then becomes compounded as the AI draws in data and progressively confirms biases within its initial coding. These unintended outcomes of the use of AI have been seen in the intelligent conversation tool reverting quickly to racist tropes, and the inability of facial recognition to adequately handle non-white faces (Ruiz, 2019). The extent to which these relatively early examples of AI add to our understanding is currently under some tension; that they are often considered by end-users to be unchallengeable and objective should be concerning for those who realise that human development has occurred through multiple scientific challenges.

Further developments in AI have begun to include self-coding programmes, further embedding initial and compounded biases. DeepMind's AlphaCode has reached a level of sophistication that means it can solve open-ended coding problems to a similar level of skill as a proficient professional coder (DeepMind, 2022). This extends the previous best example of an AI programmer—OpenAI's Copilot, which was able to complete lines of code rather than generate them from fresh (Thompson, 2022). The choice that society makes if it allows AI programmers to become mainstreamed is that essentially human choices will reside with sophisticated pieces of computer code. This would be a dramatic extension of the sort of political dystopia presented by Adam Curtis when he famously explored the impact of rational choice theory on public policy, rendering citizens as passengers to developments in society (Curtis, 2007).

Machine-learning tools and their ability to learn during their deployment has fascinating uses in speech and visual recognition, particularly in lip-reading. Visual speech recognition, which makes a highly confident prediction of what was said by analysing lip movements has obvious applications in video surveillance exploitation, from mainstream intelligence analysis through to dynamic keyword-spotting that identifies a real-time threat in a public place. At governmental level, the research into this area has been with very specialised small businesses, or research units. The announcement that Meta AI is releasing a self-supervised audio-visual speech recognition tool, free for non-commercial users, moves this technology on greatly (Meta AI, 2022). The Audio-Visual Hidden Unit BERT (AV-HuBERT) is the first such platform to model speech and lip movements together from unlabelled video data. Meta AI claims that AV-HuBERT delivers an additional 20% accuracy over the leading visual-only models, with one-thousandth of the training data. Meta AI's announced use case is for noisy factory floors where an augmented reality platform (through an updated version of Google Glass) could deliver what someone was trying to say into your ear (Meta AI, 2022). The intelligence case—not presented by Meta AI—is that it can also be used in surveillance operations, where an officer can get clear line of sight to one of the targets but not get within hearing range. Such technology further reduces the space in which an individual can enjoy privacy and increases the ability to enforce social and political norms. As the Trump era, and now the chilling of even basic freedoms in Russia, demonstrates, society needs to be very sure that political plurality is guaranteed before allowing powerful tools that can suppress this plurality to be readily available.

To that end the use of AI to create what is known as deep fake videos—that is, videos that are both highly convincing but are entirely fictionalised—has the potential to be used to create strategic effect. Deep fake technology was used in the Russian campaign against Ukraine in March 2022. A video pushed out on YouTube by the Russian government, of President Zelensky, was quickly established to be a highly convincing 'deep fake' (Burgess, 2022; Ukrainian Defence Intelligence, 2022). If the broadcast of such a deep fake was believed by a significant cleavage in society, it might well have served to undermine morale or cause Ukrainian soldiers or citizens to surrender. Whilst the impact on Ukraine would be extreme, we can easily predict smaller scale impacts of a similar nature in any developed society.

Quantum Computing

Quantum computing is a paradigm shift in computing. Based on developments found in theoretical physics around quantum mechanics, quantum computing essentially computes in 3D and harnesses the collective properties of quantum states, such as superposition, interference, and entanglement, to perform its calculations. Where classic computers work on binary systems of a state of 1 or 0, quantum systems have been simplified as being capable of holding a state that is both 1 and 0 simultaneously. Scott Aaronson describes quantum computing as the sifting and sorting of observable and non-observable answers, which is particularly useful for examining integers, which are the essence of cryptography

(Aaronson, 2021). Because of the way that quantum computers complete their calculations, IBM mooted that calculation that takes a modern desktop computer a week to complete, takes one of their quantum computers a second to do.

Currently quantum computers are not thought to be terribly useful as regular computers, such as you or I would use as a work machine but they are very adept at working through integer factorisations. There is a persuasive school of thought that state-sponsored hackers (be they government or military officers or privateers paid by governments) are engaged in the wholesale theft of private data in preparation for the day when quantum computers can decrypt the information to confer advantage (O'Neill, 2021). Currently, there are relatively few working quantum computers, partly because of the complexity of their production, partly in the scarcity of some of the components required in their manufacture, partly because of the considerable maintenance and operating conditions they require (including substantial refrigeration), and because of the relative scarcity of those able to programme them (Fukui & Takeda, 2022). Amongst NATO and EU states, quantum computers are considered to be military technology, and therefore the IP and use cases are protected by restrictions and official secrecy (Clarke & Knake, 2019). Developments in quantum computing have been heavily funded by public money, as governments were quick to realise the strategic implications of being able to break standard cryptography, following the theoretical work done on this subject in the 1990s (Hadesty, 2011; Shim & Tahan, 2016).

There are other security related applications to quantum computing: there is a growing opportunity for synthetic biology, important to understand and defend from chemical and biological threats, another area in which China has made greater strides. Similarly, there has been a use case established in radar, where quantum radar researchers achieved a 60-fold improvement in locating small drones (Lee, 2022; Zhuang & Shapiro, 2022). The use for quantum radar currently sits in the defence realm, where it will uncover stealth capabilities. What this might do is to drive the acquisition of hypersonic capabilities, where they move so quickly that being detected does not yet assist in neutralising them. Quantum radar's applicability to drones will help in disrupting criminal enterprise and the use of drones as spotters in war zones: something that will be a significant issue until the end of the Ukrainian conflict, which may well run for several years.

Quantum computing will spark a form of arms race when it comes to the opportunities and threats from synthetic biology. The NSA's Chief of Research, Gil Herrera, noted that the US was a little behind in this area of quantum computing, which suggests an avenue for NATO cooperation, and also for potential exploitation by China, which is an acknowledged leader in AI technologies (Howell-O'Neill, 2022).

Metaverse

The concept of the metaverse is still being developed and is highly contested. At essence, though, there is common ground that the metaverse is interconnected 3D virtual realities (Mystakidis, 2022). Facebook's own articulation of the metaverse is:

> The metaverse will feel like a hybrid of today's online social experiences, sometimes expanded into three dimensions or projected into the physical world. It will let you share immersive experiences with other people even when you can't be together—and do things together you couldn't do in the physical world. (Facebook, 2021)

Authentic metaverse relies upon the interconnection of independent virtual worlds, and to do this requires the creation of immersive realism in the offering, that all internet users can access it, agreed standards around identity, interoperability, and scalability, much as the original internet and Web 2.0 have enjoyed (Dionisio, Burns & Gilbert, 2013). Across the winter months in 2021 into 2022, there was a great deal of consumer activity that suggests some demand for these services, with 2 million downloads of Meta's Oculus platform in the winter holiday season, developments by Apple for their new headset, Microsoft looking to embed AR in smaller and lighter weight glasses, and Sony bringing forward details of their new eye-tracking VR headset for this year (Perez, 2022b). The need for an intermediary technology will be the major hindrance in the adoption of the Metaverse.

Facebook—as one of the world's largest social media and advertising companies—has sought to reposition its brand towards this third iteration of the internet by renaming the parent company 'Meta' (Facebook, 2021). To paraphrase business analysts, it 'bet the house' on this new version of the internet which positions individuals far closer to an augmented or alternative reality, in which they can more easily express themselves, create new communities of interest and obviously receive better targeted adverts. One issue with Facebook/Meta's version of the metaverse is that it does not appear to be a metaverse as we should understand it: it does not yet appear to be the connecting up of multiple virtual realities.

The metaverse as it has been discussed in the Euro–Atlantic area since 2020 has been heavily premised on an understanding of the internet and indeed society that is heavily influenced by Western norms. In fact, it is almost exclusively premised on the liberal social and economic values of the Global North, and the embedded challenges that are presented by the existing internet in terms of hate speech, radicalisation and harassment of identifiable characteristics, be they gender, race, religious, or any other kind of characteristics. As we move into the era of Web 3.0, the exposure to hate speech becomes more relevant. To this end, the Center for Countering Digital Hate identified—in its review of early iterations of virtual reality socialising—a hundred policy violations in less than twelve hours of exposure to it. Violations included those identifying as juveniles being exposed to graphic sexual content and being coaxed into and groomed in hate speech (Center for Countering Digital Hate, 2021). Whistleblowers have suggested that creating the space for the exchange of all ideas, including extremist ones, is part of the essential business model for all social media firms, something that all these companies publicly reject (BBC, 2020).

The metaverse will quickly present intelligence agencies with a range of new challenges. The internet as it exists today has proven to be a fertile environment for radicalisation and recruitment into extremist organisations or to prosecute violence in the name of a single issue. The metaverse is a more dangerous concept for this because it allows a personalisation of the experience—avatars will be interacting with avatars. It also allows for a three-dimensional rendering—that is, the ability to move in (virtual) space—providing a far closer experience to the analogue world. In the metaverse it will be more possible to converse, to plot and to coordinate attacks. As Elson *et al.* have noted, it will also present a greater number of targets to plotters, too: events such as religious ceremonies, same-sex weddings, or discussion groups on particular topics, will likely attract the attention of extremists seeking to disrupt and disturb (Elson, Doctor & Hunter, 2022). Similarly, the metaverse will create new opportunities for cybercriminals to develop income-generating activities through scams, through identity theft, child-sex exploitation and through counterfeiting (Lloyd, 2021). The metaverse will pose intelligence challenges in how to run covert human intelligence sources in the metaverse: Is it possible that CHIS (covert human intelligence source) in the metaverse will be individuals the handler never meets in the analogue world, and, even more stark, might bots be used as CHIS handlers? The notion of risk for informants will be different in the metaverse, less likely to result in real-world violence.

The integration of gaming into the metaverse provides opportunities for terrorists to develop parallel platforms. ISIS developed its own games to radicalise and train gamers during the 2000s. Of greater concern, however, is the integration of blockchain technologies into the metaverse through non-fungible tokens (NFTs), which serve as a proof of ownership and cryptocurrency, which are seen by most Western financial authorities as high-risk investments, rather than as stable stores of value (Fonda, 2021).

Conclusion

The technological future of intelligence is as full of opportunities as it is challenges. Societal-wide changes, such as the widespread adoption of privacy tools, improved encryption, decentralised finance, and platforms where identity is less easily established, all point toward greater challenges for intelligence agencies. Where those agencies are supported by leaps in technology—such as quantum computing, artificial intelligence, and new ways of intercepting conversations—

all point to the intelligence sector having an enhanced ability to identify and curtail threats.

These technological advancements are technology stories, and their pattern of development is not set in stone. But, placed in the contexts of intelligence, these developments are part of the wider political and ideological contest that positions the Five Eyes and much of the Euro–Atlantic area unevenly against competitors drawn from China, parts of the Indian sub-continent, Iran, North Korea, Russia and their supporters and business interests. Dominance or advantage in these developing technological areas provides an advantage against competitors, which in turn helps to protect and manage the development of liberal democratic values and the maintenance of sufficient levels of cohesion and morale to ward off threats to territorial sanctity. There is much in intelligence which is the shaping of narratives and the management of stories: the curation of values through these technological developments helps to reinforce and sustain these stories. We would do well to consider the role of storytelling and reinforcing foundational myths in security and intelligence.

References

Aaronson, S. (2021) 'What makes quantum computing so hard to explain?' *Quanta*, 8 June. Retrieved from https://www.quantamagazine.org/why-is-quantum-computing-so-hard-to-explain-20210608/, accessed 3 January 2022.

Ball, J. (2022) 'Revealed: UK gov't plans publicity blitz to undermine privacy of your chats'. *Rolling Stone*, 16 January. Retrieved from https://www.rollingstone.com/culture/culture-news/revealed-uk-government-publicity-blitz-to-undermine-privacy-encryption-1285453/, accessed 12 March 2022.

Baur, D. and Dimpfl, T. (2021) 'The volatility of Bitcoin and its role as a medium of exchange and a store of value'. *Empirical Economics*, 61 (5), 2663–2683.

BBC (2020) 'Facebook "profits from hate" claims engineer who quit'. *BBC News*, 9 September. Retrieved from https://www.bbc.co.uk/news/technology-54086598, accessed 26 December 2021.

———— (2022) 'What sanctions are being imposed on Russia over Ukraine invasion?' *BBC News*, 24 March. Retrieved from https://www.bbc.co.uk/news/world-europe-60125659, accessed 26 December 2021.

Bellingcat (2022) *How to's*. 24 March. Retrieved from https://www.bellingcat.com/category/resources/how-tos/, accessed 8 March 2022.

Bermbach, D., Lucia, S., Handziski, V. and Wolisz, A. (2021) 'Towards grassroots peering at the edge'. *Proceedings of the 8th International Workshop on Middleware and Applications for the Internet of Things* (pp. 14–17). New York, NY: Association for Computing Machinery.

Bing, C. and Satter, R. (2022) 'EXCLUSIVE iPhone flaw exploited by second Israeli spy firm-sources'. Reuters, 3 February. Retrieved from https://www.reuters.com/technology/exclusive-iphone-flaw-exploited-by-second-israeli-spy-firm-sources-2022-02-03/

Bullough, O. (2022) *Butler to the World: How Britain Became the Servant of Tycoons, Tax Dodgers, Kleptocrats and Criminals*. London & New York: Profile.

Burgess, S. (2022) 'Ukraine war: Deepfake video of Zelenskyy telling Ukrainians to "lay down arms" debunked'. *Sky News*, 17 March. Retrieved from https://news.sky.com/story/ukraine-war-deepfake-video-of-zelenskyy-telling-ukrainians-to-lay-down-arms-debunked-12567789, accessed 8 March 2022.

Campbell, D. (1988). 'Somebody's listening'. *New Statesman*, 12 August, pp. 10–12.

Center for Countering Digital Hate (2021) 'New research shows metaverse is not safe for kids'. Center for Countering Digital Hate, 31 December. Retrieved from https://www.counterhate.com/post/new-research-shows-metaverse-is-not-safe-for-kids, accessed 12 February 2022.

Chan, E. (2022) 'On "Broken nest: Deterring China from invading Taiwan" and authors' response'. *The US Army War College Quarterly: Parameters* 52 (1), 167–180.

Chouliaraki, L. (2015) 'Digital witnessing in conflict zones: The politics of remediation'. *Information, Communication & Society* 18 (11), 1362–1377.

Chrinios, C. (2022) 'Anonymous claims it hacked into Russian TVs and showed the true devastation of Putin's Ukraine invasion'. Fortune, 7 March. Retrieved from https://fortune.com/2022/03/07/anonymous-claims-hack-of-russian-tvs-showing-putins-ukraine-invasion/, accessed 8 March 2022.

Clarke, R. and Knake, R. (2019) *The Fifth Domain: Defending Our Country, Our Companies, and Ourselves in the Age of Cyber Threats*. New York, NY: Penguin.

Cooley, A., Heathershaw, J. and Sharman, J. C. (2018) 'The rise of kleptocracy: Laundering cash, whitewashing reputations'. *Journal of Democracy* 29 (1), 39–53.

Crilley, R. and Chatterje-Doody, P. (2020) 'Emotions and war on YouTube: Affective investments in RT's visual narratives of the conflict in Syria'. *Cambridge Review of International Affairs* 33 (5), 713–733.

Crown Prosecution Service (2020) *Social Media: Reasonable Lines of Inquiry.* Crown Prosecution Service, 23 November. Retrieved from https://www.cps.gov.uk/legal-guidance/social-media-reasonable-lines-enquiry, accessed 28 December 2021.

Curtis, A. (Director) (2007) *The Trap* [Motion picture].

De, N. (2022) 'Lawmakers raise alarm on crypto for sanctions evasion as experts cast doubt'. Coindesk, 2 March. Retrieved from https://www.coindesk.com/policy/2022/03/02/lawmakers-raise-alarm-on-crypto-for-sanctions-evasion-as-experts-cast-doubt/, accessed 8 March 2022.

DeepMind (2022) 'Competitive programming with AlphaCode'. DeepMind, 2 February. Retrieved from https://deepmind.com/blog/article/Competitive-programming-with-AlphaCode, accessed 8 March 2022.

Department of Homeland Security (2022) 'Feature article: Robot dogs take another step towards deployment at the border'. Science and Technology Directorate, Department of Homeland Security, 1 February. Retrieved from https://www.dhs.gov/science-and-technology/news/2022/02/01/feature-article-robot-dogs-take-another-step-towards-deployment, accessed 8 March 2022.

Deseriis, M. (2015) *Improper Names: Collective Pseudonyms from the Luddites to Anonymous.* Minneapolis, MI: University of Minnesota Press.

Dionisio, J., Burns, W. and Gilbert, R. (2013) '3D virtual worlds and the metaverse: Current status and future possibilities'. *ACM Computing Surveys (CSUR)* 45 (3), Article 34, 1–38.

Dover, R. (2022) 'Ukraine–Russia: The first shots have already been fired—in cyberspace'. The Conversation, 2 February. Retrieved from https://theconversation.com/ukraine-russia-the-first-shots-have-already-been-fired-in-cyberspace-176051, accessed 8 March 2022.

Dunn, J. amd Leibovici, F. (2021) 'Supply chain bottlenecks and inflation: The role of semiconductors. *Economic Synopses* No. 28.

Elson, J., Doctor, A. and Hunter, S. (2022) 'The metaverse offers a future full of potential—for terrorists and extremists, too'. The versation, 7 January. Retrieved from https://theconversation.com/the-metaverse-offers-a-future-full-of-potential-for-terrorists-and-extremists-too-173622, accessed 8 March 2022.

Europol (2022) 'Europol's statement on the decision of the European Data Protection Supervisor'. Europol, 11 January. Retrieved from https://www.europol.europa.eu/media-press/newsroom/news/europol%E2%80%99s-statement-decision-of-european-data-protection-supervisor, accessed 8 March 2022.

Facebook (2021) 'The Facebook Company is now Meta'. Facebook, 28 October. Retrieved from https://about.fb.com/news/2021/10/facebook-company-is-now-meta/, accessed 3 January 2022.

Fonda, D. (2021) 'Why crypto will benefit from Facebook's turn to the metaverse'. Barron's, 5 November. Retrieved from https://www.barrons.com/articles/facebook-meta-crypto-51636155729, accessed 3 January 2022.

Fukui, K. and Takeda, S. (2022) 'Building a large-scale quantum computer with continuous-variable optical technologies'. *Journal of Physics B: Atomic, Molecular and Optical Physics* 55 (1).

Gaihre, A., Pandey, S. and Liu, H. (2019) 'Deanonymizing cryptocurrency with graph learning: The promises and challenges'. *2019 IEEE Conference on Communications and Network Security*, 1–3.

Gurijala, B. (2021) 'What is Pegasus? A cybersecurity expert explains how the spyware invades phones and what it does when it gets in'. The Conversation, 9 August. Retrieved from https://theconversation.com/what-is-pegasus-a-cybersecurity-expert-explains-how-the-spyware-invades-phones-and-what-it-does-when-it-gets-in-165382, accessed 3 January 2022.

Hadesty, L. (2011) *The Quantum Frontier*. MIT Technology Review, 21 June. Retrieved from https://www.technologyreview.com/2011/06/21/258884/the-quantum-frontier-2/, accessed 3 January 2022.

Haggart, B., Tusikov, N. and Scholte, J. A. (2021) *Power and Authority in Internet Governance: Return of the State?* London: Routledge.

Halpern, S. (2022) 'The threat of Russian cyberattacks looms large'. *The New Yorker*, 23 March. Retrieved from https://www.newyorker.com/news/daily-comment/the-threat-of-russian-cyberattacks-looms-large, accessed 8 March 2022.

Helps, T., Romero, C., Taghavi, M., Conn, A. T. and Rossiter, J. (2022) 'Liquid-amplified zipping actuators for micro-air vehicles with transmission-free flapping'. *Science Robotics* 7 (63), 81–89.

Hinds, D. (2022) 'National Crime Agency: Finance'. Questions in Parliament, 10 March. Retrieved from https://questions-statements.parliament.uk/written-questions/detail/2022-03-07/135450, accessed 14 March 2022.

Horowitz, J. (2022) 'Putin's aggression leaves his right-wing fan club squirming'. *The New York Times*, 28 February. Retrieved from https://

www.nytimes.com/2022/02/26/world/europe/russia-putin-matteo-salvini-marine-le-pen.html, accessed 8 March 2022.

Howell-O'Neill, P. (2022) 'Meet the NSA spies shaping the future'. MIT Technology Review, 1 February. Retrieved from https://www.technologyreview.com/2022/02/01/1044561/meet-the-nsa-spies-shaping-the-future/, accessed 14 March 2022.

Inkster, N. (2019) 'The Huawei affair and China's technology ambitions'. *Survival* 61 (1), 105–111.

Jardine, E., Lindner, A. and Owenson, G. (2020) 'The potential harms of the Tor anonymity network cluster disproportionately in free countries'. *Proceedings of the National Academy of Sciences* 117 (50), 31716–31721.

Johnson, L., Aldrich, R., Moran, C., Barrett, D., Hastedt, G. and Jervis, R. K. (2014) 'An INS special forum: Implications of the Snowden leaks'. *Intelligence and National Security* 29 (6), 793–810.

Karatzogianni, A. and Aldrich, R. (2020) 'Postdigital war beneath the sea? The Stack's underwater cable insecurity. Figshare, University of Leicester.

Karstedt, S. (2010) 'From absence to presence, from silence to voice: Victims in international and transitional justice since the Nuremberg trials'. *International Review of Victimology* 17 (1), 9–30.

Kay, E. (2022) 'CES 2022: Better together with Android and beyond'. Google blog, 7 January. Retrieved from https://blog.google/products/android/ces2022-bettertogether/, accessed 8 March 2022.

Kayali, L. (2022) 'EU officially boots Russia's RT, Sputnik outlets'. POLITICO, 2 March. Retrieved from https://www.politico.eu/article/russia-rt-sputnik-illegal-europe/, accessed 10 March 2022.

Kethineni, S. and Cao, Y. (2020) 'The rise in popularity of cryptocurrency and associated criminal activity'. *International Criminal Justice Review* 30 (3), 325–344.

Korosec, K. and Matney, L. (2022) 'Anthony Levandowski's latest moonshot is a peer-to-peer telecom network powered by cryptocurrency'. TechCrunch, 2 February. Retrieved from https://techcrunch.com/2022/02/02/anthony-levandowskis-latest-moonshot-is-a-peer-to-peer-telecom-network-powered-by-cryptocurrency/, accessed 8 March 2022.

Kumar, S., Tiwari, P. and Zymbler, M. (2019) 'Internet of Things is a revolutionary approach for future technology enhancement: A review'. *Journal of Big Data* 6 (111), 1–21.

Lee, C. (2022) 'Entangled microwave photons may give 500x boost to radar'. Ars Technica, 7 January. Retrieved from https://arstechnica.com/science/2022/01/entangled-microwave-photons-may-give-500x-boost-to-radar/, accessed 10 March 2022.

Levi, M. (2021) 'Making sense of professional enablers' involvement in laundering organized crime proceeds and of their regulation'. *Trends in Organized Crime* 24 (1), 96–110.

Levy, I. and Robindon, C. (2018) 'Principles for a more informed exceptional access debate'. Lawfare blog, 29 November. Retrieved from https://www.lawfareblog.com/principles-more-informed-exceptional-access-debate, accessed 10 December 2021.

Lewis, P. and Evans, R. (2013) *Undercover: The True Story of Britain's Secret Police.* London: Guardian Faber Publishing.

Lloyd, T. (2021) 'Facebook's metaverse heralds a brave new underworld of metacrime'. *The New Republic*, 29 November. Retrieved from https://newrepublic.com/article/164497/facebook-metaverse-cybercrime-marc-zuckerberg, accessed 3 January 2022.

Machon, A. (2005) *Spies, Lies and Whistleblowers: MI5, MI6 and the Shayler Affair.* London: Book Guild.

McKinney, J. and Harris, P. (2021) 'Broken nest: Deterring China from invading Taiwan'. *The US Army War College Quarterly: Parameters* 51 (4), 23–36.

Mendick, R. (2022) '"Kleptocracy" unit goes after Vladimir Putin's millions of pounds of personal wealth stashed in London'. *The Daily Telegraph*, 16 March.

Meta AI (2022) 'AI that understands speech by looking as well as hearing'. Meta AI, 7 January. Retrieved from https://ai.facebook.com/blog/ai-that-understands-speech-by-looking-as-well-as-hearing/, accessed 17 February 2022.

Myers, S. L., Mozur, P. and Kao, J. (2022) 'Bots and fake accounts push China's vision of Winter Olympic wonderland. *The New York Times*, 18 February.

Mystakidis, S. (2022) 'Metaverse'. *Encyclopedia* 2 (1), 486–497. Retrieved from https://doi.org/10.3390/encyclopedia2010031, accessed 14 March 2022.

Nayar, J. (2021) The fashions of Russian conflict: The Growing Eminence of cyber warfare'. *Harvard International Review* 19 April.

Newton, C. (2022) 'How Signal is playing with fire'. The Verge, 7 January. Retrieved from https://www.theverge.com/22872133/signal-cryptocurrency-payments-encryption-invite-regulator-scrutiny, accessed 12 March 2022.

Omand, D. (2010) *Securing the State.* London: Hurst & Co.

O'Neill, P. H. (2021) 'The US is worried that hackers are stealing data today so quantum computers can crack it in a decade'. MIT Technology Review, 3 November. Retrieved from https://www.technologyreview.

com/2021/11/03/1039171/hackers-quantum-computers-us-homeland-security-cryptography/, accessed 10 January 2022.

Oxford Analytica (2022a) *Canada Trucker Protests May Alter Political Landscape*. London: Springer.

───── (2022b) 'Cyberattack blame reflects efforts to deter Russia'. *Expert Briefings*. Bingley: Emerald Publishing.

Perez, S. (2022a) 'Messenger upgrades its end to end encrypted chat experience'. TechCrunch, 27 January. Retrieved from https://techcrunch.com/2022/01/27/messenger-upgrades-its-end-to-end-encrypted-chat-experience/, accessed 10 March 2022.

───── (2022b) 'Meta's Oculus VR companion app gained ~2M downloads since Christmas'. TechCrunch, 6 January. Retrieved from https://techcrunch.com/2022/01/06/meta-had-a-good-holiday-as-its-oculus-vr-companion-app-gained-2m-downloads-since-christmas/?guccounter=2, accessed 15 March 2022.

Pickard, J. (2022) 'Government brings forward bill to tackle UK's "dirty money"'. *Financial Times*, 28 February.

Pitrelli, M. (2022) 'Anonymous declared a "cyber war" against Russia. Here are the results'. CNBC, 16 March. Retrieved from https://www.cnbc.com/2022/03/16/what-has-anonymous-done-to-russia-here-are-the-results-.html, accessed 15 March 2022.

Pomerantsev, P. (2021) 'The information war paradox'. In G. Rawnsley, Y. Ma and K. Pothong (eds) *Research Handbook on Political Propaganda* (pp. 67–79). London: Edward Elgar.

Popov, S. (2022) 'Ukraine: Why the sanctions won't topple Putin'. The Conversation, 11 March. Retrieved from https://theconversation.com/ukraine-why-the-sanctions-wont-topple-putin-178189, accessed 15 March 2022.

Quinn, B. (2021) 'Telegram is warned app "nurtures subculture deifying terrorists"'. *The Guardian*, 14 October.

Rahim, S. (2021) 'Living with Orientalism: Pakistan's nuclear community, exclusion and othering'. PhD thesis, University of Leicester.

Ruiz, C. (2019) 'Leading online database to remove 600,000 images after art project reveals its racist bias'. *The Art Newspaper*, 23 September.

Shellaker, M. (2021) 'Assessing the consequences of Brexit on UK police cooperation with the EU'. *Masters Thesis, Canterbury Christ Church University School of Law, Policing and Social Sciences.* Canterbury: Canterbury Christ Church University.

Shim, Y. and Tahan, C. (2016) 'Semiconductor-inspired design principles for superconducting quantum computing'. *Nature Communications* 7, 11059.

Spielberg, S. (Director) (2002) *Minority Report* [Motion picture].

Stevens, R. (2022) 'Bitcoin mixers: How do they work and why are they used?'. CoinDesk, 8 March. Retrieved from https://www.coindesk.com/learn/bitcoin-mixers-how-do-they-work-and-why-are-they-used/, accessed 15 March 2022.

Tang, M. (2020) 'Huawei versus the United States? The geopolitics of exterritorial internet infrastructure'. *International Journal of Communication* 14, 22.

The Guardian (2022) '"See what your friend Putin has done": Italy's Matteo Salvini confronted in Poland'. *The Guardian*, 9 March. Retrieved from https://www.theguardian.com/world/video/2022/mar/09/see-what-you-friend-putin-has-done-matteo-salvini-confronted-in-poland-video, accessed 15 March 2022.

Thompson, C. (2022) 'It's like GPT-3 but for code—Fun, fast, and full of flaws' *Wired*, 15 March. Retrieved https://www.wired.com/story/openai-copilot-autocomplete-for-code/, 12 March 2022.

Timberg, C. (2022) 'NSO offered "bags of cash" for access to U.S. cell networks, whistleblower claims'. *The Washington Post*, 1 February. Retrieved from https://www.washingtonpost.com/technology/2022/02/01/nso-pegasus-bags-of-cash-fbi/, accessed 12 March 2022.

Tuohy, J. P. (2022) 'Matter was a major star at CES 2022, but can it maintain its shine?' The Verge, 8 January. Retrieved from https://www.theverge.com/2022/1/8/22872311/matter-smart-home-ces-2022?scrolla=5eb6d68b7fedc32c19ef33b4, accessed 12 March 2022.

UK Government Office for Science (2022) *Genomics Beyond Health*. London: HMSO.

Ukrainian Defence Intelligence (2022) 'Ukrainian defence intelligence'. Twitter, 17 March. Retrieved from https://twitter.com/DI_Ukraine/status/1499157365937119235?s=20&t=PZ-g2mAfU8fqg4A98Xl3hA, accessed 15 March 2022.

US State Department (2022) 'Media Crackdown in Russia'. US State Department, Press release, 2 March. Retrieved from https://www.state.gov/media-crackdown-in-russia/, accessed 15 March 2022.

Veen, J. and Boeke, S. (2021) 'No backdoors: Investigating the Dutch standpoint on encryption'. *Policy & Internet 12* (4) 503–524.

Vengattil, M. and Culliford, E. (2022) 'Facebook allows war posts urging violence against Russian invaders'. Reuters, 11 March. Retrieved from https://www.reuters.com/world/europe/exclusive-facebook-instagram-temporarily-allow-calls-violence-against-russians-2022-03-10/, accessed 15 March 2022.

Waterson, J. (2022) 'Ofcom opens 15 investigations into RT's Ukraine war coverage'. *The Guardian*, 28 February. Retrieved from https://www.theguardian.com/world/2022/feb/28/ofcom-opens-15-investigations-into-rts-ukraine-war-coverage, accessed 8 March 2022.

Weinberg, G. (2021) 'DuckDuckGo in 2021: Building the privacy super app'. DuckDuckGo, 15 December. Retrieved from https://spreadprivacy.com/duckduckgo-2021-review/, accessed 3 January 2022.

Wilson, D. (2011) *Robopocalypse*. New York, NY: Doubleday.

Zhuang, Q. and Shapiro, J. (2022) 'Ultimate accuracy limit of quantum pulse-compression ranging'. *Physical Review Letters* 128, 010501.

10

CONCLUSION
INTELLIGENCE AS NARRATIVE AND COMPETITION

The development of networked technologies has influenced how
intelligence agencies operate, how they perceive their role, and
where they see threats to society. The ubiquity of network-enabled
technologies has shaped how citizens engage with their governments,
contributing to the erosion of trust in governments and their
institutions, both in terms of how government agencies use these
technologies and how strong and professionally presented competing
narratives have over-matched traditional sources of information and
guidance. The thinkers who surrounded the emergence of a widely
adopted internet assumed and argued that it would be a suite of
technologies that would ensure a democratisation of ideas, and a
widening of the contributor pool of thoughts and perspectives: no
longer would expertise only come from those with traditional gate-
keeper roles, like the written and broadcast media, governments,
universities, and influential book publishers. We can observe that
this, in part, did happen. The larger effect has been to see the mass
(re)production and real-world enforcement of established narratives
that privilege the power of the Anglosphere and seek to repress the
emergence of challenger states and political competitors. Where
the intelligence agencies of the Anglosphere have notably failed to

achieve this is in the inexorable rise of China and Chinese influence, usually curried through forms of investment, through the rise of anti-globalisation movements of radical environmentalists, radical and violent religious movements, and in stopping Russian state agents from supercharging the political rejectionist movements of those who have swung behind politicians such as Trump, Bolsonaro, the core of the Leave movement in the UK and Covid and vaccine denial during the first two years of the pandemic (Yan *et al.*, 2022). It is unrealistic to think that these political battles would run smoothly, but the starkness of the disjuncture in Western narratives since 2015 can be read as a demonstration of how relatively homogenous the core political ideas were in Europe prior to 2015 and how differently our competitors think about the world and about politics and competition.

What has been presented here is, therefore, an uneven topography. Some aspects of Western cultural, political, and economic life have taken on the position of a form of universalised truth. Others are at best contested, or at worst imperilled. What we can see, though, is that the networked realities of our times mean that those areas that our intelligence agencies and government have lost control of are now practically beyond recovery. The networked (re)productive effect is simply too strong to control. By contrast, those areas where control has been maintained continue to gain an outsized influence.

We can see that three sub-themes have emerged in this book, which can usefully frame our concluding thoughts. These are: disruption, dislocation and paradox.

The business of government intelligence has been disrupted by the development and widespread adoption of the internet and other networked communications. Government agencies have inflicted a disruption upon themselves by moving into data-warehousing and the analysis of large-*n* datasets, when the evidence suggests that the vast majority of this material goes unanalysed and unused, stored for the small potential of future use (McLaughlin, 2015).

The bulk collection described by Edward Snowden, and implied by studies into the behaviour of multinational internet platforms, has fundamentally compromised the ability of any of us living in the Western world to 'go off grid' or to have legitimate personal privacy.

This has impacted upon intelligence agencies and how they run field officers—no longer can an intelligence officer change/morph identity and ghost into a country. It is far more effective to bring that officer into the target country legitimately and then to have worked extensively on tradecraft. The internet age has prompted a resurgence into traditional, analogue tradecraft, including the trusty dead-letter drop.

Privacy is the pivot around which we should view many of society's largest challenges now, and into the medium term. The dangers associated with who supplies the 5G infrastructure is centred around what they could technically know about us—and the choice appears to be between Chinese suppliers and those companies that may be bought or that have special relationships with the US government—and how they could theoretically switch off or undermine critical infrastructure, creating a strategic level impact. For governments allied to the US it is a choice between the devil they know and the devil they think they know. Away from the issues of core infrastructure, data brokers have shaped what information we all see online when we use the internet. This is the nub of the contested role that Cambridge Analytica has played in discussions around elections and referenda, and the role of algorithms driving what news or bulletins we see (Hinds, Williams, & Joinson, 2020). Other forms of data broker determine what access to consumer credit we have, what we see on online search engines and, in the security and law enforcement arena, they help to model and construct profiles of offenders or adversaries and suggest the likelihood of individuals or groups committing harms (Fox & Farrington, 2018).

The New York Times, reporting about the Clearview company in America, which specialises in artificial intelligence and facial recognition, suggests that the private and public sectors are merging in their use and application of brokered data: using scraped public internet images for preventive law enforcement and security purposes (Rezende, 2020). The opportunity to curtail the actions of political activists, for example, means that such technologies are part of the reinforcement of the dominant frames of understanding. Whilst the investigation into the attack on the Capitol Buildings on 6 January 2021 has concluded, and prosecutions have started, there was an obvious and evident difference in the policing response to the Black Lives Matters protests in 2020 than there was with the far-right incursion into the heart of US Government (Borger, 2021). The backlash against Clearview has come from voices of authority, like *The New York Times*, but also from internet companies that have asked Clearview to stop scraping images from their sites, and from law enforcement agencies that have baulked at having their names revealed by an unauthorised release of Clearview's client list (Mac, Haskins & McDonald, 2020). The need to police by consent is seemingly stretched by the use of such technologies ahead of public debate and consideration by elected officials. In early 2022, the Ukrainian Defence Ministry found a disruptive purpose for Clearview software: to name dead Russian soldiers, to fill in the information void in Russia and also to undermine Russian domestic morale (Bhuiyan, 2022). The use of Clearview platforms in a war zone does also raise the prospect that similar facial recognition software could be mis-purposed to carry out targeted killings, or be mounted on drones to the same effect. The Ukrainian use of Clearview is a clever contribution to the information domain of warfare, circumventing the command and control of the state, in this case the Russian military, to deliver bad news directly to a Russian audience. This kind of change is emblematic of the sorts of direct interventions that states can make in the societies of their rivals: a key intelligence battleground in the twenty-first century.

The entrepreneurs who have worked out what data to collect, how to collect it, store it and use it, as well as how to distribute it effectively, have helped to transform modern economics (Ashmarina, Sarmento & Vochozka, 2020). In doing so, they have also helped to transform social relations and the relationship between the state, its people, and the state with peoples of other countries. The genius of Amazon's founder—Jeff Bezos—was that he realised that his commercial success would be premised upon collecting more usable data about customers than his rivals. In doing this so effectively Bezos has all but wiped out the traditional high street (Berg & Knights, 2021). The balance in the dynamic between data brokers and citizens is firmly weighted in favour of the collectors and the brokers. Those who have their data collected have virtually no actionable rights, despite the enactment of legal measures like the General Protection of Data Rights (GPDR) across the EU, and the political unease about revelations concerning intelligence agency over-reach into dragnet surveillance.

Everyday utilities and activities are run through network connections. Having no or limited access to the internet is life-limiting in our twenty-first century societies. Even if one managed to run a house and domestic finances without using the internet, the interconnected network of CCTV cameras means that the movements of an individual can be pieced together with a good degree of accuracy, even if they are not carrying a mobile telephone which—in this context—acts as a mobile tracking device, regardless of whether it is formally switched on or not (Frith & Saker, 2020). Even without a mobile phone, and with only a landline telephone, all the calls made to and from it go through computerised networks. Going shopping in a supermarket with some form of loyalty card, or a credit card, creates a myriad of datapoints about individual preferences and lifestyle choices (Davies, Green & Singleton, 2018). Going to a train station and paying in cash will result in a CCTV record being created and flagged as suspicious behaviour. This poses large challenges to agencies seeking to recruit and run human intelligence officers, in not providing obvious targets for competitor agencies, and for officers seeking not to stand out, yet not being permitted to do all the things their peer group is able to do.

The treatment of public space is a paradox. If we take the British public as our example, their desire not to have their individual spaces intruded upon by the state or other actors was considered entirely normal in the 1970s, 1980s and nearly all of the 1990s. Those who were middle aged or brought up in those decades recoil at the idea of people 'knowing their business'. Consequently, the plan of Tony Blair's government to introduce identity cards in the UK was roundly rejected by the public in 2006 (Whitley, 2009). And yet since then this same public have been content to share intimate personal details online, and to carry round mobile phones, GPS devices that can track their whereabouts in real-time and reveal more about their preferences than even they are aware of. More recently they have installed in their homes, in ever increasing numbers, devices from smart speakers that listen in for trigger words to serve their owners—and the large data harvesters that service them—to mounted video doorbells surveying streetscapes and arrivals and departures to a home, and the installation and use of dash cams in cars to record their every driving decision. And yet this same public was worried about an identity card. We shall see during the next few years whether they continue to be as vexed by the possibility of COVID passports, to show that the bearer has immunity to the virus (Bramstedt, 2020; Brown *et al.*, 2020).

The desire to maintain privacy has been repositioned by successive governments as correlating with an individual's subversive tendencies: the classic, if you have done nothing wrong, what have you got to hide? The notion that privacy rights might be a good in and of themselves seems to have disappeared from the mainstream discourse almost entirely. The secondary defence of government officials when challenged on this, is to point to the lack of resources in the intelligence and law enforcement communities that stops them being able to carry out dragnet or mass surveillance akin to the popular dystopia of Orwell's' 'Big Brother'. To say that there are not sufficient resources to carry out widespread surveillance is a barrier, but it is a weak intellectual defence, particularly as—per the previous chapter—quantum computing and artificial intelligence develop in the ways promised by their proponents, who are not designing technologies in the light of privacy concerns or privacy protections. Many have argued that quantum computing will undermine our established forms of cryptography and thus undermine our financial transactions and electronic communities, whilst others have urged caution about these near apocalyptic visions, counselling that effective mitigations have already been developed (Lindsay, 2020).

Common applications of artificial intelligence have found business use cases in the financial services and retail sectors to understand more about their customers and consequently to be able to mitigate their risks, manage supply chains and to sell more. These capabilities do illuminate the very real potential for this kind of technology to be exploited by bad actors against the public. There might be one thing worse than a surveillance society, and that is a surveillance society that relies upon exploitable or flawed technologies that are

and undermining the Western public's trust in public authorities and official information (Ognyanova *et al.*, 2020).

The distribution of public information about the work of intelligence agencies is now possible through many more forms of media than was the case twenty years ago, which in part informed Richard Aldrich and Christopher Moran's diagnosis that we are living in an era of 'regulation by revelation' (Aldrich, 2009a). The spread of outlets to distribute information is also true for those interested in pushing disinformation. Freed from the confines 'of Cold War logics, governments have greater latitude to push security resources into assessing the societal level threats we face, be it from climate change, pandemics, or economic disparities. These are productive avenues for increased analytical attention, so it is interesting that quasi-military security threats predominate. This is a choice that has been made consciously and subconsciously by policy officials working within the context of the reinforcing mix of media, politics, and industrial influences. So, not only has this been the focus out of choice, there are also contemporary examples, like Iraq, where the threat was consciously exacerbated to focus resources onto security endeavours (Porter, 2019).

The digital age promised to free people. It promised easier access to information, simpler and cheaper communications. The revolution in information technology promised greater levels of connectivity between people near to them, and those across borders, and between governments and their people. It also promised revolutions in commerce, which it has delivered to the detriment of 'bricks and mortar' retailers. But we should also observe that the information age has seen a reconsolidation of information power, through the consolidation and dominance of a select-few megalith internet platforms; a prevalence of misinformation and mental health problems caused by bad actors, uncritical publics and the 'always on' culture. It has seen a broadening of the range and number of people whose communications are intercepted and analysed by public and private agencies, and the growth of precarious employment and surveillance capitalism (Zuboff, 2019). Taken on its own terms, and placed in this context, the job of intelligence agencies has become far more complicated and diffuse, whilst the public's understanding of what intelligence is, and what purpose it serves, has hardly developed at all. So much information and yet so little understanding. It could be an epitaph of modern society, as much as Bruce Springsteen's '57 Channels (And Nothin' On)' was in the early 1990s (Springsteen, 1992).

Importantly, however, this consolidation of information retrieval and dissemination has resulted in a remarkable and yet paradoxical homogeneity in the framing logics that underpin Western societies. These unifying and singular narratives are relatively straightforward to track, but to describe them as homogeneous is paradoxical because of the strength of the splintering counternarratives they have spurred: the rejection of neoliberalism has created an uneasy set of bedfellows in jihadist extremists, the secular far-left and far-right, and protectionist populists of the centre-right and hard-right, all of whom are bankrolled by opportunist states competing with the Euro–Atlantic area. The open architecture of the internet has also provided ample opportunities for competitor and adversary states to conduct cyber and information conflicts against the West. The manipulation of elections in the US and UK by Russian state actors, which delivered strategic-level shocks to both nations, will pale into insignificance compared to the penetration of information networks and the analysis of harvested DNA by Chinese state actors: both of which are longer term enterprises (The National Counterintelligence and Security Center, 2021; Wee, 2020).

The maintenance of liberal political systems and cultures depends on understanding that our states (domestically and internationally) are created of networks or tribes of expertise and function (Van der Pijl, 2007). Furthermore, we need to understand the competitive dynamics within those tribes and between them. In both UK and US terms, the Westminster and DC bubbles do not strongly relate to the economic, political or social interests of Middle America or Middle Britain: intelligence by consent is stretched when the interests of the populous do not obviously align with the interests of the ruling clique. This mis-alignment arises through the interaction of the tribes that make up the state: the weakness that Vladimir Putin thought he detected in the NATO and EU powers was that they were incapable of creating a common position and holding to it. This was not an irrational conclusion, based on the evidence. But what he miscalculated was the extent to which the populations had tolerated the confused and sometimes seditious messaging of some political and campaigning interests, rather than fully believing in it. The political ideas, beliefs, values and behaviours that our intelligence communities protect and constantly (re)produce are emergent properties of our education, cultural inputs, shared histories, shared myths, tropes and confirmatory lived experiences. The technologies developed and used in intelligence operations, the tradecraft deployed, all go to serve the defence and projection of these political aims, and to reinforce the stories told about 'our' values versus 'their' values or outsider values. The business of intelligence is the curation of our micro- and meta-level stories, the ones that make us, 'us'.

A Final Word

Secret intelligence, as a suite of offensive and counterintelligence activities, is necessary to protect the functioning of a democratic government. This form of intelligence necessarily occasionally infringes upon the values and rights of individuals, but only when it is done with lawful purpose, in a proportionate and necessary way, with an underpinning legislative framework. What this book has demonstrated and argued is that this particular form of security intelligence activity is larger than it needs to be to meet the narrow goals of avoiding surprises, defending against adversaries, and it is overly secretive and contained. What is more, the architecture of intelligence is just as subject to economic forces as other institutions and organisations in public life. The intelligence services have followed the pattern of all government agencies in seeking to maintain and expand their resourcing platforms and to find rationales for doing so: in this case the magnitude of various threats, and the complexities in the international system. This makes them analogous to the military industrial complex that began its intellectual life as a branch of the study of political economy but which in the end became a calling card of peace campaigners. This intelligence version is also an observation of political economy, rather than of peace campaigning. I think it is possible to see another strong resonance with James Der Derian's military–industrial media–entertainment network (MIME-NET), where the form of political understanding that intelligence agencies work within flows in and out of popular cultural sources, helping to reinforce the narratives that both serve as a demand on them to act and as a justification for that action (Der Derian, 2009). What has not been laid bare up to now is the central role played by the business of intelligence in shaping and reinforcing these dominant political, economic and social narratives, and in marginalising and unpicking competing narratives.

There are considerable threats to our democracies and societies from belligerent domestic and international actors but, taken in the round, they do not represent the largest threats to our physical well-being or our way of life. Larger threats come from the dislocation of economics (the sheer number of people across the globe without access to wealth), the climate crisis (as ably shown in the winter of 2019/2020 with the rapid recurrence of once-in-a-lifetime storms, floods and fires across the globe) and the threat from pandemics (equally shown via the fitful recurrence of Ebola in parts of Africa and the COVID-19 pandemic that looks set to dwarf the 1918 Spanish flu as an epidemiological event by 2023). These are threats to our security, and they provide societal-wide insecurity, but they do not speak directly to militarised security threats, even if some of the consequences cross over into this realm. These larger threats require a different kind of intelligence response: one that is premised upon open source intelligence architecture and assessment through whole-of-government open source assessments and through public collective commons. This returns the business of intelligence closer to its original purpose, which was to provide a competitive advantage to the state and provide information to support decision making. That form of intelligence makes far greater use of open sources and experts outside the state's current intelligence community; it is also less expensive.

If we remain focused on intelligence as it is now, we can see that the trade-offs that existed a hundred years ago essentially remain the same today, albeit through new technologies. The benefits of intelligence to the mainstream of society are greater security, fewer realised threats, and a better environment to live, work and invest in, providing that a member of that mainstream does not object to the increasing levels of intrusion or to the restrictive tramlines of acceptable and unacceptable behaviours and views. The negatives for those who find themselves outside this mainstream can be stark. There has been a clear diminution of personal freedoms, and an increased chance of suffering from arbitrary government action, a slender but important difference between being surveyed and being surveyed and actioned. Politicians and the mainstream media have built a steady case and asked us to accept the adoption of maximalist positions on legally permitted intrusions. We should—instead—understand that there are productive discussions to be had on what we can do to increase the benefits we accrue from intelligence activity in terms of tasking intelligence to provide decision support across the widest breadth of government activities, whilst negating the harms of focussing ever greater powers in a narrow band of agencies and officers. It may be that in the short term this results in us effectively eschewing some benefits of the intelligence apparatus that exists today, to ensure that unintended harms are not committed and that better economic and social circumstances prevail.

The most obvious example of a technological development that promises considerable benefits to security and law enforcement agencies, but that will also deliver many unintended negative consequences to society, is the increased adoption by, and desire of, local and national government agencies to roll out facial recognition technology in our cities and towns. The problem with facial recognition technologies is that they have been shown to throw up many false positives, but also that the public remains touchingly convinced that decisions and choices determined by computers are objective. The potential negative consequences of these technologies are stark, and are unlikely—based on historical experience—to be revealed by the companies developing and marketing them, nor by the agencies seeking to utilise them. Indeed, the then Commissioner of the Metropolitan Police Service, Cressida Dick, publicly suggested, in February 2020, that as the public freely give away their images online all the time, her dragnet surveillance project (known as LFR—Live Facial Recognition) is materially similar and thus acceptable. Dick further argued that the LFR only represents a threat to those engaged in serious criminality, which is a chronic under-specification of the potential of this technology even as it is existed in 2020 (Siddique, 2020).

Whilst former Commissioner Dick complained that detractors do not understand how the technology would be used by her officers, in return she failed to understand (1) the wider context of an underpinning philosophical context where the right to some measure of value-neutral privacy is expected by citizens of any Western state; (2) the mission creep of all security technologies and the expansion of technological interventions in the law enforcement and security space that has been poorly understood and regulated by policy makers, and which has paradoxically made the recruitment and running of intelligence officers in the field more difficult; (3) the impact on social relations between citizens and between government authorities and the public. These are not necessarily the priority for a senior law enforcement or security official, but they should be for the body politic. These trade-offs should be a public and political choice, not a choice for practitioners who, for all good reasons, have been historically poor arbiters for what is appropriate and proportionate.

The weight of scholarship and government positioning tells us that intelligence exists to serve the public. Consequently, it exists to make the public safer, more prosperous, and better placed in the international system. But the public still have a poor understanding of what intelligence is for and what it does. That is not all their fault: they have been poorly served by the news media, which treats them as infants, the agencies who carefully manage the information available, academics who have focused on exciting histories, or dry analysis (and no, the irony is not lost on me here), and by popular culture, which seeks to show intelligence as omnipotent or as an echo of the glamour of quasi-special forces in the Second World War. It would be fairer and more accurate to say that intelligence exists to serve the state. More particularly it serves to protect a particular vision of a state, and a particular articulation of a value set. Protection of the public is a welcome side-product, and consequently creates a tension between the public and the security agencies.

The public have enthusiastically acquiesced in adopting technologies that provide the opportunity to increase the level of surveillance and the erosion of private spaces. Taking the small steps to opt out of and switch off tracking and sharing facilities on computers, televisions and mobile phones, and not blindly adopting panopticon technologies such as internet connected video doorbells, or smart speakers, removes some of the power that these largely unaccountable private companies have gained over the public in the last decade and which are open to intrusion by governments at home and abroad. The extent to which the dominant framing logics or pictures of reason have been created by private technology companies and venture capital firms, as a by-product of profit maximisation strategies, is evidenced in a diffuse set of literatures, each focusing on separate technical or philosophical points. When brought together this evidence appears compelling, and so one of my journal article titles from earlier in my career, 'For Queen and Company', seems more prescient now as a means by which to describe the elision between intelligence and private industry than it did then to describe the relationship between the government and the defence industrial base (Dover, 2007). Western publics have been quick to buy into always-on information services and have blindly followed the curated stories on their social media feeds (Bene, 2017). This has made them vulnerable to the disinformation campaigns of foreign states and domestic belligerents, which has created strategic shocks and has resulted in far poorer outcomes in the COVID-19 pandemic than there needed to be (Mejova & Kalimeri, 2020).

The public have the power to push for an intelligence system that is premised on providing quality information to support decisions made by domestic legislators and ministers, and to provide competitive advantage in the international system. The public could make this push, through their elected representatives and via interest groups, based on the poor understanding of, and preparations for, the latest pandemic, on the failures to address climate challenges and even in the understanding and mitigation of economic shocks. It is not at all clear, however, that the public see that they are being poorly served by the current structures, that alternative structures are possible, nor how they might effectively push for those changes. There is no collective conscience that places some of the blame for the huge public policy failures of recent times, down to the organisation of how we collect and use sensitive information. Similarly, critiques that the Anglosphere has and continues to have a negative impact on the Global South have begun to be aired, but have become subject a culture war, where such critiques are dismissed as being 'woke' (Rose, 2021). There is a better way for intelligence—but no obvious pathway to it.

References

Aldrich, R. J. (2009a) 'Regulations by revelation: Intelligence, transparency and the media'. In R. Dover and M. Goodman (eds) *Spinning Intelligence* (pp. 13–35). New York, NY: Columbia University Press.

———— (2009b) 'Beyond the vigilant state: Globalisation and intelligence'. *Review of International Studies* 35 (4), 889–902.

Ashmarina, S., Sarmento, A. and Vochozka, M. (2020) *Digital Transformation of the Economy: Challenges, Trends and New Opportunities*. Berlin: Springer.

Bene, M. (2017) 'Influenced by peers: Facebook as an information source for young people'. *Social Media+ Society* 3 (2), 1–14.

Berg, N. and Knights, M. (2021) *Amazon: How the World's Most Relentless Retailer Will Continue to Revolutionize Commerce*. London: Kogan Page.

Bhuiyan, J. (2022) *Ukraine Uses Facial Recognition Software to Identify Russian Soldiers Killed in Combat. The Guardian*, 24 March. Retrieved: https://www.theguardian.com/technology/2022/mar/24/ukraine-facial-recognition-identify-russian-soldiers, accessed 12 March 2022.

Borger, J. (2021) 'Maga v BLM: How police handled the Capitol mob and George Floyd activists'. *The Guardian*, 7 January.

Bramstedt, K. A. (2020) 'Antibodies as currency: COVID-19's golden passport'. *Journal of Bioethical Inquiry* 17, 687–689.

Brown, R. C., Savulescu, J., Williams, B. and Wilkinson, D. (2020) 'Passport to freedom? Immunity passports for COVID-19'. *Journal of Medical Ethics* 46 (10), 652–659.

Davies, A., Green, M. A. and Singleton, A. D. (2018) 'Using machine learning to investigate self-medication purchasing in England via high street retailer loyalty card data'. *PloS ONE* 13 (11), 1–14.

Der Derian, J. (2009) *Virtuous War: Mapping the Military–Industrial–Media–Entertainment Network*. London: Routledge.

Dover, R. (2007) 'For Queen and company: The role of intelligence in the UK's arms trade'. *Political Studies* 55 (4), 683–708.

Fox, B. and Farrington, D. (2018) 'What have we learned from offender profiling? A systematic review and meta-analysis of 40 years of research'. *Psychological Bulletin* 44 (12), 1247–1274.

Frith, J. and Saker, M. (2020) '<? covid19?> It is all about location: Smartphones and tracking the spread of COVID-19'. *Social Media+ Society* 6 (3), 1–4.

Harvey, D. (2007) *A Brief History of Neoliberalism.* New York, NY: Oxford University Press.

Hinds, J., Williams, E. J. and Joinson, A. (2020) '"It wouldn't happen to me": Privacy concerns and perspectives following the Cambridge Analytica scandal'. *International Journal of Human-Computer Studies* 143, 102498.

Hunter, R. (2022) 'The Ukraine crisis: Why and what now?' *Survival* 64 (1), 7–28.

Kozera, C. (2020) 'Fitness OSINT: Identifying and tracking military and security personnel with fitness applications for intelligence gathering purposes'. *Security and Defence Quarterly* 32 (5), 41–52.

Lindsay, J. R. (2020) 'Surviving the quantum cryptocalypse'. *Strategic Studies Quarterly* (Summer), 49–73.

Mac, R., Haskins, C. and McDonald, L. (2020) 'Clearview's facial recognition app has been used by the Justice Department, ICE, Macy's, Walmart, and the NBA'. Buzzfeed News, 27 February. Retrieved from: https://www.buzzfeednews.com/article/ryanmac/clearview-ai-fbi-ice-global-law-enforcement, accessed 3 December 2021.

McLaughlin, J. (2015) 'U.S. Mass Surveillance has no record of thwarting large terror attacks, regardless of Snowden leaks'. The Intercept, 17 November. Retrieved from: https://theintercept.com/2015/11/17/u-s-mass-surveillance-has-no-record-of-thwarting-large-terror-attacks-regardless-of-snowden-leaks/, accessed 3 January 2022.

Mejova, Y. and Kalimeri, K. (2020) 'COVID-19 on Facebook ads: Competing agendas around a public health crisis'. *Proceedings of the 3rd ACM SIGCAS Conference on Computing and Sustainable Societies* (pp. 22–31). New York, NY: Association for Computing Machinery.

Ognyanova, K., Lazer, D., Robertson, R. E. and Wilson, C. (2020) 'Misinformation in action: Fake news exposure is linked to lower trust in media, higher trust in government when your side is in power'. *Harvard Kennedy School Misinformation Review* 1 (4), 1–19.

Porter, P. (2019) *Blunder: Britain's War in Iraq.* Oxford: Oxford University Press.

Rezende, I. N. (2020) 'Facial recognition in police hands: Assessing the 'Clearview case' from a European perspective'. *New Journal of European Criminal Law* 11 (3), 375–389.

Rose, S. (2021) 'How the word "woke" was weaponised by the right'. *The Guardian*, 21 January.

Siddique, H. (2020) 'Met police chief: Facial recognition technology critics are ill-informed'. *The Guardian*, 24 February.

Springsteen, B. (1992) '57 Channels (And Nothin' On)' [Recorded by B. Springsteen]. Los Angeles, USA.

The National Counterintelligence and Security Center (2021) *China's Collection of Genomic and Other Healthcare Data from America: Risks to Privacy and US Economic and National Security*. Washington, DC: Director of National Intelligence.

Van den Bulck, H. and Hyzen, A. (2020) 'Of lizards and ideological entrepreneurs: Alex Jones and Infowars in the relationship between populist nationalism and the post-global media ecology'. *International Communication Gazette* 82 (1), 42–59.

Van der Pijl, K. (2007) *Nomads, Empires, States: Modes of Foreign Relations and Political Economy, Volume I*. London: Pluto.

Wee, S. (2020) 'China is collecting DNA from tens of millions of men and boys, using U.S. equipment'. *The New York Times*, 30 July.

Whitley, E. (2009) 'Perceptions of government technology, surveillance and privacy: The UK identity cards scheme'. In B. Goold and D. Neyland (eds) *New Directions in Surveillance and Privacy* (pp. 133–158). Cullompton: Willan.

Yan, K., Barbati, J., Duncan, K., Warner, E. and Rains, S. (2022) 'Russian troll vaccine misinformation dissemination on Twitter: The role of political partisanship'. *Health Communication* (January), 1–10.

Zuboff, S. (2019) *The Age of Surveillance Capitalism: The Fight for a Human Future at the New Frontier of Power*. New York, NY: Public Affairs.

NOTES

INTRODUCTION

1. Mike Goodman of King's College London and I ran three funded projects under the 'Lessons Learned' banner to try and place the emphasis on learning lessons from successful operations, rather than obsessing with those that had gone badly or were subject to public inquest or inquiry.

CHAPTER 1. 'NARRATIVE VIOLATION'

1. Whilst much maligned in the media, Cummings' work after leaving government has been as revelatory as it has been astute. His insights in the defence and security policy world have been particularly welcome.

CHAPTER 3. INTELLIGENCE AGENCIES AND THEIR OUTSIDERS

1. I have published several pieces on academic engagement with the intelligence agencies. One of these was with Michael Goodman and Martha White, and two with Michael Goodman alone. This chapter extends this work and takes the conclusions I have drawn in a completely different direction to these existing pieces.
2. The ESRC is one of the national research councils, funded centrally but administered outside of government control.
3. www.ahrc.ac.uk/innovation/knowledgeexchange/kewithpolicy makers/publications/ (accessed 16 January 2017).
4. Note that there is now a Horizon Scanning Programme team within government for whom these recommendations would uniquely apply:

www.gov.uk/government/groups/horizon-scanning-programme-team (accessed 7 November 2016).

CHAPTER 4. OPEN SOURCE INTELLIGENCE AND THE DIGITAL AGE

1.   This chapter owes a large debt to discussions with the former US intelligence officer and a leading voice for OSINT, Robert David Steele. It should be noted that, more recently, and until his untimely death in 2021, Steele had become a more controversial figure arguing that Trump had been defeated by electoral fraud, and asserting some of the agendas that have become associated with more fringe groups. This was a great shame as between 2007 and 2015—when we discussed intelligence a lot—he was an astute commentator on the value that could be added from open source intelligence, and I was pleased to work with him on this.

2.   '... every President has available to him all the information gathered by the many intelligence agencies already in existence. The Departments of State, Defense, Commerce, Interior and others are constantly engaged in extensive information gathering and have done excellent work. But their collective information reached the President all too frequently in conflicting conclusions. At times, the intelligence reports tended to be slanted to conform to established positions of a given department. This becomes confusing and what's worse, such intelligence is of little use to a President in reaching the right decisions. Therefore, I decided to set up a special organization charged with the collection of all intelligence reports from every available source, and to have those reports reach me as President without department "treatment" or interpretations. I wanted and needed the information in its "natural raw" state and in as comprehensive a volume as it was practical for me to make full use of it. But the most important thing about this move was to guard against the chance of intelligence being used to influence or to lead the President into unwise decisions—and I thought it was necessary that the President do his own thinking and evaluating... For some time I have been disturbed by the way CIA has been diverted from its original assignment. It has become an operational and at times a policy-making arm of the Government... I never had any thought that when I set up the CIA that it would be injected into peacetime cloak and dagger operations. Some of the complications and embarrassment I think we have experienced are in part attributable to the fact that this quiet intelligence arm of the

President has been so removed from its intended role that it is being interpreted as a symbol of sinister and mysterious foreign intrigue.' (Truman, 1963)

CHAPTER 5. INTELLIGENCE AGENCIES AND HYBRID WARS

1. There are unresolved issues around the creation of these 'normal' behaviours, from which outliers can be derived and noted. I was party to a heated exchange between several academic colleagues after the 7/7 attacks in 2005, in which one—who was open about his diagnosis for autism—strongly remonstrated (including with the memorable accusatory phrase 'normalist') with the other over the sorts of profiling that had resulted in the death of Jean Charles De Menezes, because he was someone who also wore a heavy coat in the summer on the tube and felt more comfortable with his hood up. The problem of creating profiles that only capture 'neutral normality' as 'safe', is deeply problematic for those impacted by conditions that render them unable to conform to the neutrally normal norms, and undermines the analytical power of the models.

2. It should be noted that a number of academics and journalists were erroneously noted on leaked documents as being part of a UK hub of experts taking part in these activities: the vast majority of them have publicly refuted the notion that they participated in these activities, and have noted their surprise at being included on the documents.

3. As scraped by the author, using an API. The set of scraped tweets may not be complete due to the vagaries of access that Twitter provides researchers, and APIs who do not subscribe to 'the full stream', something that I am told costs a six-figure sum per annum.

4. https://www.4chan.org/

5. https://www.reddit.com/

6. In two stages: first using the Stream Twitter's Application Programming Interface (API), and second using the Search API which is part of Twitter's REST API. The stream API accepts the filtering of request results, as Twitter maintains limitations in its API to the volume of data that can be retrieved within a given duration (450 requests every 15 minutes).

7. https://send.firefox.com/

8. https://onionshare.org/

CHAPTER 6. THE EVOLVING RELATIONSHIP BETWEEN INTELLIGENCE AND THE MEDIA

1. See also the accompanying chapter on open source intelligence.

CHAPTER 7. SPYING ON SCREEN

1. With eternal gratitude to Pierre Lethier for the many conversations we have had about spy cinema and for introducing me to forms of cultural production I would not otherwise have seen.
2. Pierre Lethier cites Charles Bennett and Angus MacPhail as examples of these practitioners-turned-screenwriters who worked with Hitchcock after the Second World War.

INDEX

Note: Page numbers followed by '*n*' refer to notes